Understanding
Animal Farm

The Greenwood Press "Literature in Context" Series
Student Casebooks to Issues, Sources, and Historical Documents

The Adventures of Huckleberry Finn
by Claudia Durst Johnson

Anne Frank's *The Diary of a Young Girl*
by Hedda Rosner Kopf

The Catcher in the Rye
by Sanford Pinsker and Ann Pinsker

The Crucible
by Claudia Durst Johnson
and Vernon E. Johnson

Death of a Salesman
by Brenda Murphy and
Susan C. W. Abbotson

The Grapes of Wrath
by Claudia Durst Johnson

The Great Gatsby
by Dalton Gross and
MaryJean Gross

Hamlet
by Richard Corum

I Know Why the Caged Bird Sings
by Joanne Megna-Wallace

Jamaica Kincaid's *Annie John*
by Deborah Mistron

The Literature of World War II
by James H. Meredith

Macbeth
by Faith Nostbakken

Of Mice and Men, The Red Pony, and
The Pearl
by Claudia Durst Johnson

Pride and Prejudice
by Debra Teachman

A Raisin in the Sun
by Lynn Domina

The Red Badge of Courage
by Claudia Durst Johnson

Richard Wright's *Black Boy*
by Robert Felgar

Romeo and Juliet
by Alan Hager

The Scarlet Letter
by Claudia Durst Johnson

Shakespeare's *Julius Caesar*
by Thomas Derrick

A Tale of Two Cities
by George Newlin

Things Fall Apart
by Kalu Ogbaa

To Kill a Mockingbird
by Claudia Durst Johnson

Zora Neale Hurston's *Their Eyes
Were Watching God*
by Neal A. Lester

UNDERSTANDING
Animal Farm

A Student Casebook to
Issues, Sources, and
Historical Documents

Edited by
John Rodden

The Greenwood Press
"Literature in Context" Series
Claudia Durst Johnson, Series Editor

GREENWOOD PRESS
Westport, Connecticut • London

Library of Congress Cataloging–in–Publication Data

Understanding Animal farm : a student casebook to issues, sources, and
   historical documents / edited by John Rodden.
        p.   cm.—(The Greenwood Press "Literature in context"
   series, ISSN 1074–598X)
     Includes bibliographical references and index.
     ISBN 0–313–30201–4 (alk. paper)
     1. Orwell, George, 1903–1950. Animal farm.   2. Politics and
   literature—Great Britain—History—20th century—Sources.
   3. Political fiction, English—History and criticism.   4. Fables,
   English—History and criticism.   5. Animals in literature.
   I. Rodden, John.   II. Series.
   PR6029.R8A78   1999
   823'.912—dc21   98–55338

British Library Cataloguing in Publication Data is available.

Library of Congress Catalog Card Number: 98–55338
ISBN: 0–313–30201–4
ISSN: 1074–598X

First published in 1999

Greenwood Press, 88 Post Road West, Westport, CT 06881
An imprint of Greenwood Publishing Group, Inc.
www.greenwood.com

Printed in the United States of America

The paper used in this book complies with the
Permanent Paper Standard issued by the National
Information Standards Organization (Z39.48–1984).

10 9 8 7 6 5 4 3 2 1

Copyright Acknowledgments

The editor and publisher are grateful to the following for granting permission to reprint from their materials:

Excerpts reprinted with the permission of Simon & Schuster from *George Orwell: A Personal Memoir* by T. R. Fyvel. Copyright © 1982 by T. R. Fyvel.

Excerpts from Kingsley Martin in *New Statesman and Nation*, 8 September 1945, reprinted by permission of *New Statesman*.

Excerpts from George Soule in *The New Republic*, 2 September 1946, reprinted courtesy of *The New Republic*.

Excerpts from Isaac Rosenfeld, "What I Found Most Troublesome." Reprinted with permission from the 7 September 1946 issue of *The Nation* magazine.

Personal interview by John Rodden with Russell Kirk, courtesy of Annette Y. Kirk, The Russell Kirk Center for Cultural Renewal.

Excerpts from *The Politics of Literary Reputation: The Making and Claiming of "St. George" Orwell* by John Rodden. Copyright © 1989 by Oxford University Press, Inc. Used by permission of Oxford University Press, Inc.

Excerpts from Spencer Brown, "Strange Doings at 'Animal Farm,' " reprinted from *Commentary*, February 1955, by permission; all rights reserved.

Excerpts from John Rodden, "Orwell in the USSR: Gorbachev's Glasnost," *LaSalle Magazine* (Spring 1989), reprinted courtesy of *LaSalle Magazine*.

Unpublished interview by John Rodden with Wolfgang Strauss, courtesy of Wolfgang Straus.

Unpublished interview by Cristen Carson with Elena Lifschitz, courtesy of Elena Lifschitz.

Excerpts from Arnold Blium, "Forbidden Topics: Early Soviet Censorship Directives," in *Book History* (1998), translated by Donna M. Farina, courtesy of Donna M. Farina.

Excerpts from *The Marxists* by C. Wright Mills. Copyright © 1962 by C. Wright Mills. Used by permission of Dell Books, a division of Bantam Doubleday Dell Publishing Group, Inc.

Every reasonable effort has been made to trace the owners of copyright materials in this book, but in some instances this has proven impossible. The editor and publisher will be glad to receive information leading to more complete acknowledgments in subsequent printings of the book and in the meantime extend their apologies for any omissions.

For my father and mother,
once again

Contents

Acknowledgments

Since the late 1970s, I have taught high school and college courses, the latter entitled The Quest for Community, in which Orwell's little fable, along with *1984*, has occupied a central place. My first debt of gratitude is therefore to my students, who have not just endured their teacher's preoccupation with *Animal Farm* but taught him a great deal about the book during the past two decades.

Other friends have assisted me with this book by their conversation, correspondence, technical help, or editorial suggestions: Rafe Bemporad, Janine Bukowski, Erica Carson, Michael Levenson (my benevolent intellectual "Big Brother"), Beth Macom, Nancy Maule McNally, Deanna Matthews, Arslan Razmi, Aimee Roebuck, Jack Rossi, Walter Sokel, Wolfgang Strauss, and Mary Triece. I am also indebted to my patient and scrupulous editors at Greenwood Press, including Gillian Beebe, Emma Moore, Beverly Miller, Claudia Johnson, and Barbara Rader, each of whose contributions has made this a better book.

My profound gratitude goes to the contributors to this volume: James Aune, Jonathan Rose, Bill Shanahan, and Denise Weeks. They have drawn on their expertise to place *Animal Farm* in historical context. It has been a great pleasure to work with them. I also express my appreciation to Daniel Reat, Paul and Thomas Rodden, and Craig Thompson for giving generously of their time and artistic talents to create excellent illustrations. I reserve a special thank you for Cristen Carson Reat. Not only did she add a unique dimension to this book by interviewing Russian readers of *Animal Farm* and translating material from the Russian for Chapter 6, but she also handled the permissions and indexing with exemplary professionalism.

Last but not least, I thank my parents for their unwavering support and love across the decades. Both of them are Irish-born, working-class immigrants from large families. They too, in unspoken ways, have taught me a great deal about Orwell and *Animal Farm*. Especially my father, who grew up in a family of fifteen and worked throughout the British Isles as a farm hand and unskilled industrial laborer during Orwell's lifetime, has given me a feel for the working-class conditions and values that Orwell described. My own youth in an extended working-class family possessed an emotional residue of those conditions and values. And perhaps that is why the warm, poignant glow of the animals' "quest for community" at the outset of *Animal Farm* has always resonated so deeply for me. Their close-knit affection and solidarity resemble the climate of the working-class families that Orwell met—and that I grew up in. However idealistic their attitudes, they were—and are—also real: I have witnessed them.

Introduction

John Rodden

When the British writer George Orwell submitted *Animal Farm* in 1945 to Dial Press, an American publishing house, his book was rejected with the explanation that "it was impossible to sell animal stories in the USA."

Animal Farm is subtitled "a fairy story." But is it merely a fairy tale? Or just an animal story?

The editors at Dial Press were not the only readers of *Animal Farm* to think so. Some British booksellers erroneously placed it in the "children's section" of their shops. (Orwell had to scurry around London to switch it to the "adult fiction" shelves.) Indeed, many early readers of Orwell's little masterpiece apparently did not realize that it was a brilliant work of political satire. They read the book much as did the young son of one of Orwell's friends, who reported that his boy "insisted on my reading it, chapter by chapter . . . and he enjoys it innocently as much as I enjoy it maliciously."[1]

Does it seem absurd to the readers today that the literary public of the 1940s could have read *Animal Farm* "innocently," only on the literal level? How could editors and publishers misjudge a sophisticated classic for a children's tale? How could they confuse an ingenious attack targeting the betrayal of revolution in general—and the Soviet Union in particular—for a simple animal story?

The language and form of *Animal Farm* are the keys to the an-

swer. In a certain sense, *Animal Farm* is victimized by its astonishing success as a political satire. Orwell's "simple" little book is
quite sophisticated—and likely to deceive readers into taking it too
lightly if they are inattentive to the parallels between the story and
Soviet history. And these historical issues are themselves anything
but "simple."

Animal Farm works so beautifully on its literal, surface level as
an animal story that it may lull unwary readers into staying on the
surface, thereby misleading them into missing its underlying political and historical references. Ironically, then, it is a measure of
Animal Farm's artistic excellence that it fools some readers into
taking it for an animal story.

How do the style and form of *Animal Farm* do this? The plain
language, straightforward plot, and one-dimensional characters
mask the complex subject matter and context. *Animal Farm* is
simple on the surface—yet quite subtle beneath it.

All readers—like the publishers of the 1940s that rejected the
book—think in terms of book categories when they read. For example, we classify books as fiction or nonfiction, biographies or
autobiographies—or, to refer to the present example: adult novels
or children's tales, serious fiction or animal stories.

Thus, the essential error of some readers "fooled" by *Animal
Farm* has been to mistake its genre. They see only its surface message, misreading it as nothing more than a children's tale or animal
story.

Indeed, Orwell's little book *is* both of these—on the surface.
But that is not, first and foremost, what it is. It is far more than an
uncontroversial little children's book.

Well then, what kind of book is it? And what is its form?

First, *Animal Farm* is a political allegory of the history of the
Soviet Union. (It is sometimes jokingly referred to as an "animallegory.") Traditionally, an allegory is a symbolic tale that treats a
spiritual subject under the guise of a worldly one. The word derives from the Greek *allegorein*, which means "to speak as if to
imply something other." William Langland's *Piers Plowman* and
John Bunyan's *Pilgrim's Progress* are allegories written during me-
dieval and Renaissance England, respectively, each of them a morality tale that portrays a Christian's religious quest.

Second, *Animal Farm* is an allegory written in the form of a
beast fable. The beast fable is a classical genre dating from the

Greek narratives of Aesop in the fifth century B.C. The beast fable is typically a story or poem in which the misadventures of animals expose human follies. The behavior of the animals points up human pettiness and "bestiality." We draw on existing stereotypes of beasts. Pigs have a bad name for selfishness and gluttony. Horses are slow-witted, strong, gentle, and loyal. Sheep are brainless and behave as a flock, without individual initiative. The point of departure for Orwell's fable was a statement from Karl Marx's *Economic and Philosophical Manuscripts of 1844*: "The worker in his human functions no longer feels himself to be anything but animal. What is animal becomes human and what is human becomes animal."

So Orwell adapts the literary forms of the allegory and beast fable for his own purposes. "The business of making people conscious of what is happening outside their own small circle," he once wrote, "is one of the major problems of our time, and a new literary technique will have to be evolved to meet it." Orwell's symbolic tale takes a political subject and treats it under the guise of an innocent animal story. But *Animal Farm* also has a stinging moral warning against the abuse of power.

Like most other allegories, *Animal Farm* operates by framing one-to-one correspondences between the literal and symbolic level. Its events and characters function as a simple story on the literal level. But they also operate on a symbolic level for readers who know the "code." In this case, the key code is the history of Soviet communism. Orwell subtitled *Animal Farm* "a fairy story," but the subtitle was an ironic joke. He meant that his beast fable was no mere "fairy story," but that it was happening, right then, in Stalin's Russia—and that it could happen anywhere.

Parts of Orwell's code are easy to "crack." For instance, the pigs represent the Communist Party. The pig leader Napoleon and his rival Snowball symbolize the dictator Stalin and the communist leader Leon Trotsky. Old Major is a composite of Karl Marx and Vladimir Ilyich Lenin, the major theorist and key revolutionary leader of Communism, respectively. "Beasts of England" is a parody of the "Internationale," the Communist Party song. The rebellion in Chapter 2 represents the Russian Revolution of October 1917. The Battle of the Cowshed in Chapter 4 depicts the subsequent civil war. Mr. Jones and the farmers are the loyalist Russians and foreign forces who tried but failed to dislodge the Bolsheviks, the revolutionaries led by Lenin. The animals' false confessions in

Chapter 7 represent the purge trials of the late 1930s. The false banknotes given for the corn by Frederick recall Hitler's betrayal of the Nazi-Soviet Pact of 1939. The first demolition of the windmill, which Napoleon blames on his pig rival, Snowball, is the failure of the First Five-Year Plan, an industrial plan to coordinate the Soviet economy in the 1920s that did not bring prosperity. The second destruction of the windmill by Frederick's men is the Nazi invasion of Russia in 1941. The meeting of pigs and humans at the end of the story is the November 1943 wartime conference in Tehran that Stalin, Roosevelt, and Churchill attended.

A reader who misses such allegorical correspondences may completely misread the book. Moreover, an allegory can work on different levels.

These two difficulties account for much of the confusion and controversy about *Animal Farm*. Readers who naively take it as merely an animal story miss the allegorical correspondences altogether. Readers who take *Animal Farm* merely as crude propaganda—as a vulgar diatribe against communism (or socialism)—fail to grasp the various levels on which Orwell's allegory is working.

The fact is that *Animal Farm* functions as an allegory on four levels. On the immediate verbal level, it *is* a children's story about an animal rebellion on a farm. As an animal story, the work invites readers to respond compassionately to the sufferings of vulnerable beasts. We readers identify with the suffering and oppression of the poor animals. Indeed, Orwell once explained that a scene of a suffering horse who later became the model for Boxer inspired him to conceive *Animal Farm*:

> The actual details of the story did not come to me for some time until one day (I was then living in a small village) I saw a little boy, perhaps ten years old, driving a huge cart-horse along a narrow path whipping it whenever it tried to turn. It struck me that if only such animals became aware of their strength, we should have no power over them, and that men exploit animals in much the same way as the rich exploit the proletariat. I proceeded to analyse Marx's theory from the animals' point of view.[2]

Orwell's last line makes clear the larger purpose of his story, and it suggests the other levels on which the fable functions.

Beyond an explicit, literal level, then, are three symbolic levels on which *Animal Farm* operates. First, it is an historical satire of the Russian Revolution and the subsequent Soviet dictatorship. As we have already seen, one can appreciate the precision of Orwell's allegory, which includes many exact historical correspondences between the events of *Animal Farm* and Soviet history up to 1943.

Second, *Animal Farm* is a political treatise that suggests larger lessons about power, tyranny, and revolution in general. On this level, Orwell's book has a much broader historical and political message, one that is not limited to criticism of the Soviet Union. It addresses not merely the case of the USSR but that of all nations—past, present, and future.

Third, *Animal Farm* is a fable, or a "fairy tale," as Orwell termed it. It carries a universal moral about the "animality" of human nature. For instance, by the conclusion of *Animal Farm*, some of the pigs are walking upright and wearing human clothes; they are little different from corrupt human beings. The animal farm mirrors our human world, which is sometimes referred to as "the human circus" because the various types of human personality can be compared to the character types of animals. Some humans are like pigs, others resemble sheep, still others can be compared to dogs, and so forth. On this level, Orwell's fable about human nature transcends history and particular political events. We see how the fundamental characters of animals do not change. The animals behave consistently, whether in a noble or selfish spirit, through all the changes in the story from the feudal, aristocratic, conservative farm run by Mr. Jones to the modern, progressive, radical "Animal Farm" ruled by Napoleon.

We have already quoted one of Orwell's friends, whose young son thought that *Animal Farm* was just an animal story. But the reaction of the son of another Orwell friend suggests the opposite tendency too. The friend reported that his boy, a supporter of Britain's Conservative Party, was "delighted" with *Animal Farm* and considered it "very strong Tory [conservative] propaganda." Orwell's friend concluded his letter about *Animal Farm*:

I read it with great excitement. And then, thinking it over, and especially on showing it to other people, one realizes that the danger of this kind of perfection is that it means very different things to different readers. . . . I certainly don't mean that that is a fault in the allegory. . . . But I thought it worth warning you (while thanking you very heartily) that you must expect to be "misunderstood" on a large scale about this book; it is a form that inherently means more than the authors means, when it is handled sufficiently well.[3]

So the allegorical form, as well as the complexities of international politics, contributed to misunderstandings about *Animal Farm*. Then and later, Orwell's book—as we shall see in this casebook—came to mean many different things to different people.

Some other editors of the 1940s, who saw quite clearly the political dimension of *Animal Farm*, also rejected it precisely for that reason. Indeed that was the major reason why *Animal Farm* was rejected by two dozen British and American publishers before gaining acceptance for publication. (The scarcity of newsprint during wartime was a third, important reason for its rejection by publishers.)

Given the wartime alliance among the Allies, some publishers deemed *Animal Farm* far too controversial to be published. During World War II, the Soviet Union was an ally of the United States and Great Britain. Loyal to the united war effort of the Allies, four British editors rejected *Animal Farm* because they did not want to risk offending the Soviet Union by publishing such a harsh assault on its history. In the United States, numerous editors turned it down because they were Soviet sympathizers who considered Orwell's attack on the USSR unbalanced and exaggerated.

And yet, public opinion in Britain and America changed toward the USSR in 1945–46. As the need for wartime solidarity with the USSR ended with the defeat of Germany and Japan, and as Stalin's armies aggressively occupied much of Eastern Europe, the West's cordial attitude toward the USSR cooled. Publishers became more and more willing to criticize the USSR. Its leader, Joseph Stalin, had been affectionately dubbed "Uncle Joe" during World War II. Now, with the war over, British and American policymakers judged the USSR to be their greatest threat.

Ironically, *Animal Farm* now seemed to be a prophetic book, ahead of its time. Orwell seemed to have predicted the collapse of Allied alliance and unveiled the Soviet dictatorship as the new enemy of Western democracy. *Animal Farm* seemed to forecast the upcoming international faceoff: the Cold War between the democratic West and the communist nations led by the USSR.

Another twist of ironic fate was at hand for *Animal Farm*. A book that had, just months earlier, been rejected by publishers as either an unmarketable animal story or a dangerous political book now became a runaway best-seller.

Are we prone to make a similar errors about Orwell's book? Are readers today open to missing the political dimension of *Animal Farm*? Or, at minimum, to misunderstanding the complexities of international politics at midcentury? Yes—perhaps even more so than did the book's original audience. The historical context of *Animal Farm*, which covers a quarter-century ranging from the Russian Revolution (1917) to the Allies' wartime conference in Tehran (1943), is far removed from current issues in American international relations. The first two leaders of the USSR, Vladimir Lenin and Joseph Stalin, are little more than names to many young Americans today. Even World War II feels like a vague and distant episode to many Americans, a storybook event that American high school students study in their textbooks.

Indeed, the USSR—the acronym for the Union of Soviet Socialist Republics—does not even exist today. It was dissolved in December 1991. The former republics of the Soviet Union are now separate, independent nations. Russia is just one of fifteen states of the former USSR, a member of a loose confederation of nations known as the Commonwealth of Independent States.

This volume of the Greenwood Press Literature in Context Series is written in light of these facts. It aims to bridge the historical gulf between the current American scene and those events in the first half of the twentieth century that constitute the political background of *Animal Farm*.

Perhaps more so than with most other twentieth-century works, it is vital to approach *Animal Farm* with an awareness of its context. The reason is twofold. First, the meaning and even the genre of the book are easily misunderstood without a rich appreciation of this context. Second, that context is rapidly receding as the twentieth century ends and a new millenium dawns. We are now living in the postcommunist era of the so-called New World Order.

This new era has arisen in the wake of the collapse of the Berlin Wall in 1989 and the dismantling of the Soviet Union in 1991. So anti-Communism as a major political issue in the Western nations is virtually dead.

Thus, to understand and appreciate *Animal Farm* today, we need to understand and appreciate how, in the first half of the century, Communism and anti-Communism were among the most significant issues in American and British political affairs. And to do this, we need to understand the original political background of that period, against which Orwell wrote his book.

Our historical distance makes all that difficult. But we also possess the advantage of observing this period from a broader temporal perspective. Now that the Soviet Union has receded into history, the early decades of this century are easier to examine apart from the political controversies that earlier generations had to confront.

In that regard, Orwell's fable is even more valuable for American high school students than previously. *Animal Farm* can serve as a study aid in a number of ways. It can promote an understanding of the history and international politics of the twentieth century. It can stimulate classroom discussion of distant historical events, bringing them vividly to life. It can also help explain, in greatly simplified terms, the causes of the rise and fall of the Soviet Union. Students and teachers will find that the spirit of *Animal Farm* captures both the hope and tragedy of the Russian Revolution and that it provides an introduction to a few of the major figures in the history of communism.

And *Animal Farm* is a fable that offers simple, valuable political lessons. Among them are the following:

1. Power corrupts.
2. Revolutions tend to come full circle and devour their peoples.
3. Even good, decent people are vulnerable to power hunger and leader worship.

These are the three universal themes of *Animal Farm*, and we will be examining them in detail. The succeeding chapters also address the following topics at length:

- The beast fable and allegory as works of literature
- The use of personification
- The symbolic associations of historical personages with particular animals
- Marxist theory and the basic tenets of its leading thinkers

- The history of the Russian Revolution and its aftermath
- The cultural climate in Britain and the United States during the 1940s, when the USSR was a wartime and early postwar ally, an extremely tense political period that pitted communist supporters against anti-communist critics
- The history of response to *Animal Farm* in the half-century after its publication
- The life of George Orwell and how he came to write *Animal Farm*
- The themes of the abuse of power, the high cost of pursuing revolutionary ideals, and the use of manipulation, hypocrisy, and deception by leaders and governments

The first chapter discusses *Animal Farm* as a work of literature, including Orwell's use of allegory, the beast fable, and symbols. Chapters 2 through 6 address the historical context, the intricacies of the pertinent political issues, and Orwell's biography. Chapter 7 examines recent political issues relevant to *Animal Farm*.

As we have suggested, *Animal Farm* can serve as an aid to grasping twentieth-century history, both Russian and Western. With this in mind, this book pursues an interdisciplinary focus that includes historical, biographical, literary, and political documents. One of the special features of this book are the book reviews, book excerpts, and original interviews translated from Russian and German. Until now, these documents have not been available to an English-speaking public.

The source materials for this casebook include:

- Interviews with Russian and East German readers of Orwell
- Excerpts from personal memoirs and correspondence
- Literary essays and book reviews
- Historical and political studies
- Passages from the Soviet press
- Magazine and newspaper articles
- Literary articles
- Ink drawings and illustrations

As these documents attest, *Animal Farm* emerged from and has caused political controversy—but it has also sometimes been naively misjudged as unpolitical.

Mired in historical controversy? Completely innocent politically? By examining in detail the historical and political context of Orwell's fable, we will better comprehend how and why such extremely opposed views of the book have arisen.

But let us not forget that *Animal Farm* is, first and foremost, a work of literature. As Orwell declared in his essay, "Why I Write," "*Animal Farm* was the first book in which I tried, with full consciousness of what I was doing, to fuse political purpose and artistic purpose into one whole."

We turn, then, to our initial task: to appreciate the stunning literary achievement of *Animal Farm*.

NOTES

1. Cited in Bernard Crick, *George Orwell: A Life* (London: Penguin, 1980), p. 491. Subsequent references are cited as Crick.

2. *The Collected Essays, Journalism and Letters of George Orwell*, ed. Sonia Orwell and Ian Angus (London: 1968), vol. 3, pp. 405–6. All subsequent references are to this edition and are cited as CEJL.

3. Crick, p. 491.

1

Literary Analysis of *Animal Farm*

James Arnt Aune

THE MEANING OF *ANIMAL FARM*

A literary work is an act of communication, just like a political speech or an advertisement. It is composed by an author or group of authors. It consists of a message embodied in a set of linguistic and social conventions shared by a target audience in a particular time and place. The average American, for example, can make sense of a billboard containing a picture of a cowboy and the slogan, "Come to Marlboro Country," because an association between the macho cowboy and the smoking of Marlboro cigarettes has been built up in the public mind since the company decided to stop marketing Marlboros as a "women's" cigarette in the 1950s. Other English speakers who are not familiar with the Marlboro-cowboy association will find the billboard incomprehensible. Americans who visit England will sometimes see a billboard consisting of a torn piece of purple fabric. Someone has to explain to them that the advertisement is for Silk Cut cigarettes.

Like the cigarette advertisements, *Animal Farm* was composed by an author—George Orwell, the pen name of Eric Blair. Its message is an indictment of the communist betrayal of the ideals on which the Soviet Union was founded, told in the form of a fairy story (Orwell's original subtitle for the book) or allegorical fable.

Unlike the Marlboro or Silk Cut advertisements, however, *Animal Farm* lives beyond its immediate context and target audience. Works that do that become "art" or "literature"; we might look at cigarette ads in a history book a hundred years from now, but we will look at them more as an amusing documentation of unhealthy habits than as art. Since ancient Greece and Rome, students of human communication have given the label "rhetoric" to messages that have a primarily persuasive purpose, and "poetic" to messages that have a primarily imaginative or literary purpose.

In his book on the art of rhetoric, Aristotle argued that persuasive speakers and writers accomplish their goals by using three kinds of strategies: *Logos*, or logical appeal, uses the basic beliefs and values of audiences to lead them to a conclusion desired by the persuader. *Ethos*, or ethical appeal, refers to the persuader's ability to create in the mind of the audience that he or she is a credible person with good character and with the audience's best interests in mind. *Pathos*, or emotional appeal, works by connecting an argument with the audience's passions—anger, affection, fear, and so on.[1]

As persuasion, *Animal Farm* is a powerful argument against the delusions of Soviet Communism and the dishonesty of Western intellectuals sympathetic to the Soviet Union. Its logical appeal works by reducing the argument to the level of a fairy story, something so simple and obvious that perhaps intellectuals cannot understand it. Orwell creates an omniscient narrator in the novel who tells the story simply and plainly, as if representing the character of England itself, where "such concepts as justice, liberty, and objective truth are still believed in."[2] *Animal Farm* connects with our emotions by relying on conventional identifications of animals with certain human characteristics.

A literary-rhetorical analysis that identifies persuasive strategies in a literary work needs to begin with the work's immediate context. Some literary works refer to a political or social context that no longer makes much sense to the average reader. Swift's *Gulliver's Travels* and Shakespeare's history plays are good examples. Although some background historical knowledge may aid our appreciation of these works, we can usually appreciate them today for their purely "literary" rather than "persuasive" qualities. *Animal Farm*, on the other hand, is a rare example of a great work in which the timeless literary qualities are fused perfectly with the time-bound persuasive qualities. Like all other human communication, however, *Animal Farm* has communicated meanings to audiences in different social contexts, some of which were intended by the author and some of which were not.

THE ORIGINAL MEANING OF *ANIMAL FARM*

George Orwell wrote *Animal Farm* between November 1943 and February 1944. His unpublished preface to the book explains his intentions. He was angered by the fact that "the prevailing orthodoxy" in England in 1943 was "an uncritical admiration of Soviet Russia." This orthodoxy had been promoted by the English intelligentsia for many years, and the World War II alliance between England and the Soviet Union had extended this orthodoxy to the mainstream national press as well. It was easier, Orwell wrote, to criticize Winston Churchill, the British Prime Minister, than to criticize Stalin.[3]

Orwell's efforts to get the novel published confirmed his insight. Three prestigious English publishers of varying political views (Gollancz on the left, Cape in the center, and Faber & Faber on the right) rejected the manuscript. Secker & Warburg, an obscure left-wing publisher with a history of accepting anti-Stalinist works, accepted it.

Orwell was not only what Americans today call a "liberal." He was a democratic socialist. He was convinced that an unrestrained free market leads to widespread poverty and degradation and that it also corrupts the integrity of the democratic process. Like others on the left wing of the Labour Party, he supported a generous welfare state with free health care and education, as well as support for children, the disabled, and the aged. He believed that basic industries such as energy and transportation should be owned by the people, and not run for profit. Unlike Communists, however, he believed that freedom of speech and a free press were not incompatible with the quest for greater economic equality.

Orwell's experiences as a scholarship boy in the most exclusive English public school—Eton, what Americans would call a prep school—as well as his experiences as a policeman in colonial Burma had led him to a lifelong sympathy with the underdog. When the Republican government in Spain was overthrown by Franco's fascists (allies of Hitler and the Nazis), Orwell, like many other radicals in England and the United States, went to Spain in 1938 to fight for the Republican cause. His book *Homage to Catalonia* chronicles his discovery that the Communists fighting on the Republican side were not interested in liberating Spain, but in promoting Communism at all costs. Orwell fought in an organization (Partido Obrero de Unificación Marxista [POUM]; Workers' Party of Marxist Unity) sympathetic to Leon Trotsky (the Russian revolutionary who was defeated by Joseph Stalin in the battle to succeed Lenin as leader of the Soviet Union), and the Communists seemed more interested in destroying the Trotskyists than in defeating Franco. Orwell and his wife barely escaped Spain alive.

There was plenty of evidence by 1943 that the Soviet Union's leaders had betrayed the promise of the October Revolution of 1917. The problem was that many of the most intelligent and influential figures in England either denied the evidence or refused to examine it. The October Revolution had promised to improve the standard of living of the people, especially the peasants and the working class. It had promised to create a radical democracy by placing political and economic decision making in the hands of "soviets," or local, representative councils. It promised to eliminate class privilege, promoting a truly equal society. None of these things happened. In fact, by most measures, the people were far worse off than they had been under the rule of the Czar. Millions of people died as the result of famine due to failed economic policies or from the direct order of Joseph Stalin. Freedom of speech and political dissent in any form were punished with exile to prison camps, torture, or execution. The Soviet leaders were not content just to kill opponents; they paraded them in public before the eyes of the Western press, forcing them to confess to crimes against the state. They provided a higher standard of living for Communist Party members and bureaucrats than for the ordinary workers and peasants whom they professed to make "equal." They made a deal with their archenemy Adolf Hitler.

The problem was that many intelligent people refused to see these things. This fact probably explains why George Orwell decided to point them out in the form of a fairy story, or allegorical fable. Much like the fairy tale about "The Emperor's New Clothes," *Animal Farm* tells the reader that the truth about Communism is so simple that perhaps *only* a child can see it.

The literary form of the animal fable has been used perhaps from the beginning of recorded literature. Aesop's *Fables* dramatized simple, moral points for the edification of the reader. In the educational system of ancient Rome, which was designed to teach future orator-statesmen, the very first writing and speaking exercise was to paraphrase one of these fables.[4] Later, more complex forms, called *allegories*, developed complex correspondences between fictional characters and real-life political events or moral dilemmas; Edmund Spenser's *Faerie Queene* and John Bunyan's *Pilgrim's Progress* are perhaps the two best-known examples of allegory in English. But *Animal Farm* also harkens back to a famous English satire, Jonathan Swift's *Gulliver's Travels*, a book that on the surface was a combination of travel story and animal fable, intended to express outrage at ridiculous political and philosophical attitudes popular among the English intelligentsia of his time. For most readers today, the targets of Swift's satire are unfamiliar, and the book can still be read as a commentary on the human condition as well as an entertaining story.

Orwell's allegorical satire has more direct reference to real-world people and events than these earlier examples. Part of the pleasure in reading the story, as well as educational usefulness, lies in the reader's detective work in tracking 'down the allegorical correspondences.

CHARACTERS AND EVENTS

Chart I: Characters

Animal Farm	Historical Figures
Farmer Jones	Czar of Russia
The Pigs	The Bolsheviks
Major	A combination of Marx and Lenin
Napoleon	Stalin
Snowball	Trotsky
Boxer	The working class—"Stakhanovite"
Mollie	White Russians
Moses	The Russian Orthodox and Roman Catholic church
Squealer	*Pravda*; Soviet propagandists

Napoleon's dogs	The secret police
Pilkington	England/Churchill
Frederick	Hitler (after Frederick the Great, admired by Hitler)
Minimus	Mayakovsky
Whymper	Western businessmen and journalists
Wild animals	The peasants

Chart II: Events

Animal Farm	Soviet History
The Rebellion	October Revolution (1917)
Battle of the Cowshed	The Civil War (1918–19)
Snowball's leadership	Trotsky leads Red Army
Rebellions on nearby farms	Hungarian and German communist rebellions (1919, 1923)
Revolt of the hens	Kronstadt rebellion (1921)
Napoleon's dealings with Whymper/Wellington markets	Treaty of Rapallo (1922)
Snowball's defeat	Trotsky's exile (1927)
Snowball and the windmill	Trotsky's emphasis on heavy industry
Napoleon's opposition	Stalin's emphasis on agriculture
Snowball's desire to send pigeons to nearby farms	Trotsky's "Permanent Revolution"
Napoleon's opposition	Stalin's "Socialism in One Country"
Demolition of windmill	Failure of First Five-Year Plan
Starvation	Ukraine famine (1933)
Confession of animals to aiding Snowball	Purge Trials (1936–38)
Deal with Frederick	Nazi-Soviet Pact of 1939
Battle with Frederick	German invasion (1941)
End of the novel	Tehran Conference (1943)

Other Parallels

Animal Farm	Soviet Union
Hoof and horn	Hammer and sickle

Order of the Green Banner	Order of Lenin
"Beasts of England"	"The Internationale"
Animalism	Marxism-Leninism or dialectical materialism

Mr. Jones, the cruel and drunken owner of Manor Farm, treats his animals badly. The old boar Major, shortly before his death, has a dream in which he imagines a world in which animals have overthrown their human masters. He teaches the animals a song, "Beasts of England," which expresses this yearning for a better world. He also teaches them seven commandments, warning them not to adopt human habits such as living in a house, sleeping in a bed, wearing clothes, drinking alcohol, smoking tobacco, touching money, or engaging in trade. Above all, all animals are equal.

Major has characteristics of both Karl Marx and V. I. Lenin. Karl Marx (1818–83) called for workers of the world to unite against their capitalist oppressors. He taught that the capitalists' downfall was inevitable because of inherent flaws in the capitalist economy, but it was possible for a unified working class to overthrow them now. Marx was influential on both communist and socialist parties. He never really specified how revolutionary change was to take place, and his interpreters continue to debate if his writings were responsible for the evil uses to which they have been put in communist countries.

Lenin (1870–1924) was the leader of the Bolshevik Party in its successful October 1917 revolution against the Czarist regime. He provided a theory of political change and revolution to supplement the basic Marxist indictment of the capitalist economy. His insight, first expressed in his book *What Is to Be Done?* (1902), was that the masses would never revolt on their own. The most they would ever do by themselves is organize trade unions. Only a rigidly disciplined "vanguard party" composed of the intelligentsia and "advanced" members of the working class would be able to engage in the subversive activity necessary to bring about radical social change.[5] Lenin was skeptical about the achievements of liberal democracy: freedom of speech and press, freedom of religion, and free elections. He died relatively young, disappointed in the results of his Revolution and concerned about the growing distance between Communist Party leaders and the people.

The early death of Lenin, like the death of Major, led to a power struggle between his successors: Leon Trotsky (1879–1940) and Joseph Stalin (1879–1953), who correspond to Snowball and Napoleon, respectively. Trotsky was the leader of the Red Army in the Civil War of 1918–1919, when anti-Bolshevik armies, aided by Western capitalist countries, tried to overthrow the Bolshevik regime. Like Snowball's heroism in the Battle of the Cowshed, Trotsky's leadership in the civil war made him extremely popular.

Trotsky was in favor of rapid industrialization, a program symbolized in the novel by the plan to build the windmill. Stalin, however, emphasized agricultural policy, as does Napoleon. Trotsky was in favor of exporting revolution worldwide (sometimes called Trotsky's theory of "Permanent Revolution"), while Stalin was more interested in protecting the Soviet Union from outside forces (often summarized as "Socialism in One Country"). In 1927, Stalin defeated Trotsky at the Communist Party Congress, encouraging his followers to shout Trotsky down to prevent him speaking, much as the sheep do to Snowball before he is driven off the farm. Stalin had gained control of the secret police (Napoleon's guard dogs), who continued to work against Trotsky after his exile abroad. Trotsky was finally killed (with an ax) by a Soviet agent in Mexico City in 1940.

Animal Farm was originally published in England by the firm of Secker & Warburg, which had previously issued works sympathetic to Trotsky. Orwell himself had fought with the Trotskyist POUM during the Spanish Civil War, but it is clear from his other writings that he opposed Trotsky's willingness to suspend civil liberties. The fact that the pigs (Bolsheviks) hoard all the milk for themselves early in the novel is perhaps a sign that Orwell believed that the "animalist" philosophy itself, not just the personality of Napoleon, was responsible for the defeat of the animals' hopes. One commentator on the novel, Sanford Pinsker, argues that the reader does not need to know anything about Soviet history in order to appreciate the novel; Major's original division of the world into man versus animal led to the horrors inflicted by the pigs. Any system that is based on systematic hatred of one group for another will lead to oppression.[6]

One event in the novel seems out of historical sequence: the revolt of the hens against the order to increase egg production. The event parallels the rebellion of Soviet sailors at Kronstadt in 1921, which Trotsky brutally repressed (although there are also some parallels to the peasants' revolt against forced collectivization

Snowball/Trotsky is chased out of *Animal Farm* by the dogs (the NKVD, or pre-war Soviet secret police), as Napoleon/Stalin looks on with gleeful smugness. The scene corresponds to Trotsky's expulsion from the Communist Party in 1928 and his fleeing to Mexico City, where he was murdered by NKVD agents in 1940. Created by Paul Rodden.

of their farms in 1929). Still, Napoleon is directly responsible for the evils that follow, and the events have close parallels in Soviet history up to 1943: the widespread starvation that occurs during the first winter after the rebellion corresponds to millions of deaths by starvation in the Ukraine in 1933.

Several animals falsely confessed to betraying the Animal Revolution and were torn to pieces by Napoleon's dogs. The scene corresponds to Stalin's purges, a series of show trials during 1936–38 that involved trumped-up indictments and executions of numerous Old Bolsheviks who had led the 1917 Russian Revolusion. Created by Paul Rodden.

The public trial at which animals confess to various crimes is similar to highly publicized purge trials of 1936–38. Kryuchkov confessed to a crime similar to that of the sheep who murdered an old ram "by chasing him around and around a bonfire when

An unshaven, wearied Farmer Jones, expelled from his farm by his own rebellious animals, confers with his neighboring farmers—stout, pug-nosed Frederick and bald, indolent, angular Pilkington—on how to recapture his property. The scene corresponds to Russia's maneuverings to explore possible treaties with Germany and England during the 1920s and 30s, up until Stalin did sign a mutual non-aggression pact with Hitler in 1939. Created by Thomas G. Rodden.

he was suffering with a cough." He had purposely arranged long walks and bonfires that affected Maxim Gorky's (a Bolshevik writer) weak lungs.[7]

The pile of corpses at Napoleon's feet, though shocking to the animals, is eventually accepted by them as a necessary defense of the revolution. Squealer, the archetypal Soviet propagandist (perhaps corresponding to the newspaper *Pravda*), makes the case for Napoleon. Minimus, a poet who corresponds to the Bolshevik writer Mayakovsky, writes a poem honoring Napoleon. Journalists who should have known better widely covered the show trials in the American and European press, in terms largely sympathetic to the Stalinist side, although the great American philosopher and socialist John Dewey organized an inquiry that exonerated the victims.

The various dealings with neighboring farms parallel first the Treaty of Rapallo in 1922, which led to the recognition of the Soviet Union by the Western powers. Frederick clearly represents Adolf Hitler, who greatly admired the German Emperor Frederick. Although for many years Hitler had been identified as the chief opponent of the Soviet Union, in 1939 Stalin arranged for a mutual nonaggression treaty between Germany and the Soviet Union. This startling turnabout disillusioned many Communists in the West, but once Hitler attacked the Soviet Union in 1941, Stalin became an ally of both England and the United States, and there was little criticism of him or his policies, even by conservatives. Pilkington, the other nearby farmer, is rather lazy and aristocratic, preferring hunting and fishing to active management of his farm. This portrait of Winston Churchill is distinctly negative, but fits the distaste Orwell and Labour Party supporters felt for Churchill's upper-class values.

The ending of the novel takes the reader up to the Tehran Conference in 1943, where Stalin, Churchill, and Roosevelt held a joint meeting. It is impossible, finally, to tell the difference between pig and man. This conclusion is no more flattering to Churchill and Roosevelt than it is to Stalin, but it fits Orwell's persuasive purposes as an independent socialist critic of both the Western capitalist countries and the Soviet Union. In his preface to the Ukrainian edition of the book, Orwell writes,

> A number of readers may finish the book with the impression that it ends in the complete reconciliation of the pigs and the humans. That was not my intention; on the contrary I meant it to end on a loud note of discord, for I wrote it immediately after the Teheran Conference which everybody had thought had established the best possible relations between the USS and the West. I personally did not believe that such good relations would last long; and, as events have shown, I wasn't far wrong.[8]

Orwell's sympathy for ordinary workers comes out most clearly in the portrait of Boxer, whose death is the saddest moment in the novel. (Boxer is also similar to the figure of Stakhanov, who was featured in Soviet propaganda as the "ideal" worker.) Orwell's dislike for religion is expressed in the figure of Moses, the tame raven who preaches to the animals that they will go to Sugar Candy Mountain (heaven) when they die. The reappearance of Moses late in the novel parallels the effort of Stalin to reach out to the Roman Catholic church in order to gain support for his policy toward Poland.

There are some other symbolic correspondences in the novel that are worth noting: the hoof and horn flag is like the Soviet flag with the hammer and sickle (symbolizing the workers and the peasants); the Order of the Green Banner is like the Order of Lenin; and the song "Beasts of England" is like the Communist hymn "The Internationale."

The general strategy of personification Orwell uses relies on a number of commonsense associations we have with certain animals. For example, a raven is a fairly sinister bird, but tameable by human beings in authority—an appropriate personification of religion, at least in Orwell's rather hostile view. A horse is a noble beast, one of humanity's oldest animal helpers, and Boxer and Clover are the most pleasant of the characters. Clover's effort to warn Boxer to escape from the knacker's van is probably the saddest moment in the novel. A knacker buys old horses and grinds them up for dog food or glue. At first, one might be inclined to note the "human" characteristics of Boxer and Clover, but it is really the pigs who are the most human creatures in the novel. Orwell's choice of the pig to personify the Communists' works on several different levels. Pigs are among the most intelligent barnyard animals. They do no useful labor (like horses do). They are greedy and vicious. Anyone who has lived on a farm or in a rural area has heard stories of pigs devouring small children who wander into their pens. For medical purposes, there are aspects of the pig's physiology that are very close to humans'. (Some insulin, for instance, is derived from pigs.) The vicious, greedy, and nonproductive qualities of pigs make them the ideal personification of the Marxist intellectuals who profess to speak in the name of the workers, but do nothing productive themselves except spout propaganda and engage in murder.

But it is above all the smooth development of the plot of the novel that keeps the reader's attention. There seems literally not a wasted word. A historian might have required a thousand pages to write an accurate account of twenty-seven years of Soviet history.

The newly liberated Animal Farm adopted a flag featuring the animals' body parts: a hoof and horns. The animals then proceeded to build a windmill (a symbol of Stalin's Five-Year Plan) to generate electrical power. Our drawing caricatures the windmill, which includes here the emblems of the USSR flag: the hammer and sickle, which symbolized the alliance of workers and peasants under communism. Created by Daniel Reat.

Moses the raven preaches to the animals that they will go to Sugar Candy Mountain (heaven) when they die. The raven represents the Russian Orthodox Church, whose return to the USSR was permitted by Stalin during World War II. Created by Craig Thompson.

Orwell does so in fewer than a hundred pages, and in language understandable even by young children. The simplicity of language is essential to Orwell's overall persuasive point: the Soviet Communists' actions are so obviously evil that even a child can understand them. Why cannot everyone in England and the United States see that?

OTHER AUDIENCES

Even Orwell's publisher seemed to worry about the impact of the novel. Accepted for publication in 1944, it was not actually published until August 1945, when the war in Europe had been over for three months. The book was an immediate success. It was a Book-of-the-Month Club selection in the United States. The Signet paperback edition, published in 1956, has sold several million copies. *Animal Farm* appeared as a radio play and as a cartoon (with the animals defeating the pigs at the end!). Eventually it became a school text in both England and the United States.[9]

Orwell died in 1950, at the relatively young age of forty-six, from tuberculosis. He was poor for his entire life and did not live to see the full extent of his fame and influence. His other novel about totalitarianism, *1984*, continues to be read as a powerful indictment of Communism, as well as a prophetic warning about technological invasion of privacy. As John Rodden documents in his book *The Politics of Literary Reputation*, there has been considerable debate about what would have happened to Orwell's political beliefs had he lived longer, with conservatives and radicals both claiming his legacy.

What got lost in the American reception of *Animal Farm* was the sense that Orwell was criticizing both Communism and capitalism. The Signet Classics edition, still the most widely read version, quoted Orwell's statement: "Every line I have written since 1936 has been written, directly or indirectly, against totalitarianism." What American readers did not get was the rest of Orwell's sentence: "and for democratic Socialism, as I understand it."[10] The Everyman's Library edition by Alfred A. Knopf (1993) contains more useful background information, as well as a corrected text. Just as acts of communication sometimes live beyond their immediate historical purpose and context, their actual understanding by audiences is framed by their dissemination in the mass media or in educational institutions. It was not politically safe to talk about anti-communist socialism in the 1950s in the United States— a fact that Orwell no doubt would have deplored as much as the silence about Stalin in the British press in the 1940s.

Finally, if *Animal Farm* became an instrument of Cold War propaganda by Western capitalist countries, what will future audiences with a limited historical memory of Communism make of the novel? Does it contain the seeds of the current call for animal rights? Orwell based the details of the novel on his own experience as a farmer from 1936 to 1940 (when he kept a goat named Muriel). Does the novel, as Sanford Pinsker writes, make a much more general statement about the consequences of polarizing rhetoric such as Major's? Or is it a meditation on the theme that power, no matter who wields it, is inherently corrupting?[11] If so, the enduring message of the novel would subvert Orwell's own political purposes: all efforts at radical change are doomed to fail; one should not tamper with the natural order of things. Despite the simplicity of the novel, these questions remain in the audience's mind, serving as the basis for continued meditation on the relationship between morality and politics.

TOPICS FOR WRITTEN OR ORAL EXPLORATION

1. Define the *rhetorical* and *poetic* functions of literature and communication in your own words.

2. If the rhetorical elements of a literary work outweight its poetic elements, does that mean that a work is unlikely to survive past its immediate context?

3. Why did Orwell write *Animal Farm* in the form of an animal fable? Do his intentions matter in answering that question?

4. Should schools continue to assign *Animal Farm* as an important work of literature now that the Cold War is over?

5. Do you think that your teachers and other planners of your curriculum have political purposes in mind when they assign particular books for you to read?

6. Some people have criticized Orwell for being pessimistic. Is it fair to read *Animal Farm* as cautioning against any attempt to make society more just?

7. What is the saddest moment in the novel? What is the scariest? What tools of language does Orwell use to help us feel those feelings?

8. In the 1950s there was a cartoon version of *Animal Farm* that ended up with the animals rising up against the pigs, and everyone living happily ever after. Would the book be better with a happy ending? Why or why not?

9. Learn how to use the *Reader's Guide to Periodical Literature*. Select some examples of discussions of the Soviet Union in 1938, 1943, 1953, and 1989, and compare and contrast them.

10. Is Major "responsible" for what happens later?

11. After 1989, the countries under Soviet control gained their freedom very quickly. If you were writing a new ending for *Animal Farm*, how would you discuss the 1989 events in allegorical terms?

12. Does reading *Animal Farm* make you think differently about animals? Most people eat pigs, chickens, and cattle. Most Americans do not eat horses, although our pets and Europeans do. Where did your lunch today come from?

13. Why does the novel end where it does?

14. How would you sing "Beasts of England"? Find a recording of the "Internationale." (The English popular singer Billy Bragg sings it on a recent recording.)

15. Find a copy of the Signet edition of *Animal Farm*, the recent Every-

man edition, and, if possible, the original Secker & Warburg edition and translations into other languages. What are similarities and differences in packaging?

16. Define the terms "liberal," "conservative," "Left," "Right," "Socialist," "Democratic Socialist," and "Communist." Where did the terms originate? Are their meanings different in the United States and in Europe? Have their meanings changed since the publication of *Animal Farm?*

17. Look up the terms *allegory, fable,* and *satire* in the Glossary and analyze why the terms are appropriate labels for *Animal Farm.*

18. Would things have turned out differently if Snowball had won the power struggle with Napoleon? Are there any clues in the novel itself about this issue?

SUGGESTED READINGS

Crick, Bernard. *George Orwell.* Boston: Little, Brown, 1981. The standard biography.

Letemendia, V. C. "Revolution on *Animal Farm*: Orwell's Neglected Commentary." *Journal of Modern Literature* 18 (1992): 127–37.

Meyers, Jeffrey. *A Reader's Guide to George Orwell.* London: Thames and Hudson, 1975. In Chapter 7, "The Political Allegory of *Animal Farm,*" Meyers provides an extensive discussion of allegorical correspondences between the novel and Soviet history.

Orwell, George. *The Road to Wigan Pier.* London: V. Gollancz, 1937. A journalistic account of the condition of the working class in England; perhaps the best expression of Orwell's own political beliefs.

———. *Homage to Catalonia.* London: Secker & Warburg, 1938. A moving account of Orwell's service in the Spanish Civil War and a devastating critique of communist behavior.

Pinsker, Sanford. "A Note to the Teaching of Orwell's *Animal Farm.*" *CEA Critic* (1978): 18–19.

Rodden, John. *The Politics of Literary Reputation.* New York: Oxford University Press, 1989. A discussion of the differing interpretations and political uses of Orwell's writings after his death.

NOTES

1. The best translation is Aristotle, *On Rhetoric: A Theory of Civic Discourse,* tr. George Kennedy (New York: Oxford University Press, 1991).

2. George Orwell, "England Your England," in *A Collection of Essays* (New York: Harcourt Brace Jovanovich, 1953), p. 261.

3. See Orwell's original preface (not published until 1972) to *Animal Farm*, "The Freedom of the Press," Appendix I, *Animal Farm* (New York: Alfred A. Knopf, 1993), p. 99.

4. Quintilian, *Institutes of Oratory*, Vol. I, tr. H. E. Butler (London: Heinemann, 1920), p. 157; Book I. ix.2–3.

5. V. I. Lenin, *What Is to Be Done? Burning Questions of Our Movement* (New York: International Publishers, 1969). A good introduction (in comic book form) to Marx and some of the history of Marxism is *Marx for Beginners* (New York: Pantheon, 1976).

6. Sanford Pinsker, "A Note to the Teaching of Orwell's *Animal Farm*," *CEA Critic* (1978): 18–19.

7. Jeffrey Meyers, "The Political Allegory of *Animal Farm*," *A Reader's Guide to George Orwell* (London: Thames and Hudson, 1975), p. 141.

8. Appendix II, *Animal Farm* (Knopf edition), p. 113.

9. For details, see John Rodden, *The Politics of Literary Reputation: The Making and Claiming of "St. George" Orwell* (New York: Oxford University Press, 1989).

10. The source of Orwell's statement is his essay, "Why I Write," in George Orwell, *A Collection of Essays* (New York: Harcourt Brace Jovanovich, 1953), p. 314. Julian Symons discusses the omission in his introduction to the Knopf edition, p. xvii.

11. Meyer's "Political Allegory," puts it this way: "Once in power, the revolutionary becomes as tyrannical as his oppressor" (p. 143).

2

Historical Context: Basic Tenets of Marxism
William E. Shanahan III

The mid-1800s were a time alive with socialism.[1] Radical revolutionary forces and theories could be found throughout Europe and the United States. People believed that society might change drastically and suddenly. Among these competing socialisms was Marxism, named after the provocative and insightful political theorist and philosopher Karl Marx. Marx's brand of socialism was not the only choice during this vibrant revolutionary time. Indeed, Marx himself felt the need to attack the other political theories vying for popular appeal.

The idea that the government might be radically altered or even abolished is a more distant thought today. During Marx's time and the time following him, however, this potential was recognized and accomplished. Marx and his philosophy, Marxism, changed the world, especially this century's world. The ramifications of this revolutionary theory still are being felt.

IDEOLOGICAL KEYNOTES

> It is not the consciousness of men that determines their being, but, on the contrary, their social being that determines their consciousness.[2]

To understand *Animal Farm* is at least in part to have some understanding of Marxism. After all, Animalism is the animals' Marxism. The purpose of this chapter is to provide a way into Marx's sometimes very difficult philosophy. There are many unfamiliar terms and concepts in Marxism. Its history is long and arduous. One does not need to understand this history fully in order to discern its applicability to *Animal Farm*.

The Concept of Production

Some of Marxism's basic ideological tenets include production and labor, the forces and relations of production, the bourgeoisie and the proletariat, and alienation. The cornerstone of Marx's view of the world is that humans are producers, that human history is a "history of production." Quite simply, humans produce. This, no doubt, is the experience that many of us have if we think about it. We produce an enormous amount of things. Our society is geared toward the production of objects for our consumption. We produce food. We also produce the tools necessary to produce that food. We produce vehicles to transport it, packages to contain it, stores in which to sell it, advertising to entice consumers to buy it, money for them to buy it, tools necessary to consume it, places to dispose of it. The list goes on almost indefinitely. A casual walk down any supermarket aisle demonstrates just how much we are producers. Take any product around you as you read this book: your desk, pencils, pens, paper, your shoes, clothes—anything. Now think about the sheer volume of products required to bring it to you. The list is staggering and ends from your own exhaustion rather than exhausting the list of products. In other words, you, no doubt, would give out before that list. Our brand of capitalism ensures a product list as long as our imagination.

Animal Farm is no different. Just like any functioning farm, it produces quite a bit. The animals produce different crops, including hay and corn. Apples are grown and gathered. The animals produce directly from their bodies. The hens lay eggs, and the cows provide milk. Many of the animals have offspring that are used on the old farm as produce. This changes with the change of leadership. Once the animals are "freed," they expand their range of production. The windmill is an excellent example. The animals even create a flag for their new farm. Animal Farm's inhabitants are ideal examples of Marx's producers.

This cornerstone should not be viewed, however, as something akin to fundamental human nature. Basically Marx defines humans "as a tool-making animal."[3] This is to say that tool-making is a fundamental characteristic of humans but itself is determined by other forces, specifically economic ones. Humans make tools according to the economic forces that come to bear on them. The animals also learn to use the human tools. Boxer and Clover harnessed themselves to cutters and rakes to help bring in the hay crop. Other tools, like rakes, were more difficult for the animals, but most human tools eventually get used by the animals. Tool-making is a historical process wherein the material conditions of society affect what is made, how it is used, and what ultimately is produced. This basic human trait fits nicely with humans' need to produce.

Humans also produce less tangible products besides things and objects. We are producers "of ideas, of conceptions, of consciousness." We conceive and think such that our "mental production [is] expressed in the language of politics, laws, morality, religion, metaphysics, etc., of a people."[4] Humans produce in words and in thinking much the same way that they produce objects and things. The animals on Animal Farm are no different. They produce communication with one another. The learn to produce written words. Even complex productions like political ideology—for example, the Seven Commandments—get produced by the liberated animals. They create their own slogans and songs. We produce in relationship to others and in activities both alone and together. We produce those relationships and those activities. According to Marx, if we are in the world, then we produce.

Once again, brief reflection on this point reveals its potential to help explain the world. How do we interact with one another? With society? What activity are we engaged in when we think? Talk? What happens when we make laws? Practice religion? What are you doing now as you attempt to understand Marxism? What are animals doing when they organize meetings? What about when they discuss rebellion? Devise strategy and formulate tactics?

Marx would argue that you and they are producing understanding, ideas, conceptions, and the like. These are not given, but must be worked out for one's self. No matter how much help is given, ultimately you produce your understanding. Hopefully, as you produce understanding, you also will produce relationships through which that understanding can be shared. Humans produce in many different ways, concrete and abstract. Animals, especially Orwell's, also produce in many different ways. The history of humanity is a history of production. The story of *Animal Farm* also is a story of production.

Forces, Means, and Relations of Production

The forces of production include both individuals' labor and the various means of production employed in that labor. Labor is the exercise of power that changes the value of an object. When trees are transformed into paper, for instance, human labor has changed its value from the value of a tree to the value of paper (one might wonder if value is added or subtracted in such an instance). The means of production in this example include the processing mill. So the forces of production required for the paper in this book include at least the labor and machinery used in its production. Labor itself becomes a product or object—since labor generally produces more value than it takes away, labor provides for a surplus value. This surplus value can be bought and sold. Thus, labor becomes a commodity. Labor produces value and thereby is a value. Labor and the means of production constitute the production forces.

Animal Farm is no exception. The value of the animals' labor transforms the products produced on their farm. The hay crop is an example. The animals' waste products are used to fertilize the field in order to increase its yield. The animals are exceptional weeders (especially since this work doubles as feeding). Thus, the hay crop is not hindered by undesirable plants. The animals help to till the soil, making it more receptive for the seeds. The value of the hay crop is increased as a result of the added value of the animals' labor. The example of the hay crop is repeated everywhere on the farm. Products are more valuable as a result of the animals' contributions.

Importantly, however, human (and animal) production is dependent on the material forces of a society. The forces include especially the economic forces of any given society. On Manor

Farm, the farm does not exist in a vacuum. Mr. Jones produces commodities on his farm that are exchanged with other producers for other products and capital. Even the pigs eventually decide to trade with the outside world because they are not able to produce everything that they need or desire. If an outside market for the farm products does not exist, then they would not be able to function in the same manner. We do not produce independent of economic forces, but are determined by them.

The Concept of Class

The relations of production consist in the ownership of the production forces. Marx divides society into two classes, the bourgeoisie and the proletariat. The bourgeoisie own or control the production forces, the raw materials, the property: the ruling or dominant class. The proletariat class is made up of the workers. In United States–style capitalism, this class division is prevalent. Generally the bourgeoisie own the factories and machinery, while the proletariat produce surplus value through labor. Occasionally in this version of capitalism, workers own shares in the company. Marx, however, differentiates between legal ownership and control of the production forces. Although workers may own part of a company, almost never do they control that company. Capitalism's production forces are firmly in the hands of the bourgeoisie and out of the hands of the proletariat.

The relations of production are obvious on Manor Farm. Ownership of the production forces is concentrated in the hands of the Jones. Mr. and Mrs. Jones own the farm. A rigid division of labor and class exists on the farm. Like most other farms, the workers (here, including the animals) do not control the farm's operation. They do not participate in the decision making. The physical work is done by the workers, while the intellectual work mostly is done by Jones. After the rebellion, a similar class division emerges between the pigs and the rest of the animal workers. Despite a political philosophy that should not allow one class of animals to rule over others, the pigs take on the role of the land owners. They do the thinking, and their comrades do the rest of the work. Essentially the pigs function as Mr. Jones had previously. Class division and the previous relations of production remain unchanged.

Alienation

One of the results of these relations and this class division is alienation. Labor becomes an object that exists outside the worker rather than being an essential part of who she or he is. Labor produces value in excess of wages and thus becomes a tradable commodity. Human labor is reduced to the status of a thing, not as an essential part of humanness. Labor's product is removed from the worker. What should be a satisfying, normalizing way of being in the world becomes an estranged, alien experience. Labor no longer sustains the worker, instead only providing barely enough to get by.

The animals on Manor Farm suffer intensely from this form of alienation. As Major pointed out, their lives were "miserable, laborious, and short." The Major's assessment of life paraphrases Thomas Hobbes's famous line that characterizes the lives of humanity as "solitary, poor, nasty, brutish, and short." The animals got only just enough food to survive. They had to work long hours under extreme conditions. Jones was able to make money on their toil. One of the worst aspects of this alienation occurred when an animal had offspring. This "product" was taken from the animal, usually fairly quickly. The ultimate production, birth, was denied to its producer. It is no small wonder that the animals suffered alienation of the sort Marx predicted.

A second aspect of alienation for Marx is that this production of surplus value and transformation of labor into an object works directly against the worker. The alien object "confronts" the worker in a negative fashion. The surplus value is employed by the bourgeoisie to heighten class division and distinctions, to *de*value the proletariat. Those in control use their power to keep the worker down. The more the worker produces, the worse the situation becomes:

> (. . . the more the worker produces, the less he has to consume; the more values he creates, the more valueless, the more unworthy he becomes; the better formed his product, the more deformed becomes the worker; the more civilized his object the more barbarous becomes the worker; the more ingenious labour becomes, the duller becomes the worker and the more he becomes nature's bondsman.)[5]

The proletariat provides the bourgeoisie with the means to oppress them. Obviously the worker is directly denied the products
of her or his labor. The things workers produce are the property
of the owners. So not only is the workers' labor as product denied
them, but the very thing they are producing is denied also. Capitalism, then, alienates the proletariat on two distinct levels and
uses that alienation against them. The relations of production and
the forces of production are at odds.

The production relations are certainly at odds with the production forces on Manor Farm. This second form of alienation
abounds there. The more the animals produce, the stronger Jones
becomes. He is able to buy new bits and reins. As more animals
are produced, more fields can be managed. As more fields are
worked, more animal labor is required. The animals keep producing more and more food, yet they receive less and less of it. They
frequently are cut off from their offspring, never to nurture or be
loved by them. The animals embody the worker alienation Marx
described. This alienation eventually can explode into class conflict.

Class Conflict

These relations of production under capitalism, according to
Marx, create class conflict. The way to revolution is through the
conflict between production forces and relations. At a certain
point, the producers of the products come into conflict with the
owners of the production. When this happens, society is torn up,
and an era of revolution takes place. Revolution is not so much
brought about by the proletariat as it is the result of the contra-
diction between forces and relations. The proletariat become the
agents of that revolution because the material economic forces of
society necessitate that they do so. There is a sense of inevitability
in Marx's notion of revolution. Though individual workers unite
to form a revolutionary force, they are not strictly the driving force
of that revolution. The revolutionary source area is located in society's economic forces. Humans are part of history and act within
that history. The material economic conditions of that history dictate its terms.

The revolution on Manor Farm results from the great disparity
between what is being produced and what is being distributed.

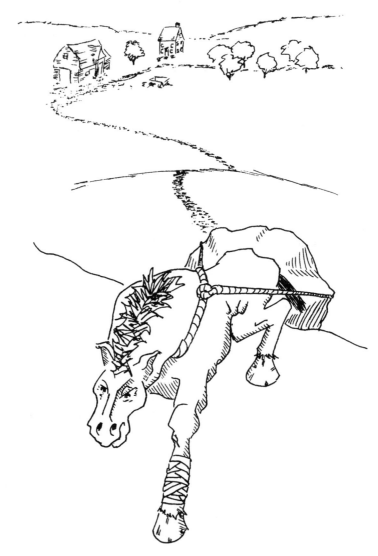

Boxer, whose mottos were "I must work harder" and "Napoleon is always right," labored even past exhaustion to build the windmill. Boxer represents the figure of Stakhanov, who was featured in Soviet propaganda as the "ideal worker." Created by Paul Rodden.

The animals could see all that was being produced, yet they were near starvation. The situation of the farm was increasingly obvious to most of the animals. Every day they made more and more food and ate less and less. Humans were working them unbelievably hard and then killing them at the end of their very difficult lives.

Mollie took a blue ribbon from Mrs. Jones' dressing table and admired herself in
the mirror. The other animals reproached her, and she soon left the farm for the
old cart life. Mollie represents Russia's counter-revolutionary forces, who prefer
life before the Bolshevik Revolution. Created by Paul Rodden.

The situation eventually became unacceptable to the animals. The
gap between what they made and what they ate resulted in the
rebellion. Class conflict raged briefly while the animals righted the
wrongs of their little society. Class conflict results when the relations and forces of production come in too great a conflict.

The Contribution of Lenin

One of Lenin's central contributions to Marxism was his belief that the spontaneous revolution needed some help. Rather than happening strictly as a result of class division, the revolution required a revolutionary vanguard which would agitate the masses and direct the course of the revolution:

I assert:

1) that no movement can be durable without a stable organization of leaders to maintain continuity;

2) that the more widely the masses are spontaneously drawn into the struggle and form the basis of the movement and participate in it, the more necessary is it to have such an organization, and the more stable must it be. . . .

3) that the organization must consist chiefly of persons engaged in revolutionary activities as a profession;

4) that in a country with an autocratic government, the more we *restrict* the membership of this organization to persons who are engaged in revolutionary activities as a profession and who have been professionally trained in the art of combating the political police, the more difficult will it be to catch the organization; and

5) the *wider* will be the circle of men and women of the working class or other classes of society able to join the movement and perform active work in it.[6]

This is one of the most controversial aspects of Lenin's works. A revolutionary vanguard—a small group of committed revolutionaries at the forefront of the revolution—flies in the face of Marx's contention that the forces and relations of production eventually would come into such conflict that revolution results. Since the vanguard aims its activities at *all* members of society, the proletariat focus of Marx is neglected. Also, the restricted membership and organizational secrecy are contradicted by the open, democratic-style participation Marx called for. Arguably, Lenin's call for a vanguard led to much of the horrible excesses in the Soviet Union over the years. Lenin was successful in his call for this vanguard.

Animal Farm provides some insight into the desirability of leading a revolution with a small vanguard. The story of rebellion on Manor Farm is begun by just such an elite band of revolutionaries: the pigs. The pigs determine the content and the direction of the revolution. They are the rebellion's architects. Rather than result-ing strictly from the forces and relations of production coming into conflict, the Animal Farm rebellion is the result largely of the pigs' initiative. Thus, the outcome of the rebellion can be traced to this revolutionary beginning. The final section of this chapter provides an analysis of what results from this Leninist approach to revolu-tionary change.

The Contribution of Stalin

Marx was helped into the twentieth century by another extra-ordinarily important figure in the history of Russia and the Soviet Union: Joseph Stalin. Stalin builds on the concept of the revolu-tionary vanguard and attempts to bring to life a "revolution from above." He argues that the Marx's world is not the world in which the Soviet Union must fight the socialist battle. Most important, according to Stalin, his country is encircled by capitalism. In Marx's time, the United States had not grown to the size and influence it enjoyed during the early twentieth century. Marx's prediction that the state would wither away after the socialist revolution could not be accomplished in the face of capitalism's power. The revolution-ary state (a direct outgrowth of Lenin's revolutionary vanguard) must remain in order to combat capitalism and direct the ongoing socialist revolution.

The revolutionary state is what grows out of the rebellion on Manor Farm. The pigs, like Stalin, refuse to give up power. They *need* to "help" the rest of the animals to succeed on their newly reorganized farm. Running a farm is a complex job, after all, just anybody cannot be expected to know how. Also just like the fledg-ling USSR, Animal Farm needs help in dealing with its surrounding neighbors who are hostile to it. Who better to handle the neigh-bors than the intelligent pigs?

Lenin's and Stalin's revolutionary theories also agreed on the need for rapid development of the country's forces of production. Since the former Russia was not economically developed, the na-tion could not provide for its members immediately after the revolution. Therefore, Stalin built on Lenin's call for increased eco-nomic and material development. He took this call much further, though. The Soviet Union would make moves to complete indus-trialization and nationalization. The goal was to bring the forces of production up to speed. Stalin went a step further and moved to large-scale, agricultural collectives, wherein small family farms were gobbled up. Eventually he hoped to make all of the farms state farms. Centralization was the chief concern of Stalin, and he brought it about rapidly through extraordinarily violent means. Stalin and his loyal followers killed tens of millions in order to accomplish his development plans.

Development of Animal Farm was one of the major debates in which the animals engaged. Napoleon argued that time would be spent best feeding the animals. Snowball made more long-range arguments in favor of the benefits that would be reaped eventually if the farm moved toward development. One of the best examples of this disagreement can be found in the windmill controversy. Should the animals spend additional time, effort, and resources on building a windmill to help reduce their workload in the future? The issues swirling around the windmill were similar to those the early Soviet Union considered.

Another of Stalin's major concerns was whether to focus on the internal problems of his country or to worry about spreading a revolution worldwide. This debate came to be known as the "Socialism in One Country" debate. Both Marx and Lenin maintained a worldwide focus. They believed that a one-country approach risked destructive nationalism and must be avoided. Stalin recognized the inability of his country to bring about such a worldwide revolution quickly and thus turned inward toward developing the Soviet Union. Although obviously still involved in international politics aimed at advancing the socialist cause, the primary focus became the industrialization and collectivization of the USSR. This focus also resulted in the death of millions through starvation. The costs of these moves were staggering.

The animals on the newly formed Animal Farm had to make similar decisions. Old Major spoke (and sang) about a *world* without humans. Snowball called for the continued attempts to spark rebellion on surrounding farms. Interestingly, Snowball both encouraged internal development and external revolutionary agitation, suggesting that the two aims are not exclusive. Should the animals worry about themselves or *all* animals?

The upshot of Stalin's revolutionary interpretation of Marxism, which he called Marxism-Leninism, was that individuals in his country were made to suffer and die. The emphasis on industrialization and collectivization led not only to the inadvertent deaths of many in the country, but also to the intentional killing of many more. In order to bring about the radical restructuring necessary for Stalin's major moves, huge groups of the individuals were unnecessary and in the way. Stalin had them killed. Revolutions from above tend to disregard those below. The revolutionary state maintained power and control to the exclusion of everyone else, including the proletariat. Socialism in one country could have meant taking care of one's own before moving on. This was decidedly not the case in the Soviet Union. The internal focus was one of centralizing and consolidating power, not helping the people. What happened on Animal Farm as a result of these Stalin-like changes? The final section on *Animal Farm*'s revolutionary doctrine will spell out the consequences.

While volumes have been written on these basic concepts of Marxism, an introductory understanding reveals the ideological roots of *Animal Farm*. Orwell's critique of Marxism is basic but forceful. He exposes some fundamental assumptions underpinning the theory and exposes them to some devastating criticism. The assumptions and criticisms are fairly straightforward and you can evaluate them. You might not be able to "decide" the issue of Marxism versus capitalism, but you should be prepared to engage in the debate.

MARXIST VIEW OF HISTORY

> The materialist conception of history starts from the proposition that the production of the means to support human life and, next to production, the exchange of things produced, is the basis of all social structure.[7]

The materialist conception of history, or *historical materialism*, is one of the most important aspects of Marxism. Production is at the center. Productive forces and relations determine the social structure. Political and societal change result when those forces and relations come into conflict. The basis of society is economic and material. This conception views history as *epochal*, that is, characterized by distinctive, separate epochs, or eras. Historical materialism is the basis of Marxism.

Production must be understood in its most basic form: subsistence, or what it takes just to survive. Individuals survive by securing their "means of subsistence." They adapt to their actual physical surroundings. According to Marx, this act is much more than simply reproducing one's physical existence. It is itself a definite "mode of production," an expression of life: "As individuals express their life, so they are. What they are, therefore, coincides with their production, both with *what* they produce and with *how* they produce. The nature of individuals thus depends on the material conditions determining their production."[8] Human nature is not fixed, but is produced by material conditions.

Animal nature is not fixed either. The animals on the farm live their lives as a result of the material conditions of production on the farm. The hens are forced to lay eggs constantly in order to produce a commodity for Jones to consume and sell. The hens would not spend so much time laying eggs if they were able to hatch and raise their chicks. Boxer and Clover would not spend their lives dragging carts around the farm if their human masters did not determine their lives for them. The Joneses *own* the horses and decide in what form of production they will engage. Even the style of labor is determined by the emphasis of the farm on livestock and agriculture. The animals' condition depends on the material conditions of the farm, not some inherent animal nature.

Marx was concerned about the real world. He labored to ensure that his approach was anchored in the real world, not in some imagined abstraction: "The premises from which we begin are not arbitrary ones, not dogmas, but real premises. . . . They are the real individuals, their activity and the material conditions under which they live, both those which they find already existing and those produced by their activity. These premises can thus be verified in a purely empirical way."[9] The legitimacy of Marxism can be found by examining the measurable world. The desirability of rebellion can be determined best by examining the world that results on Animal Farm. The importance of this need for Marx to measure cannot be fully stated without recourse through some philosophy history. Suffice it to say that he was attempting to devalue the world we carry around in our heads in favor of the world in which we walk around. Many of the philosophers of his day valued the former at the expense of the latter. Marx was responding directly to them and formulating his own way in the world.

Marxism also provided a standard according to which theories could be judged: Are they proved correct in the *real* world? Are his premises concerning human nature correct in the real world? Do material conditions produce human nature? Marx would have you examine the world to determine the answers to these questions, not some abstract philosophy. After all, according to Marx, we live in one of the most class-divisive modes of production: capitalism. Do you find that your life is determined by products? Is wealth shared and profit distributed equally among *all* those responsible for its production? Do you live in a world where the bourgeoisie and the proletariat are separate and unequal? Are there "correct" answers for these or any other questions?

Marx's Stages of Historical Development

The Tribal and Ancient Communal Stages. Marx attempts to verify his premises concerning historical materialism with empirical examples from history. By dividing history into "various stages of development in the division of labor," he focuses on the question of ownership. Who owns the means of production? Who owns labor's product? The answers to these and similar questions break down the division of labor into five stages of development: tribal or Asian, ancient communal, feudal, capitalist, and socialist:

> The first form of ownership is tribal ownership. It corresponds to the undeveloped stage of production, at which a people lives by hunting and fishing, by the rearing of beasts, or in its highest stage, agriculture. . . . The division of labour is at this stage still very elementary and is confined to a further extension of the natural division of labour existing in family. The social structure is, therefore, limited to an extension of the family: patriarchal family chieftains, below them the members of the tribe, finally slaves.[10]

This form of ownership is the most "primitive." Just as the name suggests, this stage of production is tied directly to the tribe and its means of conducting the everyday business of getting food and shelter. Marx argues that this organizational structure with the chief, the tribe, and slaves emerges from and is like the family structure where the father is chief and his wife and their children are the tribe members. The idea that the family relationship degenerates into slavery is striking and no doubt controversial. The relationship of absolute control and ownership of the children by the father is itself dangerously close to a slave relationship. The first stage of development indeed is harsh.

The second form of ownership is the ancient communal, wherein the tribes unify into larger units. These units then provide for their population through a combination of communal ownership and private property. According to Marx, this move to private property is one of the beginnings of class conflict: "The second form is the ancient communal and State ownership which proceeds especially from the union of several tribes into a *city* by agreement or by conquest, and which is still accompanied by slavery."[11] In addition to the increasing class conflict caused by an increase in private property, a division between country and town is beginning to develop. As different geographical entities are enjoined in the union of tribes, their needs and wants grow and diversify. The differing locations also put unique demands on the union. Since the towns might not be able to produce enough food for their population, they must share the responsibility of feeding their tribe with the tribes of the country. The resulting tension adds to a developing conflict between private and communal property interests. This description of the ancient communal stage of development stresses the importance of the communal arrangement for the individual tribe members. Individual power is derived from the community ownership of property. As private property increases, overall individual power necessarily decreases. The individual stake in the community is reduced as the community loses ownership and control of private property. The individual no longer derives the same benefits from the community and is less influential. Naturally, the propertied individual becomes increasingly important. Marx directly correlates the demise of community-held private property to the demise of the people in the community. This view of history supports Marx's notion that as the relations of production come in conflict with the forces of production, revolutionary social change becomes more likely.

The question of whether all are to be included in the rebellion gets raised when the dogs chase after the rats: Are the "wild creatures," like the rats and rabbits, "comrades"? The animals subsequently voted overwhelmingly that rats and rabbits indeed were comrades. Perhaps this situation replays the historical split between town and country, with the farm animals representing the concentrated town population and the wild animals representing the decentralized country. According to Marx, we must overcome that split in order to revolt successfully. Irrespective of the accuracy of the analogy, the spirit of unity among the animals is resounding.

The Feudal Stage. The third form of ownership is feudal property. Marx contrasts the previous stages of development with this one along the country-town split. He argues that "if antiquity started out from the town and its little territory, the Middle Ages started out from the *country*."[12] The reason is simple: sparse populations. Quite simply, the people were not concentrated near towns, but were spread out across the countryside. Large estates were developed in which large tracts of land were included. Along with the land came workers (here serfs). This changed the specifics of the production relationship, but many of the relations remained the same: "Like tribal and communal ownership, [feudal property] is based on a community; but the directly producing class standing over against it is not, as in the case of the ancient community, the slaves, but the enserfed small peasantry. As soon as feudalism is fully developed, there also arises antagonism to the towns."[13] Once again, the people with the power (the feudal lords) repress those without power (the serfs). The means of repression and exploitation is through the ownership of property, including the land from which production was possible. All property and power was not concentrated in the feudal system. In the towns, people who knew a trade or craft formed guilds, designed to protect their workers against the feudal system and others who threatened their livelihood, for example, industrialists. Of course, the guilds themselves set up a hierarchy of journeyman and apprentice much like the relationship of lord to serf.

The country and the town still were following similar stages of domination. Now, instead of slaves, the feudal stage of development had serfs and apprentices. The peasantry previously existed between the leaders and the slaves and so were protected somewhat from the excesses of the powerful. When the peasants are transformed into the equivalent of the slaves, they must bear the brunt of that excess. As in earlier stages, feudalism is based on small-scale agriculture, but is supplemented by a craft type of industry. This craft industry is the basis of the town guilds. Relations of production in feudalism are similar to those of earlier stages.

The conflict between these relations and the forces of production have intensified. For Marx, they now represent the possibility of revolutionary change.

The relevance of this stage of development should be obvious. This is the stage of development of *Animal Farm*. Just like Russians under the yoke of Czar Nicholas, the animals toil under the unjust leadership of Mr. Jones. The conflict between the propertied and ruling class, the farm owners, and the workers, the animals, is inevitable, according to Marx. The movement of feudal Russia to the revolutionary Soviet Union parallels that of the Manor Farm to the Animal Farm. Thus, the next stage of development was avoided by both the farm and the nation.

The Capitalist Stage. The world changes when capital begins to dominate. The relationship between serf and lord is disrupted: "The serf belongs to the land and turns over to the owner of the land the fruits thereof. The *free labourer*, on the other hand, sells himself and, indeed, sells himself piecemeal. He sells at auction eight, ten, twelve, fifteen hours of his daily life belong to him who buys them."[14] The worker does not provide labor to the capitalist but instead provides labor power. The capitalist purchases the power that workers produce. Thus, capital forms a relationship of power: "Capital is, therefore, not only a sum of material products; it is a sum of commodities, of exchange values, *of social magnitudes*."[15] The labor does not exist in a societal vacuum. Labor exists as part of an overall capitalist or bourgeois structure. Let us work with an example. A worker works for twelve hours a day for a month. This labor produces much more value than the simple product of her or his labor. This was called *surplus value*. Essentially the worker produces the owner's wealth. Capital demands the existence of a large, productive pool of labor. Capital pays the laborer for her or his work *and* produces surplus value for that labor. Since the capitalist "owns" the means of production, that value belongs to him or her. With the value of past labor, the capitalist is able to purchase more means of production, hire more laborers, and perpetuate the cycle of domination of labor by capital. Is this value invested in the interests of present or future labor? Of course not. Capital employs their profit to serve themselves, often to the detriment of labor. Nonetheless, the proletariat grows as the bourgeoisie grows. Yet again, the conditions that make possible radical change are brought about by the forces that most stand to suffer as a result of that change. Capital multiplies itself at the expense of the worker. At the same time, it multiplies the workers themselves. The proliferation of workers threatens the very existence of capital, at least according to Marx.

The Socialist Stage. The communist or socialist revolution is different from previous revolutions in that it overturns the current modes of production completely. Marx's proletarian revolution does away with "labor." The practice of labor itself, wherein the proletariat works for subsistence wages, is abolished. Rather than just adjusting the distribution of what is produced, the great revolution will eliminate the forces that led to that production in the first place. Of course, this is the stage of development the animals seek in their rebellion. The class division that resulted from previous modes and relations of production also is overcome in such a rebellion or revolution: *"The proletariat seizes political power and turns the means of production into state property.* But, in doing this, it abolishes itself as proletariat, abolishes all class distinctions and class antagonisms, abolishes also the state as state."[16] The state was necessary, according to Marxism, to handle class antagonisms. With the abolition of class, the state atrophies, withers away. The seizure of the means of production is critical, since, as we have seen, it is the cornerstone of the capitalist domination. While the bourgeoisie maintain control of production, the proletariat always will suffer at their hands. The nature of capital enlarges itself as it diminishes the worker.

That this state of affairs exists appears natural to the general population. When something happens for as long as you can remember and as long as all of the people whom you know can remember, it tends to take on the character of inevitability. Though you may not be happy with the state of affairs, overcoming them seems impossible. Situations that can be changed become unchangeable. Communism changes that situation. What used to appear natural to everyone suddenly appears created by humans and malleable by humans, if only they unite. Reality is not something fixed, but can be altered if the people who make up reality get together and change it. In fact, nothing is possible independent of individuals. The possibility opened by this perspective on reality should be obvious. If you and your family had been working as hard as possible just to make ends meet, communism lit a light at the end of that hard tunnel. Animalism did the same for the animals of Manor Farm.

The Possibility of Change

Although the language of Marx and Marxism sometimes is difficult, the concepts are fairly straightforward. The concentration of the means of production in the hands of the very few has led to the disadvantage of the many. Humans work under extreme conditions for most of their lives and end up with little to show for it by way of material well-being. They become alienated from their work, from their bosses, and, if they are not careful, from the people who mean the most to them. Eventually the disparity between what is being produced and what is being distributed becomes too great. When the conflict between the relations of production and the forces of production becomes that great, something has to give. Over the generations, changes have resulted from these class conflicts. Ultimately, however, the root cause of these conflicts has not been handled. Marx's proletariat revolution is aimed at the material and economic causes of the worker's plight. For anything to change fundamentally, superficial reform must end and radical revolution must begin. Nothing ever will change so long as the basic relationship of the bourgeoisie to the proletariat remains so asymmetrical. The only possibility of true change is in the unity of the people against their oppressors. Reality is not fixed, only entrenched. Revolution, according to Marx, is necessary and possible.

OLD MAJOR'S SPEECH AND COMMUNIST THEORY

Translating the basic concepts of Marxism into *Animal Farm* is easy. After all, Orwell was writing about the Stalinist Soviet Union, an explicitly Marxist-Leninist society. The true power of Orwell's work can be felt only in light of the excesses of that society. One need only trace out the general Marxist framework, as was done in the previous sections, to see what he is up to. Part of his strength comes from not being explicit. We can identify with the animals in the story. We feel for them when things go against them. We have hope when they overcome their master. And our hopes are dashed when the revolution ultimately fails them. This failure, according to Orwell, is the result of the revolutionary forces' going awry. Before getting to that failure, let us look at Old Major's speech and try to discern some of Marx's communist theory in Orwell's fairy story.

One possible explanation for Orwell's use of the moniker "fairy story" is provided to you in the Introduction to this book. Another possibility derives specifically from Marx's (and Engels') writings. In *Manifesto of the Communist Party*, they explain one of the reasons why they need to publish a manifesto: "It is high time that Communists should openly, in the face of the whole world, publish their views, their aims, their tendencies, and meet this *nursery tale* of the Spectre of Communism with a Manifesto of the party itself."[17] Orwell certainly read the *Manifesto* and perhaps was responding by fashioning his own "fairy story" or "nursery tale."

We are immediately alerted to the possibility that something is afoot when Major begins his speech with what has become almost a communist cliché: "Comrades . . ." Why would a pig employ such communist dogma? From the perspective of communism, the reference should make immediate sense to us: worker unity. Despite the differences among the animals, Major is suggesting, by the way he addresses them, that they are somehow united. He does not refer to the dogs or the horses differently than he does his fellow pigs. *All* of the animals are his comrades. Major repeats the reference regularly during the rest of his speech, each time invoking the message of unity. The term may have been overused over the years, but imagine the impact it might have had on this overworked, abused group of animals.

Major's first move in the speech is to describe "the nature of this life." He paints a frightening picture, replete with bare subsistence, arduous labor, and a grim future of cruel slaughter. Their plight is reminiscent of the proletarian life Marx portrayed. As with Marx, Major must grapple with the seeming naturalness of this harsh reality. He does so beautifully by first offering up their existence as the *nature* of things. One can almost see the head nodding that must have been going on among the animal audience. Once they had acknowledged the inevitability of their dire circumstances, Major pulled the conceptual rug out from under them by asking them if this state of affairs is the nature of things, if their land is too poor for a "decent life." A resounding *no* is the answer. One can almost see the heads snapping at this change of direction, followed by the slow dawning of a new reality: their world was not the way the world must be. In this new world, more of them could be fed better with less work. And they might be able to help bring about this change.

Why was it not so? they must have wondered. Major is quick to answer that the product of their labor is stolen from them by the humans. Humans are the animals' "real enemy." By eliminating humans, the animals can get to the "root" of their hunger and overwork, abolishing it forever. The focus on the product of their labor recalls Marx's emphasis on production. What is wrong with the world? The root cause of its ills can be located in labor, production, and distribution. Where Marx had the bourgeoisie, Major has Man. A common enemy emerges to unite the animals. Locating the cause outside themselves has the added benefit of not offending Major's audience by blaming them for their fate. The analogy is not strained either, since both function the same way in society by taking away or stealing labor's products. The analogy is sealed when Major maintains the focus on production. Put simply, Man does not produce. Just like capital and labor, Man requires the animals in order to survive and to flourish. Major points to the animals' essential contribution to the farm without even a hint of recompense from Man (actually lamenting their lack of ownership). The stakes are raised emotionally when the offspring are brought into it: the calves, the chicks, and the foals. Major is a forceful orator and directs his audience to the same places Marx did.

Major's litany of horrors perpetrated on animals by Man must have raised some ire as well. The litany ends with yet another vicious attack on Man. *All* the evils of the animals' lives are the result of human "tyranny." The totalizing move by Major is similar to Marx's historical materialism. *All* the evils of this life can be tied either to Man and labor's produce or to the relations and forces of production. Marx's materialist reduction of the world's many different aspects into one is the same as Major's with humans. Both attempt to include everything in their explanation of what is wrong with the world.

Fortunately for his audience, Major offers a way out: get rid of the humans, and their labor's product would become their own. They would be "rich and free" almost overnight—but their task would not be completed. They must work constantly with all their might to overthrow the humans. Major's message is clear: rebellion. Once again, note the focus on labor's produce. The result of getting rid of Man, the reason for the rebellion, is to get back their produce. The world is righted when labor regains its produce. Freedom and wealth are dependent on it. Also, this time Major mirrors the Marxist belief that rebellion could come "almost overnight." Also like Marx, Major is careful not to present a timetable for this rebellion. Rebellion does not follow the will of humans and animals, but is dictated by the relations of labor to its produce.

Major summarizes his arguments by laying out the rebellious animals' duties—basically, the rejection of all that is Man: the way he walks, his vices, where he sleeps, and the like. Major reiterates the totalizing claim that all human habits are "evil." Finally, he echoes a familiar sentiment that "all animals are equal" (22) and should be afforded equal respect and protection. Marx similarly argues that communism is based on equality. Of course, many other political programs and philosophies have endorsed such equality. The division between animals and Man roughly mimics that between the classes in Marxism. Major is erecting (or revealing, depending on how one looks at it) class barriers. Class division is at the heart of both Marxism and Animalism. Man and the bourgeoisie must be overcome if animals and the proletariat are to survive at anything more than their subsistence level.

Major concludes by recounting a dream that he had the previous night. He dreamed of an earth free from Man. This possible future is set out in a song called "Beasts of England." In it, all the indignities and worse heaped on animals by Man would be eliminated. The song is essentially a utopian vision of the world after the rebellion, a "golden future time." Food will be of higher quality and more plentiful. The water and air will be purer and sweeter. The song is a cautionary tale as well, calling for continued labor toward that time. Freedom is promised as the reward, if only they work. This should remind us of historical materialism: the relations of production will eventually, and perhaps inevitably, come into such conflict with the forces of production that a revolution will occur. Just wait. Many accuse Marx of a similar brand of utopianism. Despite his explicit attacks on utopian socialism, Marx left out much of how to get to his golden future time. One of the principal challenges from the anarchists was leveled at how the state would wither away after the revolution. As it turns out historically, this concern was not unfounded. Arguably, much of what went wrong in the Soviet Union is the result of the state's failure to wither away. Both Marx and Major sang a similar song concerning the road to their future times.

Major's speech is filled with communist theory (and songs). The similarities between his ideas and those described earlier in this chapter are striking. Production and labor are the focal points for Marx and Major. Both orient around a common enemy theme and reduce all of the complexities of that enemy to a single negative entity. Both equality and freedom are heralded as justifications for the hard work necessary for a revolution. Historical materialism and the eventual conflict between forces and relations of production bringing about revolution govern the course of life on the farm and in the factory. Orwell's farm reflects Marx's England as clearly as Mollie looking at her reflection in the drinking pool.

DOCTRINE OF REVOLUTION IN *ANIMAL FARM*

Animal Farm's revolution fails miserably. The revolutionaries ultimately betray their comrades. Is this inevitable in revolutions? Does power eventually corrupt all revolutionaries? Can there be a successful revolution in the face of "human" nature? Are we doomed to live in the world of our predecessors, or is this a story of hope? Is Orwell spelling out the dangers rather than predicting their inevitability? Ask yourself: Is revolutionary change possible in your society? Look to Orwell and *Animal Farm* for some possible answers.

The setting immediately should strike the increasingly astute Marxist reader. Mr. Jones's farm is indicative of the situation Marx described as the third stage of class division's development: feudalism. The peasant serfs on Jones's land are obviously the animals. The farm is "owned" by Jones, and he uses his control of the forces of production to subjugate the animals much the same way the feudal organizations associated to subject the producing class. The animals produce value from themselves (milk, eggs, offspring) and from the land (tilling, fertilizing, harvesting). The value produced for Jones is in excess of what he would have without the animals. As Major aptly points out, this value is not returned to the animals, who are given barely enough food to survive. So, the productive relationship between the animals and Jones is similar to that of serfs to feudal lords. This class division sets the stage, historically and in *Animal Farm*, for revolution or rebellion.

When would the rebellion against Jones happen? The next three months were filled with much "secret activity." Although the animals could not know when the rebellion would take place (in fact, there was no reason to think that it would occur within their lifetime), they believed that it was up to them to prepare for it. The emphasis on secrecy immediately recalls Lenin's revolutionary vanguard. Just like Lenin, the burden of the revolution falls squarely on the shoulders of the more *intelligent* animals. He argues that "it is much easier for demagogues to side-track the more backward sections of the masses."[18]

The comparison between Lenin's and Orwell's revolutionary doctrine is startling. Historical materialism is not sufficient to bring about the rebellion. Instead, rebellion requires "public exposures" and agitation by a small cadre of revolutionaries. Since the pigs were considered to be the most clever farm animals, they were responsible for teaching and organizing the other animals. Power was quickly being consolidated into an exclusive intelligentsia of pigs. The pigs held meetings, raised consciousness, combated the natural fears and concerns about such a radical change. They even gave their revolutionary doctrine a name: Animalism.

An inevitable part of any attempt to instigate rebellion is to fight the counterrevolutionary forces that arise to preserve the status quo. The raven presents a traditional religious response to calls for change in this world: the promise of a better life in the next world (here, Sugar Candy Mountain). Much like the atheism of Marxism, Animalism had to expose such heavenly rewards as fantasy. The pig-led revolutionary vanguard successfully started the rebellious wheels rolling. As with Lenin's contribution, what is in doubt is not the ability of the vanguard to start revolutions, but where they end up.

Like most other revolutionary actions, the Manor Farm uprising was sparked by a sudden, powerful event: the failure to feed the animals. They stormed the food stores and began to take what they believed was owed to them. This, as is the way, encountered violent retaliation from the humans who had caused the situation in the first place. Without knowing it, they were pouring gasoline on a fire. The animals' revolutionary pumps had been primed by all the talk of rebellion and refused to take the harsh treatment at the humans' hands. They turned their anger and frustration on the humans and drove them from the farm. Quickly the aggression was redirected toward the tools of oppression that had been used to do much violence to them over the years. Whips, castration knives, riding gear, and the rest were destroyed in the animals' revolutionary rage. The successful overturning of the farm hierarchy was accomplished quickly and severely.

Alienation, which had been the constant refrain of their prerebellion farm days, was replaced by the song of contentment. The animals realized immediately that they still had to work, but their new work was satisfying. No longer did they toil in slavery for a tyrannical farmer. Although the hay must be harvested, the bounty would remain in its rightful place. The produce of the animals' labor was the sole property of the animals themselves. Bringing in the harvest became a point of honor instead of a chore. Not surprisingly, the time required to bring in the harvest was reduced drastically. Also not surprisingly, the amount of theft was reduced to nothing with a corresponding rise in the yield. There was more leisure time, and everything seemed better. Worker alienation had been all but eliminated. The animals were happy.

Part of becoming a newly formed revolutionary force involves creating a sense of belonging, a sense of honor in the new organization. The animals, in a further attempt to do away with the previous regime, changed the name of the farm from Manor to Animal Farm. A certain amount of pageantry is required to demonstrate unity and respect for the new community. The animals, led by the pigs, fashioned a flag and established a new ceremony involving flag raising and much singing. The ceremonies became more complicated over time, expanding to include military decoration and commemorative firing of a firearm. The community celebrated its new-found independence with an appropriate amount of festivity.

No new community is complete without new direction. The direction was to come, naturally, from the vanguard. The pigs continued their secretive ways. They learned to read and write in secret. With this new skill, they were able to control the community's direction. They designed seven commandments, largely out of Major's speech. They came up with a slogan: "Four legs good, two legs bad." Not all of their secrecy and influence was quite so seemingly innocuous. Milk was taken, at first secretly and then openly. Justification was provided by more exclusive knowledge:

science. The vanguard took the apple crop in order to remain properly nourished. They continued their organizational activities by attempting to organize the animals into committees. Open debate was paid lip-service and dominated by the articulate, intelligent pigs. Eventually *all* farm *policy* was formulated by the pig vanguard. Of course, a vote was held, but within the pig-dominated forum. Such busy, important animals could not be expected to work in the fields.

The vanguard was refusing to give up its power, exactly what opponents of Lenin's vanguard had feared. The pigs protected their privilege through a combination of secrecy and loaded public discussion. The animals thought they were governing themselves instead of being governed secretly by a group that was supposed to atrophy postrebellion.

All rebellions and revolutions must fight the responses from those who cling to the past. Obviously there were outside forces aligned against the new union. The pigs controlled the means of communication with the outside world: the pigeons were excellent messengers. The vanguard continued in its role to spread the word of the rebellion, propagating a constant stream of revolutionary "information." Afraid of the changes on old Manor Farm, the neighboring farmers started circulating information on their own. Each side claimed that the other was lying about the situation on Animal Farm. Increasingly the pigs escalated their rhetoric to include stories that they knew to be false. The war of words became a shooting war when the animals successfully defended their land against the invaders in the Battle of the Cowshed. Violence and killing were coming home to roost.

Early on, Napoleon had stashed away a litter of puppies from Jessie and Bluebell, secretly raising them for untoward purposes. When they were old enough, Napoleon used them as a dictator would use his or her military. First, they were used to drive his only major competition for sole farm leadership, Snowball. Then fear and intimidation became their method of operation. Public debates were not required when the leader was always "right." Any dissent could be handled easily by a group growl from the dogs—funny how quickly animals agree when they are threatened with maiming and death. The new regime took over so smoothly that the other animals soon forgot about it. The new tools at Napoleon's disposal, not to mention his ability to conduct affairs openly, allowed him to initiate a rule of iron discipline. The threat of violence succeeds beautifully in a community supposedly built on trust and cooperation.

Napoleon's new regime rapidly went about reversing most of the gains the early revolutionaries made. The workweek was increased regularly. Although work was voluntary, harsh penalties were meted out for exercising that right. Food was decreased gradually, until eventually reaching prerebellion days. Eggs were stolen. Retirement was never granted. How could such a state of affairs be allowed to happen? Why did the other animals not resist? How could they not know what was happening to them?

One of pivotal moves made by the pig vanguard, still alive in Napoleon, was to control history—to revise it as they saw fit. Napoleon literally changed history. Since history is written, they simply rewrote it. Take, for example, the Battle of the Cowshed. Snowball was one of the heroes of the battle and received a newly invented medal, "Animal Hero, First Class." Napoleon first told the animals that Snowball's contribution was not as great as previously believed and that the medal may not have been deserved after all. The leader of the battle became Napoleon, whose great accomplishment in the battle was to *thwart* Snowball. The medal changed hands. Napoleon received two, and Snowball never received any. The pellet wounds Snowball suffered at the hands of the invaders became teeth marks inflicted by Napoleon. Though resisted briefly, these revisions were accepted by the largely illiterate group of animals with poor memories. Those who could read or remembered things differently could always tell the dogs. Napoleon did not limit his historical flair to just the Battle of the Cowshed. Like any good revolutionary who does not want to lose power, he cast his historical net far and wide. The specific list is not as relevant as the practice of controlling history, information, and truth.

Napoleon was able to exercise this control by controlling what was written and read. The seven commandments had been written on the barn along with their motto. The inability of many animals to read the barn was exacerbated by the willingness of Napoleon (and Squealer) to *rewrite* the wall by literally adding on phrases to the commandments. For example, "No animal shall kill any other animal" has the phrase "without cause" appended to it. The effect of this change and others like it is to allow previously proscribed behavior. The commandments become their opposites. When one event or enemy can be reversed overnight, anything goes. And Napoleon went for it. Animals were killed. Confessions were manufactured. Boxer was sent to the slaughterhouse! Eventually memory fades. Literacy declines. Generations die. The world can change in a generation. Who was Boxer?

The lessons to be learned about revolutions and rebellions sometimes require stories. Orwell's story depicts how a revolution can betray and destroy those it was meant to help. The simplicity of the story does not belie a shallow critique of Stalinism and Marxism. Rather, such simplicity allows us to see the danger more clearly. Without a lot of detail or theory, Orwell makes astute, insightful observations about the dissolution of revolutionary hope and promise and the ease with which rebellion can end up repeating the errors of its previous oppressors, with the tyranny of the oppressors becoming the tyranny of the oppressed. The fears concerning Lenin's revolutionary vanguard are fulfilled with brutality and a vengeance. The pageantry of ceremony degenerates into the laughable self-aggrandizement of pomp and foolery. Secrecy and exclusion beget deceit and bigotry, intimidation and violence, fear and pain. Power may not corrupt, but it gives power to the corruption. Truth, reality, and the world are open for interpretation. History is written, usually by the winners. No matter how much things appear to remain the same, they change. Revolution and rebellion are serious forces and should not be entered into lightly or without both eyes open. This tale, in part, is aimed at opening eyes to the magnitude of the power. Be careful.

THE TOTALITARIAN STATE

The animal rebellion on Manor Farm degenerated into the totalitarian state of Animal Farm. Many commentators other than Orwell have written about the dangers of totalitarianism. Actually, the literature on totalitarianism is large and growing. Today's world provides ample evidence that such political nightmares are not exclusively concerns of the past. Despite the fall of the Soviet Union and the reunification of East and West Germany, there exist many political hot spots that could devolve into totalitarian regimes. One need only look to areas formerly "protected" under the Soviet Union's vast ideological umbrella to get a glimpse of these dangers. Ethnic, racial, and religious animosity long suppressed by those regimes is erupting in Europe. A casual glance at any day's newspaper can speak to the horror that is still a part of our world. Animal Farm is a microcosm of what could happen almost anywhere.

• • •

One of the great treatises on totalitarianism is Hannah Arendt's *The Origins of Totalitarianism*. Arendt traces the roots of twentieth-century totalitarianism to the rise of anti-Semitism and imperialism in the nineteenth. The resulting totalitarianism of Nazi Germany and Stalinist Russia is examined in great detail. The various ways those with totalitarian leanings are able to take over and maintain control are fleshed out. The power of this work is its ability to draw parallels between totalitarian regimes and nontotalitarian governments, to locate both societal and individual causes of totalitarian takeovers of nontotalitarian states, and to present readers with the knowledge and understanding necessary to avoid such disastrous pitfalls in the future.

The passage excerpted below focuses on several of the themes developed earlier in this chapter. Arendt seizes on the secret alliance of forces as one of the primary ways that totalitarian regimes gain and consolidate power. She highlights centralization of power and suppression of dissidents, aspects prominent in *Animal Farm*. This should recall for you Lenin's revolutionary vanguard. Moving the conspiracy into broad daylight allows almost limitless power since everything is apparently above-board. Napoleon attempts a similar move when he unmasks his own power structure with the emergence of his own military: the dogs. The rule of iron discipline follows quickly on the heels of that revelation. Stalin and Napoleon were in charge.

The leader is the center of the totalitarian movements. This center allows for enormous abuse of authority. The major avenue for this abuse is through lying. The vanguard and its leader grossly, and at times obviously, distort the truth for their advantage. In fact, a gullible and cynical populace welcomes lying. Much like the illiterate animals with poor memories, the masses welcome any word from their leader. After all, the leader brought about revolutionary change and represents the only hope of not returning to the previous, intolerable regime. Propaganda is the way of totalitarian movements and governments. Interestingly, Arendt repeats the exact language of Boxer, only in the context specifically of Hitler and generally of all all totalitarian leaders: "The Leader is always right."

This brief excerpt should demonstrate the relevance of Orwell's fairy story to world politics. We should not be too quick to limit its critique of revolutions and rebellions to only Stalinist Russia. If nothing else, Nazi Germany also is implicated. More than that, however, is the need for us to be on guard in the world at large. Remember that the Nazis gained power through constitutional, democratic means. We also must be on guard against grouping *all* revolutions together. Orwell is not indicting the possibility or potential benefit of revolutionary change. Rather, we must enter such engagements with some understanding of what terrible consequences might result and be prepared better to avert them.

The world Arendt describes is remarkably similar to life on Animal Farm. Lying is one of the dominant communication tools employed by the pigs. The hierarchical structure of a totalitarian state Arendt describes is identical to the one on Animal Farm, from the tight inner circle of pigs around Napoleon, to the party loyalists like Boxer, and on to the "fellow-travelers" just along for the ride. Squealer is an example of the inner circle, the chief orchestrator of the lying and expected to speak the new party line as if it were always that way. "Napoleon is always right" was one of Boxer's favorite sayings and the slogan for Napoleon's revolution. Even when some of the animals suspected something was up with, for example, the Seven Commandments, they eventually were convinced by their Leader, Napoleon. Arendt could have been describing Animal Farm.

FROM HANNAH ARENDT, *THE ORIGINS OF TOTALITARIANISM*
(New York: Meridian Books, 1973; original, 1951)

The chief value, however, of the secret or conspiratory societies' organizational structure and moral standards for purposes of mass organization does not even lie in the inherent guarantees of unconditional belonging and loyalty, and organizational manifestation of unquestioned hostility to the outside world, but in their unsurpassed capacity to establish and safeguard the fictitious world through consistent lying. The whole hierarchical structure of totalitarian movements, from naive fellow-travelers to party members, elite formations, the intimate circle around the Leader, and the Leader himself, could be described in terms of a curiously varying mixture of gullibility and cynicism with which each member, depending upon his rank and standing in the movement, is expected to react to the changing lying statements of the leaders and the central unchanging ideological fiction of the movement. . . . The machine that generates, organizes, and spreads the monstrous falsehoods of totalitarian movements depends again upon the position of the Leader. To the propaganda assertion that all happenings are scientifically predictable according to the laws of nature or economics, totalitarian organization adds the position of one man who has monopolized this knowledge and whose principal quality is that he "was always right and will always be right." To a member of a totalitarian movement this knowledge has nothing to do with truth and this being right nothing to do with the objective truthfulness of the Leader's statements which cannot be disproved by facts, but only by future success or failure. The Leader is always right in his actions and since these are planned for centuries to come, the ultimate test of what he does has been removed beyond the experience of his contemporaries.

• • •

Leszek Kolakowski is a former professor of the history of philosophy at the University of Warsaw who has written extensively on Marxism. The short article excerpted here is an insightful look at the inescapable need of totalitarian regimes to rely on the lie as means of controlling the individual totally. Both he and Arendt agree that lying is an integral aspect of totalitarianism. Kolakowski takes the analysis one step further, arguing that this defining characteristic could lead to its demise. Since the regime needs lying to control the mental as well as the physical, reality needs to be controlled. Kolakowski defends reality's ability to defeat ideology and lying. The "real" world might have the potential to help end certain totalitarian regimes by exposing and exploiting their essential failure to control reality. His defense does not claim to be able to predict future events.

This excerpt is especially relevant for us. The Marxism-Leninism in *Animal Farm* is implicated directly in this article. When describing totalitarianism, Kolakowski stresses the importance of production, class division, social justice, slogans, and the ability to transform memory overnight (as in Orwell's *1984*). The devastating consequences to the animals in the story are given theoretical explanation in the article. The tragic effects of Animalism's views on truth similarly are provided with philosophical underpinnings. Additional historical contextualization lends credibility to *Animal Farm*'s critique of Stalinism. Finally, Kolakowski brings the story and the history up to the recent past by discussing Poland. His article speaks directly to our analysis of *Animal Farm*.

FROM LESZEK KOLAKOWSKI, "TOTALITARIANISM AND THE VIRTUE OF THE LIE"
(Sidney Hook, *Marx and the Marxists*
[Princeton, NJ: Van Nostrand, 1955; reprint, 1984])

Total power and total ideology embrace each other. The ideology is total in a much stronger sense, at least in its claims, than any religious faith has ever achieved. Not only does it have all-embracing pretensions, not only is it supposed to be infallible and obligatory; its aim (unattainable, fortunately) goes beyond dominating and regulating the personal life of every subject to the point where it actually replaces personal life altogether, reducing human beings into replicas of ideological slogans. In other words, it annihilates the personal form of life. This much more than any religion has ever prescribed.

Such an ideology explains the specific function and specific meaning of the *lie* in a perfect totalitarian society, a function so peculiar and creative that even the word itself, "lie," sounds inadequate. . . . Let us consider what happens when the ideal has been effectively achieved. People remember only what they are taught to remember today and the content of their memory changes overnight, if needed. They really believe that something that happened a day before yesterday and which they stored in their memories yesterday, did not happen at all and that something else happened instead. In effect, they are not human beings any longer. Consciousness *is* memory. . . . Creatures whose memory is effectively manipulated, programmed, and controlled from outside are no longer persons in any recognizable sense and therefore no longer human.

This is what totalitarian regimes keep unceasingly trying to achieve. People whose memory—personal or collective—has been nationalized, become state-owned and perfectly malleable; they have been deprived of their identity; they are helpless and incapable of questioning anything they are told to believe. They have been transformed into dead objects.

TOPICS FOR WRITTEN OR ORAL EXPLORATION

1. Have a debate with one or more of your classmates on the desirability of a Marxist revolution in the United States. Resolved: That the U.S. government should become Marxist.

2. Compare and contrast the political lying prevalent in totalitarianism and the of lying of which recent U.S. presidents have been accused (for example, Clinton or Nixon).

3. Research one of the radical revolutionary theories competing with Marxism during the nineteenth century (for example, utopian socialism or anarchism). Make arguments for why your alternative is more desirable than Marxism.

4. Create your own utopian vision of what society should look like. Include details about economic, political, and cultural features.

5. Some people argue that the failures of actual Marxist regimes do not invalidate Marx's philosophy and political theory. Discuss this issue in the light of Marx's emphasis on empirical proof.

6. Watch a movie about some revolutionary event. Write a newspaper-style review of it. Emphasize its political and revolutionary elements.

7. Defend totalitarianism as a system of government. Why might it be desirable? For society? For individuals? You may use arguments that actual totalitarians made or make up your own.

8. Compare and contrast the revolutionary activity taking place in the United States and France during 1968. No revolution took place. What went wrong for the revolutionaries? What went right for the government?

9. Write a "fairy story" with some political insight and analysis contained in it. Provide sufficient detail to allow your reader to understand your message. Try to make your story engaging and persuasive.

10. Examine a product from a Marxist perspective. Learn about its relations and forces of production. Find something out about the proletariat and bourgeoisie involved in its production. How does this perspective help you to understand the product better? Does this perspective suggest anything about what to do to improve the product?

11. Create a timetable of events in the 1986–88 Iran-Contra scandal in the Reagan Administration. What do later events reveal about earlier claims that President Reagan and others made? Is it necessary to lie in order to carry out the duties of political office? What about if one is involved in the military (for example, Oliver North)?

12. Compose your own revolutionary song. Use the music from some other song, or write your own. The listener should be able to understand what is being attacked and what is being defended. This song should inspire its listeners at least to consider your revolution.

SUGGESTED READINGS

Hook, Sidney. *Marx and the Marxists: The Ambiguous Legacy*. Princeton, N.J.: Van Nostrand, 1955.

Lenin, V.I. "What Is to Be Done?" In *Essential Works of Lenin*. Ed. Henry M. Christman. New York: Dover, 1966.

Tucker, Robert C., ed., *The Marx-Engels Reader*. 2nd ed. New York: W.W. Norton, 1978.

NOTES

1. Robert C. Tucker, ed., *The Marx-Engels Reader*, 2d ed. (New York: W.W. Norton, 1978), p. xxxiii.

2. Karl Marx, "Marx on the History of His Opinions," in *A Contribution to the Critique of Political Economy*, in Tucker, pp. 4–5.

3. Sidney Hook, *Marx and the Marxists: The Ambiguous Legacy* (Princeton, N.J.: Van Nostrand, 1955), p. 21.

4. Marx, *The German Ideology*, in Tucker, p. 154.

5. Marx, *Economic and Philosophic Manuscripts of 1844*, in Tucker, p. 73.

6. V. I. Lenin, "What Is to Be Done?" In *Essential Works of Lenin*, ed. Henry M. Christman (New York: Dover, 1966), pp. 147–48.

7. Friedrich Engels, *Socialism: Utopian and Scientific*, in Tucker, pp. 700–701.

8. Marx, *Ideology*, in Tucker, p. 150.

9. Ibid., p. 149.

10. Ibid., p. 151.

11. Ibid.

12. Ibid., p. 152.

13. Ibid., p. 153.

14. Marx, *Wage Labour and Capital*, in Tucker, p. 205.

15. Ibid., pp. 207–8.

16. Engels, *Socialism*, in Tucker, p. 713.

17. Marx and Engels, *Manifesto of the Communist Party*, in Tucker, p. 473; my emphasis.

18. Lenin, pp. 147–48.

3

The Russian Revolution and Joseph Stalin

Jonathan Rose

> For the past ten years or so I have been convinced that the destruction of the Soviet myth was essential if we wanted a revival of the Socialist movement. . . . I thought of exposing the Soviet myth in a story that could be easily understood by almost anyone and which could be easily translated into other languages. However the actual details of the story did not come to me for some time until one day (I was then living in a small village) I saw a little boy, perhaps ten years old, driving a huge cart-horse along a narrow path, whipping it whenever it tried to turn. It struck me that if only such animals became aware of their strength we should have no power over them, and that men exploit animals in much the same way as the rich exploit the proletariat.
>
> I proceeded to analyse Marx's theory from the animals' point of view.
>
> —George Orwell, preface to the Ukrainian edition of *Animal Farm*, 1947

Animal Farm may be the most effective and widely read political satire ever written. Its success can be attributed largely to its simplicity. Written in elementary English, it distills the early history of the Soviet Union to its basic outline. Orwell admitted that for the sake of telling his story, he rearranged some of the facts of that history and reduced their complexity. Nevertheless, one must admire his skill in explaining the essence of the Soviet experiment and exposing its betrayal by Joseph Stalin.

As a committed socialist, Orwell did not mean to discredit the ideal of equality, or to dismiss the possibility of a true socialist revolution. He admired the original vision of Karl Marx, represented in *Animal Farm* by Old Major. Marx saw the workers, or proletarians, the true producers of all wealth. But the capitalists, or bourgeoisie, owned the means of production—land and industry. They consequently earned enormous profits while the workers were left with a subsistence wage at best. Marx predicted that eventually the proletariat would become so numerous and so impoverished that it would rise up against the capitalist system, destroy it, and create a communist utopia.

Marx was somewhat vague about how socialism actually would work, but he clearly believed in state control of all major economic institutions: land, banks, industries, communications, transport. The new regime would abolish the class system and realize Marx's great ideal of economic justice: "From each according to his ability, to each according to his need!"

Marx believed that since only a large and politically aware proletariat could carry out a socialist revolution, it would happen first in one of the industrialized countries of the West. Yet the first Marxist state was established in 1917 in Russia, a country that was just beginning to industrialize. Although there were large concentrations of industrial workers in a few big cities, such as Moscow and Petrograd (now known as St. Petersburg), most Russians were still peasants.

Vladimir Ilyich Lenin is not represented by any character in *Animal Farm*, though he led Russia into a Marxist revolution as the leader of the Bolshevik party. A dogmatic and dictatorial intellectual, he claimed to be an undeviating disciple of Marx. In reality, he revised Marxist theory in ways that proved fateful for the regime he would create. His Bolsheviks were an underground, frankly conspiratorial party open only to professional revolutionaries. Marx had envisioned Communism as a more open and democratic movement. True, Marx had sometimes spoken of the necessity of a "dictatorship of the proletariat," but if the proletariat constituted the mass of the population, that might simply amount to majority rule enhanced by temporary emergency powers during a revolutionary crisis. But Lenin argued that no political party could operate openly in the repressive atmosphere of Czarist Russia, and he knew that a Marxist party was not likely to win an election in a country with relatively few industrial workers. Therefore, in Russia the dictatorship of the proletariat became the dictatorship of the Party, which became the dictatorship of Lenin.

Russia under its last Czar, Nicholas II, was not unlike Manor Farm under Mr. Jones. Narrow-minded and incompetent, Nicholas was an autocrat who refused to make any meaningful concessions to democracy. He proved incapable of exercising effective leadership in World War I. Inept generals, military reverses, rising prices, and food shortages led, in March 1917, to food riots and army mutinies in Petrograd. Unable to cope with the deteriorating situation, Czar Nicholas abdicated. Czarism was not actually overthrown; like Communism in 1989, it collapsed under its own weight.

Lenin was in exile in Switzerland in early 1917, and he was surprised by this turn of events. He hurried back to Petrograd, where a Provisional Government was attempting to steer Russia toward free elections. That brief experiment in democracy would be aborted in November 1917, when Lenin mobilized the Bolsheviks to seize power and begin the construction of the first Communist state.

Chapter 3 of *Animal Farm* might suggest that the first years of the Soviet regime were a golden age of peace, prosperity, and equality. In fact, it was a period of terrible warfare and privation. The Bolsheviks had to wage a civil war on several fronts against the White armies, which aimed to overthrow the revolution. Britain, France, Japan, and the United States all dispatched armed forces to intervene in the conflict. The Communists subjected workers to military discipline and confiscated food from the peasants, who often destroyed their crops rather than turn them over to the Red Army. The Bolsheviks won the civil war, but Lenin's disastrous economic policies brought about a near-total collapse of industrial production and a famine that killed as many as 3 million Russians. Only massive humanitarian aid from America prevented the starvation of millions more.

In the face of economic catastrophe, Lenin reversed course in 1921 and proclaimed the New Economic Policy (NEP). He permitted a partial return to capitalism: although the state remained in control of heavy industry, smaller businesses could now be privately owned. Rather than confiscate food from the peasants, the state now simply taxed them a certain percentage of their crop and allowed them to sell the rest on the open market. The NEP restored a measure of prosperity to Russia, though the rise of a new entrepreneurial class (or NEPmen) also brought about a return of economic inequality. When they first took power, the Bolshevik leaders had voted themselves a wage equal to that of a skilled worker, but soon there would be large pay differentials separating the Communist elites from the proletariat they professed to represent.

One of the first acts of the young Soviet regime was to create a secret police: the All-Russian Extraordinary Commission for the Suppression of Counterrevolution, Sabotage and Speculation, popularly known as the Cheka. By the end of 1920 it employed 250,000 full-time agents and had executed more than 50,000 people. (In contrast, the last czars had carried out an average of seventeen executions a year for all crimes.) Lenin had one answer to all the problems that the new government faced: "Apply the terror—shooting on the spot—to speculators." He called for "the arrest and shooting of takers of bribes, swindlers, etc." He ordered Bolsheviks to "instantly introduce mass terror, shoot and transport hundreds of prostitutes who get the soldiers drunk, ex-officers, etc."

Was this the utopia Karl Marx envisioned? Would he have approved of mass murder? Marx did sometimes discuss the need for "revolutionary terror," though he seems to have had in mind the Reign of Terror that followed the French Revolution in 1793–94, Fighting a desperate war against foreign powers and against counterrevolutionaries within their own borders, the French republic executed 40,000 "enemies of the people." Although many innocent individuals died, the French Terror only lasted about a year, ending when the military situation improved and the revolution was more secure. Marx believed that the bourgeoisie might attempt to destroy the socialist revolution, and to prevent that he was willing to use terror—as a temporary measure.

But the Soviet Terror became permanent and institutionalized. It increased relentlessly even when the civil war had been won and the Communist regime was less threatened from within. The Cheka was transformed into the OGPU, then the NKVD, and with each reincarnation it acquired more arbitrary and sweeping powers. Each of the three men who created the Soviet Union—Lenin, Leon Trotsky, and Joseph Stalin—used terror without remorse, though Stalin was by far the most murderous of the three.

In other respects Trotsky and Stalin, who appear in *Animal Farm* as Snowball and Napoleon, respectively, were strikingly different personalities. A brilliant Jewish intellectual and an electrifying speaker, Trotsky had organized the Red Army practically from scratch and led it to victory against the White armies. After Lenin, he was by far the best-known member of the Politburo, the chief executive body of the Communist Party.

The least known was Joseph Stalin. While most Bolshevik leaders belonged to the middle-class intelligentsia, he alone was of peasant stock. He had been born in Georgia, a small nation conquered by Czarist Russia in the nineteenth century, and he spoke halting Russian with a Georgian accent. His only advanced education was in a Russian Orthodox seminary, which expelled him for Marxist activities. Although he played only a minor role in the 1917 revolution, he was named General Secretary of the Communist Party in 1922.

At first the General Secretary was just that—a secretary in charge of party correspondence and communications. It seemed the logical job for Stalin. Unlike Lenin and Trotsky, he could not discuss Marxist theory on a sophisticated level, but he could efficiently handle reams of dull paperwork. This position, however, allowed Stalin to quietly gain control of the rapidly expanding Soviet bureaucracy, placing his supporters in key positions. In 1923, Lenin warned the Communist Party that Stalin was too rude and brutal to trusted with power. But after Lenin died a year later, Stalin used his base of support to outmaneuver Trotsky in the struggle for succession.

Another reason for Stalin's triumph was his advocacy of "Socialism in One Country." All Marxists, including Marx himself, had expected that the revolution, when it came, would be a world revolution. After seizing power in Russia, Lenin and Trotsky bent every effort to incite communist revolts in other countries—much like the pigeons in *Animal Farm*, who are dispatched to preach

Napoleon/Stalin reviews the Soviet army at the close of *Animal Farm*, now that Animal Farm (the U.S.S.R.) is an established success and the windmill is built. Created by Craig Thompson.

the gospel of Animalism to other farms. However, every attempt to spread Communism beyond the borders of the Soviet Union failed.

Leon Trotsky refused to postpone the dream of "Permanent Revolution." Russia, he argued, was a backward country incapable of completing the socialist revolution on its own. With a small industrial base, a very small educated class, and a predominantly peasant population, Russia would inevitably revert to the autocracy and inefficiency that had characterized Czarism. His strategy therefore was to promote revolution among workers in the more advanced nations of the West: once they had overthrown their capitalist masters, they would assist their Russian comrades in building socialism. However, after years of bloodshed and hunger, many Communists felt that their limited resources and energies should be spent first on rebuilding the Soviet Union rather than on dubious schemes for world revolution. It was Stalin who argued that Russia could go it alone, and his position certainly appealed more to the Russian sense of national pride.

Stalin and Trotsky also clashed over economic issues. The NEP

Squealer (Pravda) rewrites the Seven Commandments of Animalism that had been printed in the barn, including the last commandment. The other animals suspect—but cannot prove—that the repainting is the handiwork of Napoleon/Stalin. The scene corresponds to Stalin's repeated betrayals of the principles of socialism and its promise of universal equality. Created by Daniel Reat.

had brought idle industrial capacity back into production, but virtually nothing had been invested in new plant and equipment. All economies, capitalist or communist, need capital to grow. Obviously no capitalist would invest in the Soviet Union, and the Soviet state had no money to invest. Trotsky proposed a radical solution

to this dilemma. All Russian farmland, now owned mostly by individual peasants, would be organized into large collective farms.
Tractors and other modern equipment would be used to boost
agricultural productivity. The state would take the surplus produce, sell it on the world market, and use the hard currency to
purchase industrial equipment. In a dispute that paralleled Snowball's and Napoleon's debate over the windmill, Stalin warned that
Trotsky's scheme would disrupt the relative calm and prosperity
of the NEP. Many rank-and-file Communists, who remembered the
disastrous economic policies of the Civil War period, were inclined
to agree with Stalin.

In this context, it is significant that Orwell chose the name "Napoleon" for the pig who represents Stalin in *Animal Farm*. The
French Revolution of 1789, like the Russian Revolution of 1917,
had started out with an enthusiastic vision of human equality. In
France, however, the revolution was ultimately taken over and betrayed by Napoleon Bonaparte, a military dictator who proclaimed
himself emperor. The Bolshevik leaders were educated men who
knew their history, and they feared that their own revolution might
fall victim to what they called "Bonapartism." But who among them
would play the role of Bonaparte? Who could equal Napoleon as
a military genius and a charismatic orator? Who, like Napoleon,
talked grandiosely of conquering Europe and imposing a new order on it? Who shared Napoleon's ambition and hunger for power?
The obvious answer in every case was Leon Trotsky—the architect
of the Red Army, the apostle of world revolution. Stalin appeared
to be less of a threat, the dark horse of Bolshevik politics. He struck
most Communists as a modest and self-effacing man, reassuringly
dull, inarticulate but good at paperwork, not inclined to gamble
on high-risk political adventures. Few expected him to become a
Soviet emperor far more tyrannical than Napoleon.

For all those reasons, Stalin was able to garner support among
Communists and defeat Trotsky in the struggle for power. Trotsky
was expelled from the Party in 1927, then banished to Central Asia,
then exiled from the USSR. All the while, he publicly protested
Stalin's betrayal of the revolution. But when Trotsky was still
Lenin's right-hand man, he had proclaimed that the Party was infallible and that all dissent and "factionalism" should be ruthlessly
crushed. Now Stalin was able to turn his own words against him.

The removal of Trotsky left Stalin to face a deteriorating economic situation. The state had been trying to purchase food cheaply from the peasants who produced it, but since the peasants could buy few consumer goods with their paper rubles, they were increasingly reluctant to sell their produce. By 1927 state purchases of grain were two million tons less than needed, and Soviet cities once again faced the prospect of severe hunger. To gain control of the food supply, Stalin embarked on a radical and ruthless policy of forcing peasants into collective farms. This, he grandly predicted, would boost agricultural production by 150 percent, and the surplus would be used to finance a crash program of industrial development, the First Five-Year Plan.

All this was a more extreme version of the plan that Trotsky had proposed and Stalin had denounced just a short while ago. Back then, Stalin had opposed the plan in order to discredit Trotsky politically. Now that Trotsky was gone, he could adopt it as his own. Anyone who favored a more moderate policy could be denounced and removed from power.

Millions of peasants, however, refused to give up their land to collective farms. In what was virtually a second Russian civil war, the Red Army attacked resisting villages with artillery and machine guns. Peasants often slaughtered their animals and burned down their farm buildings rather than surrender them to the Soviets. The *kulaks*—the richest and most productive farmers—were targeted for particularly brutal treatment. Contrary to Stalin's confident predictions, agricultural production plummeted. Since the Soviets were at the same time exporting more food to earn hard currency, the inevitable result was a man-made famine. Five million people starved to death or were executed; an equal number were forcibly shipped to Siberia or other underdeveloped areas.

Against the advice of his economic planners, Stalin demanded that the Five-Year Plan increase the output of heavy industry by 330 percent. Such unrealistic goals, along with inept centralized planning, led to enormous waste and inefficiency. Bureaucrats in Moscow misallocated resources. Sometimes factory buildings were constructed without the proper equipment—equipment that, it turned out, had been left to rust at some faraway railway siding. Unskilled Russian workers often could not operate sophisticated machinery. Industrial managers were assigned production quotas and tried to fulfill them at all costs, without regard for quality control.

By the end of 1932, Stalin proclaimed that the Five-Year Plan had overfulfilled its goals and cited reams of production figures to prove his point. Soviet economic statistics were notoriously exaggerated and unreliable, but there is no question that the First Five-Year Plan succeeded in building a large industrial base. For the first time in history, Russia was truly an economic superpower. The Soviet people had been promised that the new steel mills and power plants would dramatically raise their living standards. In fact, most of them were now worse off, having worked long hours and sacrificed consumer goods to fulfill the plan. Industrial output was used to build more industry, expand the Red Army, and support a growing privileged class of bureaucrats and Party members—the pigs of *Animal Farm*. As for the proletarians, they were urged to follow the example of Alexei Stakhanov, a coal miner who (it was claimed) had mined many times his assigned quota of coal. All workers were now expected to become "Stakhanovites" and achieve ever higher levels of output. In fact they were treated like military draftees: compelled to work wherever they were ordered at wages fixed by the state, and subject to harsh punishment for unwarranted absenteeism or failure to fulfill production targets. Slipshod work was often treated as sabotage, for which a worker could receive the death penalty.

Thus, the economic modernization of Russia brought with it a crescendo of political terror. The regime could not admit that agricultural collectivization and the Five-Year Plan were flawed in any way and blamed failures on "saboteurs," "slackers," "spies," even agents of the exiled Leon Trotsky. The Cheka under Lenin had murdered opponents of the Communists, but not Communists themselves. Its successor, the NKVD, would extend the terror up to the highest ranks of the Party. In December 1934, Leningrad Party boss S. M. Kirov was assassinated, probably by the NKVD on orders from Stalin, who wanted to eliminate a popular rival. The murder also gave Stalin a deadly political weapon: anyone he wanted out of the way could now be accused of complicity in the murder, even if there was no evidence. Before he was finished, as many as half a million of "Kirov's assassins" had been shipped to forced labor camps.

Although Stalin no longer faced any real internal opposition, the momentum of terror increased relentlessly, driven by his deep-seated paranoia. In 1936 came the first of the show trials, in which sixteen prominent and loyal Communists publicly confessed to unbelievable crimes—spying, terrorism, and plotting with Leon Trotsky. Though no evidence other than the confessions was produced, all sixteen were immediately executed. About 70 percent of the Party leadership ultimately became victims of what would be known as the Great Purge. So sweeping was the terror that of all the delegates at the 1934 Party Congress, less than 2 percent attended the next congress five years later. The purge killed most of the top army and naval commanders, and victimized half of the officers in the armed forces. Intellectuals who tried to speak out against the terror were eliminated; those who survived were cowed into servile adulation of Stalin. Millions of innocent people were herded into a vast network of *gulags* (forced labor camps) in Siberia and other remote regions. Those arrested included many research scientists whose talents could not be wasted, so some *gulags* were equipped with sophisticated laboratories, where the scientists could continue their work. Finally, in 1940, the terror claimed its most famous victim: Leon Trotsky, assassinated by one of Stalin's agents in Mexico City.

Adding up all of the individuals who were shot in the purges, perished in the inhuman conditions of the *gulag*, starved to death in the famines created by Soviet economic policies, some historians have estimated that Stalin may have killed as many as twenty million people. We will never know the exact number, but we can say this with certainty: Joseph Stalin was one of the most notorious mass murderers of all time, in the same company as Adolf Hitler.

Hitler was Stalin's most deadly adversary. He had taken power in Germany in 1933, promising to rebuild the armed forces and destroy what he called "Jewish Bolshevism." Belatedly Stalin realized he would need allies to meet the growing Nazi threat. In 1934 he ordered a dramatic about-face in Soviet foreign policy. Once he had vilified all the capitalist nations of the West; now he proclaimed that any enemy of fascism was a friend of the Union of Soviet Socialist Republics (USSR). The Soviet Union joined the League of Nations (the precursor of the United Nations) and proposed a policy of "collective security," allying with Britain and France to counter Nazi aggression.

But Western leaders did not trust the Communist dictator. They were not quite ready to shake the bloody hand of Joseph Stalin who, until very recently, had called for the destruction of the capitalist powers. They also doubted that the Red Army, devastated by the purges, was an effective fighting force. When negotiations with Britain (Pilkington in *Animal Farm*) and France proved unproductive, Stalin decided that he could get a better deal from Hitler (represented by Frederick). On 23 August 1939 the world was stunned to learn that the two archenemies had signed the Nazi-Soviet Pact. They agreed to a nonaggression treaty, provisions for trading war materiel, and a secret protocol to divide much of Eastern Europe between them.

Up to this point, many Communists and Communist sympathizers throughout the world had regarded the USSR as a bulwark against fascism. For them the Nazi-Soviet Pact, on top of the Great Purge, was profoundly disillusioning. Soviet intelligence as well as Western leaders warned Stalin that Hitler was preparing to double-cross him. He refused to listen until 22 June 1941, when Nazi Germany and the other Axis powers launched a surprise attack on the USSR.

In the first months of the war, the German army swept from victory to victory, surrounding and capturing hundreds of thousands of Red Army troops. Nazi forces advanced to the very outskirts of Moscow and Leningrad, halted finally by the brutal Russian winter and stiffening Soviet resistance. Initially the invading Germans had often been welcomed as liberators, so brutal had been the iron rule of Stalin. But attitudes changed when it became apparent that the Nazis were treating occupied Russia as a vast colonial empire, in which the natives were reduced to virtual slavery. Guerrilla armies of partisans organized to harrass the Germans behind the front lines. Stalin knew that the Russian people would fight more enthusiastically to protect their motherland than to defend Communism, so he played down ideological propaganda and made appeals to patriotism. Once he had suppressed the Russian Orthodox clergy (Moses the raven in *Animal Farm*); now he permitted them to preach sermons in support of the war effort. "The Internationale," the old Communist anthem, was (like "Beasts of England") replaced with a more patriotic song. The turning point in what Russians called "The Great Patriotic War" was the battle of Stalingrad, which ended in February 1943 with the encirclement and surrender of an entire German army. Over the next two years the Red Army pushed the Nazis back across half of Europe, capturing Berlin in May 1945. The end of the war was celebrated with dancing in the streets of Moscow and Leningrad, but the cost of victory was appalling. As many as twenty-five million Soviet people had died, and an equal number were homeless. Industrial production was down by 30 percent, and the country was close to starvation.

Moreover, the USSR had won the war in alliance with the great capitalist powers of the West, the United States and Britain. The British Prime Minister, Winston Churchill, had once advocated the overthrow of the Bolshevik regime, but in 1941 he promised all aid to fight their common enemy, Nazi Germany. British seamen ran gauntlets of German bombers to ship essential war supplies to the Soviets. In turn, Stalin ordered Communists in Britain and other allied nations to drop their revolutionary agitation and support the common struggle against Nazism. In 1943 the "Big Three"—Stalin, Churchill, and U.S. President Franklin D. Roosevelt—met in Tehran to plan war strategy and discuss the shape of the postwar world. George Orwell had this summit conference in mind when he wrote the last chapter of *Animal Farm*, where the pigs and humans become indistinguishable. Was not Stalin now parleying on equally friendly terms with "bourgeois democracies" he had once promised to overthrow?

"I personally did not believe that such good relations would last long," Orwell recalled in 1947; "and, as events have shown, I wasn't far wrong." In the final scene of *Animal Farm*, Napoleon and Pilkington are furiously accusing each other of cheating at cards. The elimination of Nazi Germany would bring to the surface all the old animosities between the USSR and the Western powers. They were soon locked in a bitter and protracted Cold War, which continued with varying degrees of mutual hostility until the collapse of the Soviet Union in 1991.

PROLETARIAN DEMOCRACY AND DICTATORSHIP

Lenin laid out the Bolshevik program on the eve of his seizure of power in 1917. He promised a "proletarian democracy" that, unlike the "bourgeois democracies" of the West, would truly represent the interests of the toiling masses. However, a "dictatorship of the proletariat" would be necessary to protect the new socialist regime from counterrevolutionaries. Since the Bolshevik party presumed to rule in the name of the proletariat, and since Lenin exercised increasingly rigid control over the Bolsheviks, the practical result was a dictatorship of Lenin and the party leadership. Plans had been underway before the revolution to elect a Constituent Assembly, but when the vote went against the Bolsheviks, they immediately suppressed the first and (until the collapse of Communism) the only Russian experiment in democracy.

Lenin was a passionately committed revolutionary who lived quite frugally, but Communist elites (like the pigs of *Animal Farm*) soon established themselves as a privileged class, enjoying special access to scarce goods and services.

FROM V. I. LENIN, *THE STATE AND REVOLUTION*
(Sidney Hook, *Marx and the Marxists* [Princeton, NJ: Van Nostrand, 1955; original, 1917])

The state is the product and the manifestation of the irreconcilability of class antagonisms. When, where, and to what extent the State arises, depends directly on when, where, and to what extent the class antagonisms of a given society cannot be objectively reconciled. . . . The substitution of a proletarian for the capitalist State is impossible without a violent revolution. . . .

We are not Utopians, we do not indulge in "dreams" of how best to do away *immediately* with all management, with all subordination: these are anarchist dreams based upon a want of understanding of the tasks of a proletarian dictatorship. . . . No, we want the Socialist revolution with human nature as it is now; human nature cannot itself do without subordination, without control, without managers and clerks. But there must be submission to the armed vanguard of all the exploited and laboring classes. . . .

. . . It is constantly forgotten that the destruction of the State involves also the destruction of democracy; the withering away of the State also means the withering away of Democracy. At first sight such a statement seems exceedingly strange and incomprehensible. Indeed, perhaps someone or other may begin to fear lest we be expecting the advent of such an order of society in which the principle of majority rule will not be expected—for is not a Democracy just a recognition of this principle?

No, Democracy is not identical with majority rule. No, Democracy is a *State* which recognizes the subjection of the minority to the majority, that is, an organization for the systematic use of *violence* by one class against another, by one part of the population again another.

Democracy for an insignificant minority, democracy for the rich—that is the democracy of capitalist society. . . .

The dictatorship of the proletariat . . . cannot produce merely an expansion of democracy. *Together* with an immense expansion of democracy—for the first time becoming a democracy for the poor—the dictatorship of the proletariat will produce a series of restrictions of liberties in the case of oppressors, exploiters and capitalists. We must crush them in order to free humanity from wage-slavery; their resistance must be broken by force. It is clear that where there is suppression there must also be violence, and there cannot be liberty and democracy.

. . . In this connection the special measures adopted by the Commune and emphasized by Marx are particularly noteworthy: . . . the lowering of the payment of *all* servants of the State to the level of the *workmen's wages*. Here is shown, more clearly than anywhere else, the *break*—from a bourgeois democracy to a proletarian democracy; from the democracy of the oppressors to the democracy of the oppressed; from the . . . suppression of a given class to the suppression of the oppressors by the whole force of the majority of the nation—the proletariat and the peasants. . . .

The control of all officials, without exception, by the unreserved application of the principle of election and, *at any time*, recall; and the approximation of their salaries to the "ordinary play of the workers"— these are the simple and "self-evident" democratic measures, which harmonise completely the interests of the workers and the majority of peasants; and, at the same time, serve as a bridge, leading from Capitalism to Socialism.

TERRORISM AND COMMUNISM

George Orwell was not the first to recognize that the Russian Communists had betrayed the ideals of democratic socialism. As early as 1919, German socialist Karl Kautsky spoke out against Lenin's regime. Communist repression, carried out by the Cheka, was already more severe than the old Czarist autocracy it had replaced. On the other hand, the terror that Stalin unleashed in the 1930s would be far more lethal.

FROM KARL KAUTSKY, *TERRORISM AND COMMUNISM*
(Sidney Hook, *Marx and the Marxists* [Princeton, NJ: Van
Nostrand, 1955; original, 1919])

Bolshevism has, up to the present, triumphed in Russia, but Socialism has already suffered a defeat. We have only to look at the form of society which has developed under the Bolshevik regime, and which was bound to develop, as soon as the Bolshevik method was applied. . . .

Originally they were whole-hearted protagonists of a National Assembly, elected on a strength of a universal and equal vote. But they set this aside, as soon as it stood in their way. They were thoroughgoing opponents of the death penalty, yet they established a bloody rule. When democracy was being abandoned in the State they became fiery upholders of democracy within the proletariat, but they are repressing this democracy more and more by means of their personal dictatorship. They abolished the piece-work system, and are now reintroducing it. At the beginning of their regime they declared it to be their object to smash the bureaucratic apparatus, which represented the means of power of the old State; but they have introduced in its place a new form of bureaucratic rule. They came into power by dissolving the discipline of the army, and finally the army itself. They have created a new army, severely disciplined. They strove to reduce all classes to the same level, instead of which they have called into being a new class distinction. They have created a class which stands on a lower level than the proletariat, which latter they have raised to a privileged class; and over and above this they have caused still another class to appear, which is in receipt of large incomes and enjoys high privileges. . . .

The absolutism of the old bureaucracy has come again to life in a new but, as we have seen, by no means improved form; and also alongside of this absolutism are being formed the seeds of a new capitalism, which is responsible for direct criminal practices, and which in reality stands on a much lower level than the industrial capitalism of former days. It is only the ancient feudal land estate which exists no more. For its abolition conditions in Russia were ripe. But they were not ripe for the abolition of capitalism. . . . Moreover, this loss of liberty is not compensated for by increase of prosperity. . . .

The economic, and with it also the moral, failure of Bolshevik methods is inevitable. It can only be veiled over if it should end in a military collapse. No world revolution, no help from without could hinder the economic failure of Bolshevik methods. The task of European Socialism, as against Communism, is quite different, namely, to take care that the moral catastrophe resulting from a particular *method* of Socialism shall not lead to the catastrophe of Socialism in general; and, further, to endeavor to make a sharp distinction between these methods and the Marxist method, and bring this distinction to the knowledge of the masses. Any Radical-Socialist Press must ill understand the interests of social revolution, if it really imagines it serves those interests by proclaiming to the masses the identity of Bolshevism and Socialism. . . .

Among the phenomena for which Bolshevism has been responsible, terrorism, which begins with the abolition of every form of freedom of the Press, and ends in a system of wholesale execution, is certainly the most striking and the most repellant of all. It is that which gave rise to the greatest hatred against the Bolsheviks. . . .

Shooting—that is the Alpha and Omega of Communist government wisdom. Yet does not Lenin himself call upon the "intelligentsia" to help him in the struggle against the rogues and the adventurers? Certainly he does; only he withholds from them the one and only means that can help, namely the *freedom of the Press*. The control exercised by the Press, in every respect free and unimpeded, alone can keep in check those rogues and adventurers who inevitably fasten on to any Government which is unlimited and in its powers and uncontrolled. Indeed, often through the very lack of the freedom of the Press these parasites thrive the more.

LEON TROTSKY DEFENDS TERRORISM

In a reply to Kautsky, Leon Trotsky openly defended the use of terror against "counterrevolutionaries." Later, Stalin would turn the same arguments against Trotsky and his supporters.

FROM LEON TROTSKY, *DICTATORSHIP VS. DEMOCRACY*
(Sidney Hook, *Marx and the Marxists* [Princeton, NJ: Van
Nostrand, 1955; original, 1922])

Kautsky, in spite of all the happenings in the world today, completely fails to realize what war is in general, and the civil war in particular. . . .

The problem of revolution, as of war, consists in breaking the will of the foe, forcing him to capitulate and to accept the conditions of the conqueror. . . . The bourgeoisie itself conquered power by means of revolts, and consolidated it by the civil war. In the peaceful period, it retains power by means of a system of repression. As long as class society, founded on the most deep-rooted antagonisms, continues to exist, repression remains a necessary means of breaking the will of the opposing side.

. . . The question as to who is to rule the country, i.e., of the life or death of the bourgeoisie, will be decided on either side, not by references to the paragraphs of the constitution, but by the employment of all forms of violence.

. . . The more ferocious and dangerous is the resistance of the class enemy who have been overthrown, the more inevitably does the system of repression take the form of a system of terror. . . .

The working class, which seized power in battle, had as its object and its duty to establish that power unshakeably, to guarantee its own supremacy beyond question, to destroy its enemies' hankering for a new revolution, and thereby to make sure of carrying out Socialist reforms. Otherwise there would be no point in seizing power.

. . . The revolution does require of the revolutionary class that it should attain its end by all means at its disposal—if necessary, by an armed uprising; if required by terrorism. A revolutionary class which has conquered power with arms in its hands is bound to, and will, suppress, with rifle in hand, all attempts to tear the power out of its hands. Where it has against it a hostile army, it will oppose to it its own army. Where it is confronted with armed conspiracy, attempt at murder, or rising, it will hurl at the heads of its enemies an unsparing penalty. Perhaps Kautsky has invented other methods? . . .

Or, perhaps, Kautsky wishes to say that execution is not expedient, that "classes cannot be cowed." This is untrue. Terror is helpless—and then only "in the long run"—if it is employed against a historically rising class. But terror can be very efficient against a reactionary class which does not want to leave the scene of operations. *Intimidation* is a powerful weapon of policy, both internationally and internally. War, like revolution, is founded on intimidation. A victorious war, generally speaking, destroys only an insignificant part of the conquered army, intimidating the remainder and breaking their will. The revolution works in the same way: it kills individuals, and intimidates thousands. In this sense, the Red Terror is not distinguishable from the armed insurrection, the direct continuation of which it represents. The State terror of a revolutionary class can be condemned "morally" only by a man who, as a principle, rejects (in words) every form of violence whatsoever—consequently, every war and every rising. For this one has to be merely and simply a hypocritical Quaker.

"But in that case, in what do your tactics differ from the tactics of Czarism?" we are asked, by the high priests of Liberalism and Kautskianism.

You do not understand this, holy men? We shall explain to you. The terror of Czarism was directed against the proletariat. The gendarmerie of Czarism throttled the workers who were fighting for the Socialist order. Our Extraordinary Commissions shoot landlords, capitalists, and generals who are striving to restore the capitalist order. Do you grasp this . . . distinction? Yes? For us Communists it is quite sufficient.

LESS SOCIALISM, MORE REPRESSION

Lenin's New Economic Policy permitted a partial and temporary restoration of capitalism in Russia, but greater economic freedom brought with it more political repression. Many Communists feared that the rise of a new class of entrepreneurs, the NEPmen, would undermine the revolution completely. Left-wing critics of the Bolsheviks—Karl Kautsky in Germany, Otto Bauer in Austria, the Menshevik and Socialist Revolutionary parties in Russia—could now say that they had been right all along to distrust the new regime, which was betraying the ideals of the revolution. Lenin felt threatened both by Russia's new capitalists and rival socialists. He therefore tightened the screws of dictatorship, even though the White armies had been defeated and Russia was finally beginning to enjoy modest prosperity and peace.

FROM V. I. LENIN, SPEECH TO THE ELEVENTH CONGRESS OF
THE RUSSIAN COMMUNIST PARTY
(Sidney Hook, *Marx and the Marxists* [Princeton, NJ: Van
Nostrand, 1955; original, 1922])

The other day I read an article . . . on a new book by Otto Bauer (who was our teacher at one time, but who, like Kautsky, became a miserable philistine after the war). Bauer now writes: "They are now retreating to capitalism: we have always said that the revolution is a bourgeois revolution."

And the Mensheviks and Socialist Revolutionaries, all of whom preach this sort of thing, are astonished when we say that we shall shoot those people who say such things. They are amazed; but surely it is clear. When an army is in retreat, a hundred times more discipline is required than when the army is advancing, because during an advance everybody presses forward. If everybody started rushing back now, that would spell disaster—immediate and inevitable.

Precisely at such a moment, the most important thing is to retreat in good order, to fix the precise limits of the retreat, and not to give way to panic. And when a Menshevik says, "You are now retreating; I have been advocating retreat all the time, I agree with you, I am your man, let us retreat together," we say in reply, "For the public advocacy of Menshevism our revolutionary courts must pass sentence of death, otherwise they are not our courts, but God knows what."

They cannot understand this and exclaim, "What dictatorial manners these people have!... The revolution has gone too far. What you are saying now we have been saying all the time; permit us to say it again." But we say in reply: "Permit us to put you before a firing squad for saying that. Either you refrain from expressing your views, or, if you insist upon expressing your political views publicly in the present circumstances, when our position is far more difficult than it was when the Whiteguardists were directly attacking us, we shall treat you as the worst and most pernicious White Guard elements." We must never forget this.

SOCIALISM IN ONE COUNTRY?

In their contest for power in the mid-1920s, Stalin and Trotsky clashed over the issue of "Socialism in One Country." This excerpt from Trotsky's writings may suggest why his position alienated the Party's rank-and-file. He appeared to disparage the Soviet Union as a hopelessly backward country. Stalin's argument—that a communist state could be built without assistance from the West—undoubtedly appealed more to Russian patriotism.

FROM LEON TROTSKY, "THE THIRD INTERNATIONAL
AFTER LENIN"
(Sidney Hook, *Marx and the Marxists* [Princeton, NJ: Van
Nostrand, 1955; original, 1937])

For the proletariat of every European country, even to a larger measure than the USSR . . . it will be most vitally necessary to spread the revolution to neighboring countries and to support insurrections there with arms in hand, not out of any abstract considerations of international solidarity, which in themselves cannot set the classes in motion, but because of those vital considerations which Lenin formulated hundreds of times—namely, that without *timely* aid from the international revolution, we will be unable to hold out. . . .

. . . The theory of socialism in one country inexorably leads to an underestimation of the difficulties which must be overcome and to an exaggeration of the achievements gained. One could not find a more anti-social and anti-revolutionary assertion than Stalin's statement to the effect that "socialism has already been 90 percent realized in the USSR." This statement seems to be especially meant for a smug bureaucrat. In this way one can hopelessly discredit the idea of socialist society in the eyes of the toiling masses. The Soviet proletariat has achieved grandiose successes, if we take into consideration the conditions under which they have been attained and the low cultural level inherited from the past. But those achievements constitute an extremely small magnitude on the scales of the socialist ideal. Harsh truth and not sugary falsehood is needed to fortify the worker, the agricultural laborer, and the poor peasant, who see that in the eleventh year of the revolution, poverty, misery, unemployment, bread lines, illiteracy, homeless children, drunkenness, and prostitution have not abated around them. Instead of telling them fibs about having realized 90% socialism, we must say to them that our economic level, our social and cultural conditions, approximate today much closer to capitalism, and a backward and uncultured capitalism at that, than to socialism. We must tell them that we will enter on the path of *real* socialist construction only when the proletariat of the most advanced countries will have captured power; that it is necessary to work unremittingly for this, using both levers—the short lever of our internal economic efforts and the long lever of the international proletarian struggle.

In short, instead of the Stalinist phrases about socialism which has already been 90% accomplished, we must speak to them in the words of Lenin:

"Russia (the land of poverty) will become such a land (the land of plenty) if we cast away all pessimism and phrasemongering; if clenching our teeth, we gather all our might, strain every nerve and muscle, if we understand that salvation is possible *only* along the road of international socialist revolution that we have entered."

STALIN'S DICTATORSHIP OF THE PROLETARIAT

Citing Lenin as a source of infallible inspiration, Stalin developed the theory of the dictatorship of the proletariat in its most absolute form. Note from the following excerpt that Stalin was a plodding and repetitive public speaker who conspicuously lacked the intellectual depth and electrifying oratorical skills of Lenin and Trotsky.

FROM JOSEPH STALIN, *PROBLEMS OF LENINISM*
(Sidney Hook, *Marx and the Marxists* [Princeton, NJ: Van
Nostrand, 1955; original, 1953])

The state is a machine in the hands of the ruling class for suppressing the resistance of its class enemies. *In this respect* the dictatorship of the proletariat does not differ essentially from the dictatorship of any other class, for the proletarian state is a machine for the suppression of the bourgeoisie. But there is one *substantial* difference. This difference consists in the fact that all hitherto existing class states have been dictatorships of an exploiting minority over the exploited majority, whereas the dictatorship of the proletariat is the dictatorship of the exploited majority over the exploiting minority.

Briefly: *the dictatorship of the proletariat is the rule—unrestricted by law and based on force—of the proletariat over the bourgeoisie*, a rule enjoying the sympathy and support of the laboring and exploited masses. (Lenin, *The State and Revolution.*)

From this follow two main conclusions:

First conclusion: The dictatorship of the proletariat cannot be "complete" democracy, democracy for *all* for the rich as well as for the poor; the dictatorship of the proletariat "must be a state that is democratic *in a new way (for* the proletariat and nonpropertied in general) and dictatorial *in a new way (against* the bourgeoisie)." . . . Under capitalism there are no real "liberties" for the exploited, nor can there be, if for no other reason than that the premises, printing plants, paper supplies, etc., indispensable for the actual enjoyment of "liberties" are the privilege of the exploiters. Under capitalism the exploited masses do not, nor can they ever, really participate in the administration of the country, if for no other reason than, even under the most democratic regime, under conditions of capitalism, governments are not set up by the people but by the Rothschilds and Stinnesses, the Rockefellers and Morgans. Democracy under capitalism is *capitalist* democracy, the democracy of the exploiting minority, based on the restriction of the rights of the exploited majority and directed against this majority.

Second conclusion: The dictatorship of the proletariat cannot emerge as the result of the peaceful development of bourgeois society and of bourgeois democracy; it can emerge only as the result of the smashing of the bourgeois state machine, the bourgeois army, the bourgeois bureaucratic machine, the bourgeois police.

WHY THE SOVIET STATE DID NOT WITHER AWAY

Karl Marx and his collaborator, Friedrich Engels, held that the state was simply the machinery that the ruling class used to repress the laboring class. Once the socialist revolution had abolished classes, government would no longer be necessary and would soon wither away. Under the Soviets, exactly the opposite happened: state power became increasingly oppressive and murderous. Stalin therefore had to explain why the socialist utopia had to be postponed. Not until after Mikhail Gorbachev took power in 1985 would the USSR "wither away"—something neither Gorbachev nor any other Soviet leader had intended or foreseen.

FROM JOSEPH STALIN, *PROBLEMS OF LENINISM*
(Sidney Hook, *Marx and the Marxists* [Princeton, NJ: Van Nostrand, 1955; original, 1953])

It is sometimes asked: "We have abolished the exploiting classes; there are no longer any hostile classes in the country; there is nobody to suppress; hence there is no more need for the state; it must wither away.— Why then do we not help our socialist state to wither away? Why do we not strive to put an end to it? Is it not time to get rid of the state, as so much lumber?"

Or again: "The exploiting classes have already been abolished in our country; socialism has in the main been built; we are advancing toward communism. Now, the Marxist doctrine of the state says that there is to be no state under communism.—Why then do we not help our socialist state to wither away? Is it not time we relegated the state to the museum of antiquities?"

These questions show that those who ask them have conscientiously memorized certain tenets of the doctrine of Marx and Engels about the state. . . . Consider, for example, the classical formulation of the theory of the development of the socialist state given by Engels:

> As soon as there is no longer any class of society to be held in subjection; as soon as, along with class domination and the struggle for individual existence based on the anarchy of production hitherto, the collisions and excesses arising from these have also been

abolished, there is nothing more to be repressed which would make a special repressive force, a state, necessary. The first act in which the state really comes forward as the representative of society as a whole—the taking possession of the means of production in the name of society—is at the same time its last independent act as a state. The interference of the state power in social relations becomes superfluous in one sphere after another, and then ceases of itself. The government of persons is replaced by the administration of things and the direction of the processes of production. The state is not "abolished," *it withers away*.

. . . Well, but what if socialism has been victorious only in one separate country, and if, in view of this, it is quite impossible to abstract oneself from international conditions—what then? Engels' formula does not furnish an answer to this question. As a matter of fact, Engels did not set himself this question, and therefore could not have given an answer to it. Engels proceeds from the assumption that socialism has already been victorious more or less simultaneously in all countries, or in a majority of countries. . . .

But it follows from this that Engels' general formula about the destiny of the socialist state in general cannot be extended to the particular and specific case of the victory of socialism in one separate country, a country which is surrounded by a capitalist world, is subject to the menace of foreign military attack, cannot therefore abstract itself from the international situation, and must have at its disposal a well-trained army, well-organized penal organs, and a strong intelligence service, consequently, must have its own state, strong enough to defend the conquests of socialism from foreign attack.

THE BRAVE NEW WORLD OF SOCIALISM

How did the Soviet regime persuade its people to accept so much privation and tyranny? It was not solely a matter of terror. Communist propaganda promised that once the Soviet Union had built up its economic base and defeated world capitalism, it would create a workers' utopia. High technology would transform nature, abolish hard manual labor, and provide wealth and leisure for all. Although Communists dismissed the Christian concept of heaven as "the opium of the people," they offered the Russian people an alternative myth—a vision of a heaven on earth. These dreams seem pathetically grandiose today, but millions of Soviet people believed in them and worked enthusiastically to make them a reality.

As Leon Trotsky described it, socialism would create a perfectly planned scientific society. Note his contempt for the unplanned quaintness of old Russian villages, his disdain for the natural beauties of the Russian countryside. Communist planning did build new urban areas, as Trotsky predicted; now they are vast stretches of monotonous, crumbling apartment blocks. Stalin did construct a base of heavy industry; those factories and mines are today poisoning the Russian environment with unchecked pollution. The eventual collapse of the Soviet regime came about partly because that industrial plant, devoted largely to producing weapons, failed to provide the consumer goods that Stalin and Trotsky both promised.

FROM LEON TROTSKY, *LITERATURE AND REVOLUTION*
(Sidney Hook, *Marx and the Marxists* [Princeton, NJ: Van
Nostrand, 1955; original, 1957])

There is no doubt that, in the future—and the farther we go, the more true it will be—such monumental tasks as the planning of city gardens, of model houses, of railroads, and of ports, will interest vitally not only engineering architects, participators in competitions, but the large popular masses as well. The imperceptible, ant-like piling up of quarters and streets, brick by brick, from generation to generation will give way to titanic constructions of city-villages, with map and compass in hand. . . . Architecture will again be filled with the spirit of mass feelings and moods, only on a much higher plane, and mankind will educate itself plastically, it will become accustomed to look at the world as submissive clay for sculpting the most perfect forms of life. . . .

. . . The present distribution of mountains and rivers, of fields, of meadows, of steppes, of forests and of seashores, cannot be considered final. . . . Man will occupy himself with re-registering mountains and rivers, and will earnestly and repeatedly make improvements in nature. In the end, he will have rebuilt the earth, if not in his own image, at least according to his own taste. We have not the slightest fear that this taste will be bad. . . .

The new man, who is only now beginning to plan and to realize himself, will not contrast a barn-door for grouse and a drag-net for sturgeons with a crane and a steam-hammer. . . . Through the machine, man in Socialist society will command nature in its entirety, with its grouse and its sturgeons. He will point out places for mountains and for passes. He will change the course of the rivers, and he will lay down rules for the oceans. The idealist simpletons may say that this will be a bore, but that is why they are simpletons. Of course this does not mean that the entire globe will be marked off into boxes, that the forests will be turned into parks and gardens. Most likely, thickets and forests and grouse and tigers will remain, but only where man commands them to remain. And man will do it so well that the tiger won't even notice the machine, or feel the change. . . .

. . . The passion for mechanical improvements, as in America, will accompany the first stage of every new Socialist society. The passive enjoyment of nature will disappear from art. . . .

. . . Having rationalized his economic system, that is, having saturated it with consciousness and planfulness, man will not leave a trace of the present stagnant and worm-eaten domestic life. The care for food and education, which lies like a millstone on the present-day family, will be removed, and will become the subject of social initiative and of an endless collective creativeness. Woman will at last free herself from her semiservile condition. . . .

. . . Man will become immeasurably stronger, wider and subtler; his body will become more harmonized, his movements more rhythmic, his voice more musical. The forms of life will become dynamically dramatic. The average human type will rise to the heights of an Aristotle, a Goethe, or a Marx. And above this ridge new peaks will rise.

SOVIET CENSORSHIP POLICIES

While promising a utopian future, the Soviet regime rigorously suppressed news about the privations and injustices that its citizens faced every day. Westerners have always known that there was censorship in the USSR, but only recently have Russian scholars been allowed to investigate government archives and write openly about the subject. Their research reveals, in unprecedented detail, how Soviet censorship worked. Following is an excerpt from a study by Arlen Blium, an eminent Russian librarian whose father was shot in 1938. Blium sees all too clearly the similarities between the Soviet Union and the totalitarian societies imagined by George Orwell in *Animal Farm* and *1984*. His research shows that the bureaucratic machinery of censorship was already in place by the mid-1920s, even before Joseph Stalin gained absolute power. The press was controlled—in incredible detail—by the Central Directorate for Literary and Publishing Activity, known by the abbreviation "Glavlit."

FROM ARLEN VIKTOROVICH BLIUM, "FORBIDDEN TOPICS:
EARLY SOVIET CENSORSHIP DIRECTIVES"
(Trans. Donna M. Farina, *Book History* 1 [1998]: 271–280)

To stop criticism definitely, a special directive for censors was published in 1925: "It is forbidden to publish any article, notice, or announcement calling attention to the work of agencies responsible for controlling material before and after publication." . . . Directives such as this immediately became the most widespread and effective method of control. They were sent to all the local censorship branches and looked like this:

People's Commissariat of Education
Central Directorate for Literary and Publishing Activity ("Glavlit")
14 October 1924

To all provincial and regional censorship agencies.
To all political editors and representatives of Glavlit in printing offices, publishing houses, newspapers and magazines.

. . . Glavlit suggests that information about price policies or concrete steps taken in pricing should not be permitted in the press. This ban applies to policies for the whole Soviet Union and for individual regions; it covers information about prices paid not only by the grain-procuring organizations, but on the entire procurement market.

These directives were all strictly classified. "Secret" (or "Strictly Secret"); "Urgent" invariably appears at the top of each one. They were "to be strictly executed." Any failure to do so was investigated at the highest level and led to sanctions against the censors involved "along Party and administrative lines." The huge apparatus of Glavlit agencies became larger with each passing year. They were strictly guided by instructions from above and by the Glavlit directives; they had to display their vigilance and class consciousness by purging from print everything that the hand of Glavlit had not yet touched. This had to be done quickly, even before the appearance of the corresponding Glavlit directive, by "considering the local situation," in response to the latest news, with guidance from Party documents and materials from the newspapers.

From time to time, separate censorship directives were combined in special "Lists of information, classified as secret and not to be disseminated, for the preservation of the USSR's political and economic interests." The first of these lists appeared in 1925, in the form of a sixteen-page brochure stamped "Top Secret"; each list was numbered. I was able to examine several of them in the archives; for example, no. 8 . . . contains ninety-six points or "positions" that were prohibited from publication. We need cite only a few to show just how cruel and all-encompassing censorship had become under these new conditions:

§1. Statistics on homeless and unemployed elements of the population, and about counterrevolutionary raids on government institutions.

§2. Clashes between the authorities and peasants during the implementation of tax and fiscal measures; also conflicts caused when citizens are drafted for compulsory work.

§62. Information about sanitary conditions in places of incarceration.

§82. The publication of crime statistics, the party affiliation of accused persons, and the number of court decisions calling for the death penalty are not permitted.

§91. The publication of news about suicide or cases of mental derangement caused by unemployment and hunger are forbidden.

In compliance with "The List," "information about the availability of medications" in pharmacies and "information about help to regions suf-

fering from crop failures" was also barred from publication. . . . Due to
"the exacerbation of the class struggle," more sections were added to the
expanded and revised "List" of 1927. These sections forbade information
"about *unrest, strikes,* disorder, demonstrations, discontent, . . . among
workers and peasants." An extremely interesting footnote to this section
reads: "Information about strikes at *private* businesses . . . can be published." Clearly, it was necessary to compromise private enterprise, since
the Politburo had already decided to curtail the NEP. An indication of
what was in store can also be seen in those points of the 1927 "List" that
seem to prepare censors for the coming show trials of the late 1920s and
early 1930s. . . . It was forbidden to publish material about "the number
of political crimes," "the dissolution of bourgeois and kulak councils and
sanctions against them," and "administrative deportations of socially dangerous individuals or groups." Of course, information about the political
trials of "saboteurs" was published in the newspapers, but this was done
only with the approval of Party authorities. Independent initiative was
not tolerated.

The existence of OGPU concentration camps was a carefully guarded
secret, as this directive from 1926 shows:

> Glavlit.
> 13 May 1926
> Secret. Directive to all provincial censorship agencies and political
> editors.
>
> Numerous articles have appeared recently in the periodical press
> about the OGPU Solovetsky concentration camps and the life of the
> prisoners. Moreover, these articles are based on a variety of sources.
> Glavlit suggests that articles such as these should not appear in the
> press without the permission of the OGPU's special division. . . .

Glavlit repeatedly issued directives ordering stricter control over information pertaining to "Kremlin secrets" and Kremlin leaders. Beginning
in 1924, directives stamped "Top Secret" ordered the local press to with-
hold information "about trips planned by members of the USSR Government and Russian Communist Party Central Committee." The ban
included information "about scheduled stops and places where speeches
would be made." It was forbidden to "send out reporters and photog-
raphers, etc., without the consent of the OGPU." Such information could
appear in the newspaper only if "there is no mention of the time and
place the person is supposed to appear." (One wonders how this could
have been carried out in practice!)

All publications mentioning buildings that *could* be visited by Kremlin
leaders (and not only the Kremlin buildings themselves) entered into the
censors' sphere of attention. In the 1925 "List," there was even a special

section (§95) about the Kremlin buildings: "The publication of information, either modern or historical in nature, about the Kremlin, Kremlin walls, exits and entrances, etc., is forbidden without the consent of the Kremlin Commandant." Because it was so frequently visited by Kremlin leaders, the Bolshoy Theater had always been considered the "court" theater. Now it too had to be shrouded in secrecy:

Glavlit.
29 June 1926
Secret. Directive to all political editors of Glavlit.

Until the repairs on the State Bolshoy Theatre are completed, Glavlit suggests that information on their progress should not be published. When the repairs are finished, information may be published only with the consent of the Kremlin Commandant, Comrade Peters.

. . . In "the year of the great turning point" [1929], coinciding with Stalin's fiftieth birthday and the beginning of the "mustachioed man's" unprecedented elevation, Glavlit issued numerous directives. These ordered the "canonization" of the Leader's image—everything that might damage it had to be dissociated from it. This treatment even extended to physical images of Stalin, such as photographs. For example, a special directive was published on 20 December ordering the local authorities "to make sure that official portraits of Stalin used photos received only from . . . the Russian Telegraph Agency. The publication of other portraits or photos is not permitted."

The names of Stalin's political opponents began to be purged even before this, around 1925–26. This included the name of his greatest opponent, Leon Trotsky. . . . The censors' directive forbade published photographs of "enemies of the people." In addition, their names had to be accompanied by appropriate epithets that were sanctioned and approved at the highest level. Later on, after a hate campaign was conducted in the press, these names had to diappear completely from print. . . . This was also a sign that soon the person would physically disappear, as often happened during the years of the Great Terror. The rewriting of history had begun. . . .

The country's real economic situation had to be shrouded in absolute secrecy. Under no circumstances could the censoring agencies allow descriptions of calamities, especially starvation. From its debut in 1923, . . . Glavlit issued warnings about the possible publication of material on economic topics; these warnings even covered works still *in preparation* and discovered by the censoring agencies through intelligence sources. For example, the following secret directive appeared on 26 June 1923:

According to our sources, a certain A. Vainshtein wants to publish his research on taxes levied on the rural population. This scholarly research attempts to show that taxes under the Soviet regime are an extreme burden. If a manuscript like this is submitted by any publishing house, it should not be passed for publication.

The era of total secrecy now began. As time went on, this was carried to absurd heights. The aforementioned "Secret Lists" consisted largely of articles concerning the preservation of "military secrets" (the stationing of troops, armaments, etc.). While this is not so unusual, in actual practice completely harmless pieces of information were declared secret. Likewise, information that had never been secret before was now classified as "economic secrets." For example, in the 1920s information about the export of wheat was carefully concealed, not to ensure a profit for the USSR on the world market but to hide from the public the fact that wheat was being exported. It is well known that the export of grain continued during the 1930s, even during the year of horrible starvation in the Ukraine (1933): this the public should never suspect.

Many directives instructed: "Until further notice, statistics about the year's harvest should not be published. This includes general figures on the harvest, individual crops or areas." . . . In 1928, the censor of the newspaper *The Pskov Bell* received a reprimand for letting . . . slip into print . . . a plan to export mushrooms from the Pskov region. The same censor was also reprimanded for allowing the newspaper to publish information on the procurement of flax, leather hides, and fur skins. . . .

The directives prohibited the most unexpected things. For example, there was a ban on advertising foreign goods in the press. The following Glavlit directive, stamped "Top secret," was released in 1925:

> This is to inform you that advertisements by foreign companies for the following products are not desired in the Soviet press: (a) knitted articles; (b) footwear; (c) cosmetics; (d) fabric for making vestments; (e) ready-made clothing and underwear; (f) food; (g) clocks and watches; (h) needles; (i) various household articles; (j) irons, kerosene stoves, etc.

This order did not result from fear of unwanted competition from foreign goods on the domestic market (in spite of a few economic improvements during the first years of the NEP, almost none of the products mentioned above were available). Rather, the directive stems from ideological considerations: the Soviet people should not even suspect that things that had vanished from the stores after the Revolution were being produced in abundance in the "decaying West."

The censorship agencies were constantly protecting the Soviet people's peace of mind: they did not need to know about natural disasters (there should not be any calamities of nature under socialism), train wrecks, factory explosions, or the like. . . .

15 November 1926
Secret.

The Leningrad Provincial Censorship Agency suggests that steps be taken so that no information whatsoever about train wrecks on the Northwestern Railroad appears in print, without the knowledge and consent of the OGPU's Political Control.

. . . The "List" even prohibited information on epidemics or medical assistance in districts where disasters occurred.

The creation of Glavlit resulted in an effort to hide the truth that bordered on paranoia. As we know, this practice continued for many decades and at times resulted in tragic consequences for the population. The practice was curtailed only in May 1986, when the authorities were forced to inform the public about the Chernobyl nuclear catastrophe. Even then, the urge to conceal did not disappear all at once: disclosures about Chernobyl were delayed and incomplete. (An even greater catastrophe of this type occurred in the South Urals in 1957, but an overwhelming majority of the Soviet people only learned of it thirty years later). "Ignorance Is Strength." This party slogan from Orwell's novel [1984] was completely adopted by the real, nonfictional "Ministry of Truth."

TOPICS FOR WRITTEN OR ORAL EXPLORATION

1. "The point of *Animal Farm* is that all revolutions are futile: they will inevitably produce a new tyranny as oppressive as the one they replaced." Do you agree or disagree?

2. Explain why allegory is a particularly effective method of political satire.

3. Is *Animal Farm* solely and simply a story about the Soviet Union, or are its lessons relevant to other societies as well? Provide illustrations and examples to defend your answer.

4. In writing *Animal Farm* Orwell did not exactly follow the history of the Soviet Union. Was he justified in doing so? Explain why a writer of historical fiction might take liberties with the historical record.

5. According to most estimates, Joseph Stalin's regime was as murderous as Adolf Hitler's. Why has political terror been carried out in the twentieth century on a scale unheard of in earlier eras?

6. Karl Marx defined socialist equality in these terms: "From each according to his abilities, to each according to his needs." Can this ideal ever be achieved? If so, how? If not, why not?

7. Does *Animal Farm* help to explain why the Soviet Union collapsed in 1991?

8. Can *Animal Farm* be read as a tract for animal rights? If it is wrong to exploit and oppress working people, is it equally wrong to exploit and oppress farm animals?

9. Try writing an allegory of your own—one that addresses any political issue of your choice.

4

George Orwell and the Road to *Animal Farm*
Denise Weeks

EARLY YEARS

Eric Blair, the boy who would become George Orwell, was born in India in 1903 and died in England in 1950, just five years after he became famous around the world as the author of *Animal Farm*. Throughout his life he struggled with the weak and tubercular lungs that would finally fail him, but his illness was not correctly diagnosed until the year before he died. Like Boxer in *Animal Farm*—who eventually dies from overexerting himself and injuring his lungs—Orwell was a determined fighter. Unlike Boxer, of course, he was not an illiterate "beast" who could remember only four letters of the alphabet at a time. But many events in Orwell's life led him to identify strongly with the people whom Boxer represents: the working classes.

Orwell returned to England with his mother and siblings at a young age, and he spent his boyhood in a small country town. On regular family outings and long walks through fields and woods, Orwell's love of the outdoors and animals took root. He cherished the times he spent fishing at nearby ponds and rivers, and he loved dogs, cats, rabbits, and guinea pigs. Later in his life, when he was a schoolteacher, he would lead his pupils on exploratory walks, perhaps hoping to instill in them the same fondness for the out-

During the 1930s, George Orwell farmed a small plot in Wallington, outside London, where he grew his own crops and raised animals. This scene imagines Orwell's farm animals looking on as he types the manuscript *Animal Farm*. Created by Paul Rodden.

doors that he experienced. He eventually had his own small farm complete with goats, chickens, and a dog named Marx (an affectionate and ironic tribute to Karl Marx).

Orwell's concern for animals was a constant throughout his life. In *Animal Farm* his appreciation of the better qualities in animals is apparent in his treatment of strong and unwavering Boxer, kindhearted Clover, the cynical donkey, Benjamin, and the hardworking ducks and hens. Pigs do not fare so well under Orwell's scrutiny, nor do the sheep. The pigs' intelligence in *Animal Farm* allows them to rule the farm ruthlessly. The sheep, on the other hand, cannot think for themselves and can be trained to bleat whatever slogan the pigs want them to. ("Sheeplike" was an adjective Orwell once applied to the British—suggesting that they too would accept whatever they were told.) Orwell's interest in animals, whether it be his own dog, Marx, or the more objectionable pigs in neighbors' farms in Wallington, most likely gave him the confidence to use animals as characters in his allegorical novel.

As a boy, Orwell was interested in words and the stories he could create with them. He explained in the essay "Why I Write," "From a very early age, perhaps the age of five or six, I knew that when I grew up I should be a writer" (435). He also added, "I knew that I had a facility with words and a power of facing unpleasant facts" (435). A talent with words and an ability to face unpleasant facts describe very well the young man who would grow up to write *Animal Farm*. Among the "unpleasant facts" that he would face in his life were his early school experiences at St. Cyprian's, where Orwell found the educators cruel and harsh. Orwell would later describe the environment at the school as cold and inhumane. He also reported that its power-hungry "leaders" reinforced class distinctions and believed education was nothing more than cramming students' heads full of facts.

It was at St. Cyprian's that Orwell first encountered the kind of authoritarian system that he would later satirize in *Animal Farm*. He did not experience anything nearly as savage as what Napoleon inflicted on the farm animals, of course, but he saw in the school the same kind of oppressive system that dehumanized—*animalized*—those who came in contact with it.

We can imagine that in writing certain sections of *Animal Farm*, Orwell might have been drawing on memories of his early schooling and combining them with his adult awareness of the insidious nature of political propaganda and ideological indoctrination. What is education in *Animal Farm* if not indoctrination? Under Snowball, who is benign in comparison with Napoleon, education is bureaucratic. Committees are formed for every aspect of farm life, and all the farm animals are taught to read (though there is nothing to read but the principles of Animalism written on the barn doors). For the wild animals (rats, birds, the cat), there is a committee set up for "re-education." With masterful irony Orwell describes the results of Snowball's efforts. The cat rejoins the Re-education Committee, but only, apparently, so that she can catch more birds. What the cat gets out of its "re-education" is that it is possible to use the empty slogan, "All animals are now comrades," against other animals. So far from equality and true comradeship are they that the cat sees only how it can take advantage of others. The sparrow too is not convinced by the propaganda and knows to keep its distance.

Under Napoleon, the more ruthless of Animal Farm's early leaders, education becomes a much more powerful tool. First Jessie and Bluebell's puppies are taken away to be educated as savage killers who will protect Napoleon and take care of his "enemies." Then, at the end of the book, Squealer takes the sheep away for their private lessons. What are they taught? To turn everything on its head: to reverse everything that Animalism was supposed to stand for. They come back from their lessons just in time to bleat their accompaniment to the spectacle of the pigs walking on their hind trotters: "Four legs good, two legs *better*" (122).

All of Orwell's early school experiences, first at St. Cyprian's and later at Eton, contributed to his development as a critic of systems. Throughout his young life and into adulthood, wherever Orwell found institutions or systems trying to control the thoughts and actions of its followers, Orwell also found reasons to speak out against tyranny. He would do this most eloquently in his first bestseller, *Animal Farm*.

Orwell's secondary school experiences at Eton, a school roughly equivalent to a private American high school, may have further reminded him of the unfair class system that determined one's place in British society, but it also prepared Orwell for a scholarly future. To be accepted into Eton at all was proof of Orwell's distinctive intelligence, but it was a distinction that Orwell later downplayed. He did not, for instance, use the advantage such an education afforded him to prepare himself for a scholar's life; instead, upon graduating from Eton he decided to take a post with the Indian Imperial Police in Burma. Surprisingly, the young man who knew he was destined to be a writer chose instead to work for the British Empire. He would discover later that he was trading one oppressive system for another, but as a policeman he had the unhappy experience of *enforcing* rather than *following* the system's rules.

WORKING FOR THE EMPIRE

One might expect a budding artist—a youth with intelligence and a yearning to write books—to take the most advantage of his opportunities. For young Orwell, however, the opportunities he sought did not lie in the traditional pursuits. Experience interested him more than formal education. It is possible, too, that the traditional university education would have been too elite for Orwell. Although he was not from a poor family, he had not grown up in the class that traditionally went to the country's most prestigious schools. Eton had the distinction of preparing some of Britain's best minds, and Orwell might have felt that by pursuing a path available to so few, he was cutting himself off from the world of the common man and the working classes that he would later champion.

By most accounts, India did not provide Orwell with the experience he desired. He became disenchanted with the empire: the militaristic nature of his job, which he described with poignant detail in his essays "Shooting an Elephant" and "A Hanging," did not suit the young artist. He began to see that imperialism was a self-serving, rigid system that brought out the worst in people— both the rulers and the ruled. His job as a policeman put him into situations where he experienced firsthand the kind of brute power and arrogance he would later use as a model for Mr. Jones and Manor Farm. In India, as at St. Cyprian's School, Orwell experienced the injustice of authoritarian systems that strive for efficiency at all costs. Such systems, Orwell argued, were inevitably corrupt. They take what might originally have been good ideas and turn them into rigid, destructive patterns. This idea gets played out in *Animal Farm* when Major's ideas for a revolution, originally meant to liberate the animals, get turned into a "complete system of thought" named Animalism. This authoritarian system ultimately gives complete power to Napoleon. In *Animal Farm* Orwell is not yet exposing the evils of totalitarianism; that would be explored in his next best-seller, *1984*. He is instead simply warning against what could happen, even to England, if it were to be seduced by the rhetoric of Soviet socialism.

The relationship between rulers and ruled, and the systems that sustained these unjust relationships, continued to interest Orwell during his time in India and would become a touchstone for much of his political writing.

BECOMING A WRITER

Leaving his position in India to become a writer struck Orwell's middle-class family as a somewhat reckless move. As far as making a living goes, serving the empire was far more lucrative than being a writer. As a novelist and journalist, Orwell would start to make the kind of money he made as a police officer only after the publication of *Animal Farm* in August 1945. When he left India and started writing full time in 1927, that was still eighteen years away. So how did he live? Meagerly. The image we have of starving artists fits the young Orwell perfectly. His experiences after returning from India included periods of poverty, "tramping" (staying in homeless shelters with other vagabonds), going hungry, and even getting arrested. But these were not *unfortunate* experiences for Orwell; rather they served as research. Putting on dirty trousers and sleeping in the Salvation Army gave Orwell a way to enter a world he could never participate in as an educated, middle-class man, much less a policeman. And living among the poor, even if on his own terms and for short periods only, seems to have been a way for Orwell to expiate his guilt and long-pent-up frustration at having worked for the British Empire. As he would say about his escape from his position in India years later, "I felt that I had got to escape not merely from imperialism but from every form of man's dominion over man. Failure seemed to me to be the only virtue. Every suspicion of self-advancement, even to 'succeed' in life to the extent of making a few hundreds a year, seemed to me spiritually ugly, a species of bullying" (*Road* 138). But Orwell was not devoid of ambition, and he worked tirelessly at his writing.

Guilt at having worked as an agent for the empire may be one reason that Orwell immersed himself in poverty and deprivation. Another reason might be found in the times themselves. Among many liberal writers in the 1930s, there was a growing conviction that the "common man"—the working classes and the poor— needed better representation. Artists were recognizing that no one wrote about the poor with any compassion or understanding. Although he was not yet politically active in the late 1920s and early

1930s, Orwell shared this concern for the working classes and would address their problems and needs in many of his books and essays. In *Animal Farm*, for instance, his concerns over class inequality and the living and working conditions of the poor are made apparent by Mr. Pilkington. Near the end of the book, when the pigs have dressed themselves in Mr. Jones's clothes and are dining with the neighboring farmers, Mr. Pilkington raises his glass in a toast: "If you have your lower animals to contend with . . . we have our lower classes!" (126). What did Pilkington approve of in Napoleon's treatment of his "lower animals"? Discipline, orderliness, and the nearly slavelike working condition of the animals. Orwell had observed the same treatment of the poor and working classes on several occasions in his life. Now, in his fiction, he could create a fantasy story that would show the cruelty inherent in systems that oppressed the "lower class."

The difference between reality and fiction in Orwell's work has long been a topic of debate for Orwell critics. His two most famous novels, *Animal Farm* and *1984*, are obviously fiction because they are stories: they have characters, settings, and a plot. They are not straightforward accounts of anything Orwell experienced directly. But does that mean that they are not about reality, that they do not treat the reality that Orwell knew and experienced? This is where the difference between reality and fiction in Orwell's work becomes blurred.

Orwell's first book, *Down and Out in Paris and London* (1933), is different from *Animal Farm* and *1984* in that it is a documentary rather than a novel. It documents—in other words, notes, records, and observes—the experiences Orwell had in Paris after his return from India. He moved there hoping to begin his career as a writer, which he did by publishing a few articles, but he ended up working as a dishwasher and spending a few days without any money at all. The book also describes a short period of time he spent "tramping" in and around London with the regular down-and-out crowd. Although the details he recounts in the book did not always happen exactly as he records them, for the most part, the book is a true account of what he witnessed and experienced over a period of several years. What is important about this first book for an understanding of *Animal Farm* is that Orwell is beginning to develop the famously clear prose style that characterizes the writing in *Animal Farm*. Observation, telling it like it is, honesty: these characterize the style Orwell developed in his early work and perfected throughout his career.

Although the journalistic *Down and Out in Paris and London* was an important first venture for Orwell, it did not prove a success. In fact, it almost never made it to print because of Orwell's persistent lack of faith in his own talent. Upon finishing the work and trying unsuccessfully to find a publisher, Orwell eventually handed the manuscript over to a friend with the instructions to throw it away. Luckily for Orwell, his friend disregarded his directions and instead sought out an agent she thought would take an interest in the work. She was persistent, and eventually successful. Orwell's new agent soon had an agreement with Victor Gollancz, a publisher. (The relationship between Gollancz and Orwell would prove fruitful for both, but it would never be easy. Gollancz would help Orwell by offering him the commission to Orwell's next successful documentary, *The Road to Wigan Pier*, but he would also publicly critique Orwell's politics and be the first publisher to reject *Animal Farm*.) So even after his first book was published, he continued to feel that he was not a "real" writer yet—that he had to write fiction to achieve his ultimate goal. With the publication and success of *Animal Farm* twelve years later, Orwell was no longer "becoming" a writer but had "become" one.

BECOMING A NOVELIST

Orwell's second book, a novel titled *Burmese Days*, did more than his first book to establish his career as a writer. Novels sold better than nonfiction or documentary texts, and they awarded their authors greater prestige. What this second book did for Orwell was provide him a more popular vehicle for self-expression while also giving him the opportunity—in print—to work through the negative experiences he had had in India. The violence and cruelty that Orwell had observed in British authorities, in the Indians they ruled, and in himself are shown in the character sketches in this novel. One can see the origins of *Animal Farm* in this book in the way the system in *Burmese Days* poisons relations between characters. Genuinely caring relationships are impossible in a climate that forces competition and power struggles. Imperialism, like the authoritarian St. Cyprian's, Orwell may have been arguing, brings out the worst in human relationships.

In 1932–1933, when Orwell was inserting his ideas about the failings of imperialism into his first novel, he had not yet observed the larger failings of Stalin's socialism. Ten years later, when he began *Animal Farm*, he had observed quite enough. By that time, too, Orwell would have mastered both the style of his writing and the format for its expression. His style would reflect the straightforward reporting voice that he continued to develop in his nonfiction writing, and the format would be the novella, and in particular, the beast fable or fairy story. The novel, after all, had a much broader appeal to reading audiences, and the novel was better suited for Orwell's fantasy story about talking barnyard animals and pigs that could read and write. Although written as a novel, the story has at its base a very factual, straightforward, reportorial voice that Orwell had used in his first book and had developed throughout his career.

BECOMING A SOCIALIST

In the research and writing of two other books from the 1930s, *The Road to Wigan Pier* (1937) and *Homage to Catalonia* (1938), Orwell found the content for his art. With his first book he had begun to develop his style; with his second book he found a format for his work; and by 1936 he discovered his subject matter. As he explains in his essay "Why I Write," "Every line of serious work that I have written since 1936 has been written, directly or indirectly, *against* totalitarianism and *for* democratic socialism, as I understand it" (440). He notes also that his goal after 1936 was to "make political writing into an art." In *The Road to Wigan Pier* and *Homage to Catalonia*, he worked toward achieving the goal that would be completed in *Animal Farm*.

What had such a dramatic effect on Orwell's outlook? In 1935, Victor Gollancz, Orwell's publisher, asked Orwell to travel to northern England to write about the living conditions and status of the unemployed there. Because Orwell's first book treated this same subject in a different context, Orwell must have seemed a natural choice for the work. Although admittedly only vaguely political up to that point, Orwell took the commission and set out to document the lives of the working class (employed and unemployed) in and around Wigan, England. As Gollancz would write in his foreword to the account, the first half of the book is a "terrible record of evil conditions, foul housing, wretched pay, hopeless unemployment and the villainies of the Means Test: it is also a tribute to courage and patience" (Foreword xi). The second half of the book, however, was less favorably received (xii). What disturbed Gollancz was Orwell's shift in attention from the workers' lives to the socialists' efforts to help them. Gollancz did not appreciate that Orwell was criticizing socialist methods and theories, but Orwell's point was that "before you can be sure whether you are genuinely in favor of Socialism, you have got to decide whether things at present are tolerable or not tolerable, and you have got to take up a definite attitude on the terribly difficult issue of class" (*Road* 121). The problem, as Orwell saw it, was that socialists were not facing the class issue head on and were alienating the very people they were trying to reach. Gollancz, a staunch socialist, did not respond well to Orwell's challenge.

What Orwell saw and experienced in industrial northern England was a turning point in his life and writing. He became aware of his own political consciousness and his need not only to criticize but also to do something *for* the causes he believed in. By the late 1930s, there was something very definite to act against: fascism. In Germany, Hitler's Nazi party had been in power since 1933; Italy was now ruled by the dictator Mussolini; and in Spain, Franco's totalitarian regime would overthrow the government in 1936. All of these crises, and their ramifications for England, compelled Orwell to look critically at his own involvement in contemporary events. What he saw during his trip to Wigan was an exploited but nearly invisible class of people. He also began to think about his own responsibility in keeping those people down, and he saw the failures of political parties that did nothing concrete to help.

But it was not enough for Orwell to simply be *against* systems he did not support; he felt too that he needed to be *for* something. The something he is for in *The Road to Wigan Pier* is a reformed, more effective democratic socialism. He states this argument most strongly when he makes the almost prophetic point that "we are at a moment when it is desperately necessary for left-wingers of all complexions to drop their differences and hang together" (220).

Orwell would observe the same problem among the left when he went to Spain a year later, and he would satirize this propensity for infighting in *Animal Farm*. After the first rebellion, as Manor Farm is being transformed into Animal Farm, Snowball and Napoleon do everything but "hang together." Snowball and Napoleon always take different sides in debates, for example, and eventually Napoleon runs Snowball off the farm and later defames him by calling him a traitor. Hanging together—the oppressed fighting the oppressors—was at the base of Orwell's ideal for a more effective socialism, and in *Animal Farm* he showed how corruption and abuse of power made achieving such a state impossible.

In his desire to be actively *for* something, Orwell found a cause in the Spanish Civil War. It is important to understand how significant this war was for all Britons, Europeans, and the rest of the world. Politically engaged artists and writers in England had been aware of the spread of fascism since 1933, but apart from writing about injustice and urging social action, there seemed to be little they could do. Spain changed that. To Orwell and many other writers and artists, Spain was a turning point. Here was a country not buckling beneath totalitarian forces but defending itself against them. Here was a simple case of wrong versus right, of fascism versus democracy—or at least that is how it appeared to Orwell in the fall of 1936.

The year 1936 was eventful for Orwell. He spent the first part of it researching *The Road to Wigan Pier*; in March he moved to the small village of Wallington, where he moved into a small farm house; in June he married his sweetheart, Eileen O'Shaughnessy; and in December he went to Spain. Each of these events has some bearing on the publication of *Animal Farm* nine years later. The observations he made while researching *The Road to Wigan Pier* urged him to declare his stand for democratic socialism. Moving to Wallington returned Orwell to the country living he had enjoyed so much as a child and gave him the opportunity to have a garden, goats, dogs, and chickens. His experiences with these animals and his knowledge of farming show in the detail he includes in *Animal Farm*. (Interestingly, too, the small house and farm that he occupied there had previously been an experimental farm named "Manor Farm.") His wife, Eileen, some critics have suggested, helped Orwell as he drafted and revised his book, and she was very supportive of his daring efforts. Going to Spain gave Orwell a glimpse of a "socialist utopia" that—like the ephemeral utopia in *Animal Farm*—is ultimately betrayed.

When Orwell arrived in Barcelona, he was assigned a position with the militia group called the Partido Obrero de Unificación Marxista (Workers' Party of Marxist Unification)—POUM, for short. His role would be like every other soldier's in the unit: when a large enough group had formed, they would be sent to the front to defend northern Spain from Franco's loyalist guards. To Orwell, whose aim in coming to Spain was to fight fascism, the divisions between the parties on the left had not yet revealed themselves.

Indeed, what Orwell saw in Barcelona was unlike anything he had ever seen before. The anarchists, the group of fighters comprising mostly the working class, were in control of the city. Here is Orwell's description in *Homage to Catalonia*, the book that details his experiences in Spain:

> It was the first time that I had ever been in a town where the working class was in the saddle. . . . Every shop and café had an inscription saying that it had been collectivized . . . waiters and shop-walkers looked you in the face and treated you as an equal. . . . And it was the aspect of the crowds that was the queerest thing of all. In outward appearance it was a town in which the wealthy classes had practically ceased to exist. Except for a small number of women and foreigners there were no 'well-dressed' people at all. Practically everyone wore rough working-class clothes, or blue overalls or some variant of the militia uniform. (4–5)

Coming so recently from his own country, where the class distinctions were obvious and entrenched, this spirit of equality struck Orwell as "a state of affairs worth fighting for" (5). He also wrote, "I believed that things were as they appeared" (5).

What Orwell first observed in Spain appeared better than it really was. Barcelona appeared to be a great brotherhood of common men fighting a common enemy, and it appeared that the sympathizers who had come from all over Europe to join the fight had no motive but to defeat fascism and promote freedom. And though his experience in Spain ultimately taught him otherwise, it seemed that the unified fighting represented a simple and necessary response to an absolute evil. But Orwell observed that the men in the Spanish militias did not seem like "real" soldiers and that the war was at times rather slow. Despite any disappointment he felt at not seeing more action, however, he continued to believe that he was contributing to a worthwhile cause.

If the fighting on the battlefield did not impress Orwell as very serious, it was at least serious enough that Orwell ended up getting shot. Although his injury ended his career as a soldier in the Spanish Civil War, it did not end his participation in the political battles that surrounded it.

Unbeknown to Orwell, tensions between the communist and anarchist factions in the war had been building for some time. By early 1937, while Orwell fought with the POUM, the USSR-backed communists had begun spreading rumors that the POUM militia, not followers of Stalin, were in fact part of Franco's army. They called the POUM both "Trotskyists" and "Franco's Fifth Column," hoping to call their loyalty into question. Because Franco was their common enemy, these charges were quite serious. In May, the communist-supported government forces banned the POUM newspaper and in mid-June outlawed the party altogether and started arresting its leaders. The plea Orwell had made in *The Road to Wigan Pier*—that "we are at a moment when it is desperately necessary for left-wingers of all complexions to drop their differences and hang together"—could not have found better justification than in the events that unfolded in Spain that spring.

By June 1937, Orwell realized that things were not as they had appeared in January, and he recognized that he had been partially blinded by his own zeal to fight *against* fascism and *for* "common decency." He realized too that he had believed the newspaper accounts he had read at home and had not recognized that events in Spain were more political than moral. The complexities of the political machinations in Spain, the left's infighting, and the true nature of the workers' uprising had not been discussed in newspaper accounts back home, and Orwell, like other well-meaning readers, had believed the oversimplified reports that most papers published. Orwell surmised that the misinformation campaign was made possible by the government's interest in keeping the truth hidden. More than a simple fight between two parties representing good and evil, Orwell began to see that the Spanish Civil War was being waged by at least three groups: two that wanted to "win" in order to preserve the status quo (Franco's loyalists and the Communists), and one that wanted revolution (the anarchists).

The fascists, though a real presence throughout Europe and in part behind Franco's military uprising, were not as important in the war as had been argued in the newspaper accounts of the war. The evil specter of fascism had been thrown around in the press so often that the conflict in Spain had been reduced to simple black-and-white terms. What was more important than identifying the enemy as the outsider, the invader, the evil fascist, as Orwell saw it, was the recognition that fascism, communism, imperialism, and democratic capitalism all had in common a desire to maintain the status quo. Instead of representing a strong counter to fascism, then, communism under Joseph Stalin (and democratic capitalism and imperialism in the United States and Britain) was too invested in making money to allow workers to gain too much power. What was happening in Spain, Orwell discovered, was far more radical than citizens fighting off an enemy who threatened their way of life. What the workers in the anarchist (and POUM) parties were doing was spearheading a revolution that would change the country's base of power. Though ostensibly part of the same leftist movement as the anarchists, the Communists, who were supported and armed by Stalin, had a very different agenda for Spain.

Because Orwell had come to Spain with papers endorsed by socialists rather than Communists and because he had been a member of a militia not sanctioned by the Communists, it meant that when the POUM was outlawed, Orwell was in serious danger. He and his wife, Eileen, who had been working in Barcelona, had to escape the country to avoid arrest and imprisonment. Other members of the party had already been killed, and a friend of theirs would remain in prison for another eighteen months. The events that Orwell experienced that year in Spain meant something else too. They were a deciding factor in Orwell's development as a political thinker and writer. As he would later write in his essay "Why I Write," "The Spanish war and other events in 1936–7 turned the scale and thereafter I knew where I stood. Every line of serious work that I have written since 1936 has been written, directly or indirectly, against totalitarianism and for democratic socialism, as I understand it" (440). Many of those "serious lines" would make up his best-selling fable, *Animal Farm*.

That the inspiration for *Animal Farm* was born out of Orwell's experience in the Spanish Civil War cannot be overemphasized. *Homage to Catalonia*, which Orwell wrote about those experiences, should be a primer for students of *Animal Farm*. It contains the lessons Orwell learned about political deception, propaganda, and the corrupting influence of power. Of course, the figures for *Animal Farm* would take shape in Orwell's imagination later, as events during World War II cast an even harsher light on the USSR and Stalin's betrayal of socialism. But it is important to note that it was at this point in his life, too, when Orwell realized that his best writing grew out of his desire to fight injustice and to make political writing an art. Here was the old tension (journalistic writing versus literature), but with a new twist. Whatever he wrote, whether editorials, essays, nonfiction, or novels, it would have to grow out of his political purpose.

Although 1937 was the year Orwell gained this new sense of himself as a writer with a purpose, he did not become a dogmatist, preaching one sermon only. From the time he left Spain until he began writing *Animal Farm*, in fact, he changed his political outlook substantially. He first joined, then quit the Independent Labour Party; he initially endorsed, then condemned pacifism; and at the start of World War II, he recognized that his patriotism was even more powerful than his anti-imperialist skepticism. In the same spirit that urged him to join the fight in Spain, Orwell wanted to serve the British army in 1939. His suffering health forbid it.

Orwell felt that it was his duty to do something during the war to help defeat Hitler, and because he was unable to serve with his body, he took what writing jobs he could to keep busy. These included writing reviews, articles, and essays, for all of which Orwell continued to sharpen his skills as observer and develop his talent as a plain-speaking social and political critic.

The most significant work Orwell published during the war was a book-length essay, *Lion and the Unicorn*. Here Orwell outlined his most optimistic hope for Britain during England's most devastating period of the war. While London was being bombed, Orwell wrote of the great opportunity for radical change the war afforded England. This war, Orwell argued, gave the British the unique chance to practice a Leninist concept called "war-communism" that would allow them to sweep out the old order and move toward a specifically British brand of social democracy.

In arguing this position, Orwell took pains to show that he was not simply against the current government, but that he was for positive social change. He did not advocate a revolution simply for the sake of throwing out the old, but offered a six-point plan whereby Britain could adopt a democratic socialist form of government that would abolish Britain's class-based system of privilege.

These were some of the same ideas Orwell had tackled in his documentary accounts of the "down and out" in Paris and London and later in *The Road to Wigan Pier*. Now, by 1941, Orwell's political views had been strengthened by his observations of world events. He had noted how the British government had responded slowly and negligently to the events that led up to World War II. He had seen how left-leaning intellectuals were sold on Soviet propaganda for the "workers' state" even while Stalin consolidated his totalitarian power through ruthless purges and show trials. He had seen in Spain both the possibilities for a truly classless society and its betrayal and ruin by the Communists. And he had seen how the totalitarian regime in the Soviet Union could hide or rationalize all of its criminal acts under the guise of progress. His understanding of their deceit would be demonstrated years later, in *Animal Farm*, when he has the pigs rationalize their "scientifically proven" need for milk and apples. Squealer, who is always sent out to calm any doubts the animals may have about the pigs' rules and behavior, tells the animals that milk and apples are abolutely essential for the pigs' health. They eat the milk and apples to maintain their strength, Squealer tells them, not because they enjoy them.

The Orwell writing in 1941 that "what is wanted is a conscious revolt by ordinary people against inefficiency, class privilege, and the rule of old" (*Lion* 86) was a much wiser writer than he was a decade earlier when he wrote that there was "a sort of heavy contentment" and simplicity associated with poverty (*Down and Out* 91). No longer could Orwell romanticize the life of the poor; by 1941 it seemed to Orwell that the class system in Britain, and the government that sustained it, made England vulnerable. "We cannot win the war without introducing Socialism," Orwell urged, "nor establish Socialism without winning the war" (*Lion* 94). The most important element of Orwell's call for a democratic socialism was that it be a *British* socialism rather than a *Soviet* socialism. It should not be based on Marxism, which was the basis for the Soviet model, or follow the pattern adopted by Nazi Germany. A British form of socialist democracy, Orwell felt, had to embrace and reflect the peculiarities of British civilization, which, according to Orwell, was full of "anachronisms and loose ends."

Although it may seem that a call for action of this magnitude—this urgent plea for revolution—would indicate an overly critical or negative frame of mind on the part of its author, Orwell was, in fact, quite enthusiastic about the possibilities for positive change during the war. But his hope for revolution did not in any way undermine his larger support for Britain during the war. He was not like so many on the left who were merely against fascism or imperialism; he wanted to do all he could to help Britain defeat Hitler.

Orwell's desire to help the war efforts were thwarted by his continuing poor health. Never able to serve as a soldier, he decided to do what he could at home. In 1941 he accepted a position with the British Broadcasting Corporation (BBC) as an announcer and program developer for the Indian section of the empire service. This was a radio program that covered political and literary topics of possible interest to Indian listeners. The goal of the programming, according to BBC officials, was to provide "positive" propaganda for Indian listeners who were also being bombarded by German propaganda that threatened to turn India against Britain. It is ironic that Orwell should end up back in the service of the empire, working under the severe hand of Britain's Ministry of Information (which would appear in *1984* as "Miniform").

Orwell had accepted the BBC work with the hope that it might help the wartime effort, but he eventually grew dissatisfied with the drudgery of bureaucracy and the censors' control over his broadcasts. He ultimately felt, too, that his efforts were being wasted and that few people were listening. He did gain something from the experience, however, and that was the model for Squealer, the pigs' main propagandist.

When Orwell left the BBC in 1943, he began the period of his career that would lead to his lasting fame. He began working as literary editor and columnist for the *Tribune*, and in November 1943 he began writing *Animal Farm*.

Orwell's position at the *Tribune* could not have been more perfect for him. He had politically like-minded colleagues, flexible work hours, and the freedom to write on any topic of his choosing in his weekly "As I Please" column. On subjects ranging from roses to revolution, Orwell fine-tuned his craft as a political and social observer. The "anachronisms and loose-ends" that he had said characterized British civilization in *The Lion and the Unicorn* here came under his weekly scrutiny. Writing most often with the humor and sharp wit that would characterize *Animal Farm*, Orwell's weekly columns contributed to his growing reputation as a plain-speaking friend of the common man. Never tolerant of jargon or difficult phrasing, Orwell worked even harder in his column to write clearly, intelligently, and with purpose. Orwell did have his critics. Unlike the censors at the BBC or the publisher Victor Gollancz, however, the *Tribune*'s editors supported Orwell's work and were not intimidated by his open castigation of Soviet Russia and those who continued to support it. In one sharply worded critique he wrote: "Don't imagine that for years on end you can make yourself the boot-licking propagandist of the Soviet regime or any other regime, and then suddenly return to mental decency. Once a whore, always a whore" (qtd. in Crick, 305). Orwell might have replaced *whore* with *pig*, as *Animal Farm* was, by the early 1940s, already in Orwell's mind as an idea for a next novel. "Boot-licking" would fit right in with the more deceptively benign picture Orwell paints of Squealer, the "brilliant talker" with "twinkling eyes" whose persuasive manner could turn black into white (26). The language in *Animal Farm* is less offensive, perhaps, than that used in his "As I Please" column, but no less pointed. Orwell had no tolerance for those who manipulated language for their own ends, especially those who managed to convince themselves of necessity of their own lies.

While Orwell's political views became sharper and more focused, his mastery of the English language and his love of literature also continued to grow. Colleagues of Orwell could not help but recognize his facility with language and the clarity of his thought; many of his friends recall the long monologues he had delivered during which he would talk a subject through from beginning to end without pausing or stumbling (or letting anyone else get a word in). The same thing was true of his writing; he could sit down and compose his entire "As I Please" column in a single session, with no corrections needed. It is perhaps not surprising, then, that the entire composition of *Animal Farm* took him only a few months and was written at the same time he was working as editor and columnist.

Animal Farm, finished in February 1944, represents the culmination of Orwell's growth as a political thinker and writer from 1936 to 1944. In it, he turns political writing into an art. This beast fable, seemingly simplistic in style and approach, was as politically sophisticated and well written as anything Orwell had done to date. It was a daring project, too, in that sentiments in early 1944 were still strongly in favor of the Soviet Union. It turned out that this "fairy story"—as the book jacket identified it—was too bold a critique of the Soviets' betrayal of the Russian Revolution for most publishers. In fact, despite Orwell's increased success as a writer by 1944, he did not find a publisher for *Animal Farm* for an entire year. Gollancz, the publisher of his first book, refused it, stating that he could not "possibly publish . . . a general attack of this nature" (qtd. in Crick, 312). Though disheartened at the timidity of the publishers who refused the book, Orwell, along with Eileen, knew the book was a success. Usually always a harsh critic of his own fiction, Orwell trusted that in this book, written so differently from his previous nonfiction works, would work. And it did—and still does.

While the most immediate "explanation" of *Animal Farm* can be found in the parallels between the pigs at Animal Farm and the leaders of the Soviet Union (as shown in Chapter 1), Orwell's own explanations of the book add to our understanding of its context and origins. Orwell's experiences in Spain were the turning point in his career from aspiring novelist to political writer. This is not to suggest that he stopped caring about literature, but that he began to work harder to fuse the political and artistic in his writing. The two ideas he carried with him from Spain were, first, that a truly classless society like the one he experienced in Barcelona was something worth fighting for; and second, that the communist leaders of the Union of Soviet Socialist Republics (USSR) had betrayed the socialist revolution. Both of these ideas find expression in Clover's unvoiced thoughts about the state of Animal Farm as she contemplates the violence that has occurred since Old Major first inspired them to revolt. Instead of freedom and equality, the animals now experience fear and bloodshed. These ideas are also spelled out at the end of *Animal Farm*, when Napoleon goes so far in his attempts to rewrite history that he denies that there had ever been a revolution at all. This, for Orwell, was the real betrayal: the denial of the revolution itself, the desire for the status quo, the mere replacement of one set of rulers for another. This was something that Orwell had experienced firsthand in Spain and had seen again and again in reports on the Soviet Union. Orwell, through the vehicle of his "animal" story, was one of the few writers brave enough to expose the lie.

What served as an even more immediate catalyst for *Animal Farm* was an observation Orwell made long after his return from Spain:

> On my return from Spain I thought of exposing the Soviet myth in a story that could be easily understood by almost anyone and which could be easily translated into other languages. However the actual details of the story did not come to me for some time until one day (I was then living in a small village) I saw a little boy, perhaps ten years old, driving a huge cart-horse along a narrow path, whipping it whenever it tried to turn. It struck me that if only such animals became aware of their strength we should have no power over them, and that men exploit animals in much the same way as the rich exploit the proletariat. (Qtd. in Crick, 309)

In recalling his inspiration, Orwell provides as vivid and powerful an image as the book itself leaves in a reader's mind: the cruel boy, the suffering horse; the ruthless Napoleon, the gentle but strong Boxer. The misery of the animals' lives is described well by Old Major, who, when he calls them together to tell them his dream, states: "Let's face it: our lives are miserable, laborious, and short. We are given just so much food as will keep the breath in our bodies . . . and the very instant that our usefulness has come to an end we are slaughtered with hideous cruelty" (18).

Orwell's idea that animals who understood their strength could overpower their oppressors also gets realized in *Animal Farm*. The revolution, occurring spontaneously after the animals get whipped for helping themselves to the food they had been deprived of, totally surprises Jones and his men because they had never experienced anything like it before: "This sudden uprising of creatures whom they were used to thrashing and maltreating just as they chose, frightened them almost out of their wits" (29). Both the sight of the boy whipping the horse and the story it inspired are seemingly simple, too, but it is due to Orwell's talent as a writer—his economy of style, matter-of-fact tone, and command of the English language—that a complex political situation could be made into a highly readable and relevant modern fable.

BECOMING IMMORTAL

This biographical sketch describes Orwell as a man destined to write *Animal Farm*. All of his major life experiences led him to it. But that is not the complete story, for we all know that Orwell went on to write *1984*. Does the road to *Animal Farm* end in 1945? No. Where *Animal Farm* ends, *1984* begins. It is important that readers not separate these books into different categories because one is about "animals" and the other is a darker, more "realistic" look at the future. Readers who look closely will see that *Animal Farm* ends with the pigs in control of "Manor Farm" (no longer "Animal" Farm after the pretense of equality has been abandoned), and *1984* begins with similar rulers more firmly entrenched. Where *Animal Farm* shows the dangers of tyranny and authoritarian systems, *1984* shows what must happen under a well-developed totalitarian system.

It is important to remember, too, that when Orwell finished writing *Animal Farm* in 1944, World War II had not yet ended and England was still allied with the USSR. Orwell could see where things were headed, but the finale to the war had not yet sealed the fate of the world's great superpowers. *1984* was the logical and necessary sequel to *Animal Farm*. The first book signaled the warning—this could happen to us!—and the second book, published just before Orwell died in 1950, played out the inevitable consequences of allowing it to occur.

TOPICS FOR WRITTEN OR ORAL EXPLORATION

1. Debate the inclusion of *Animal Farm* in the curriculum for eighth-grade English class.

2. Following Orwell's model in *Animal Farm*, satirize a contemporary political event by creating your own "beast fable." What animals would represent the different people? How would you describe them? Where would the story take place?

3. Recount an episode in which you witnessed a cruelty similar to what Orwell observed when he saw a young boy whipping his horse. Write a brief documentary account of the episode.

4. Create a dialogue between Napoleon and Snowball on the topic of education.

5. Explain what Orwell means when he says that after 1936–37 he knew where he stood.

6. Describe the propaganda that Orwell satirizes in *Animal Farm*. Who delivers it? What is its intent?

7. Can you identify any positive or negative contemporary propaganda? Where do you see it? What is its intent? Is it successful?

8. Debate the issue of *Animal Farm* as propaganda.

9. Bridging the gap between political writing and artistic writing was important to Orwell. Identify contemporary writers who try to do the same. Comment on their similarity or differences to Orwell.

SUGGESTED READINGS

Crick, Bernard. *George Orwell: A Life*. London: Secker & Warburg, 1980.

Gollancz, Victor. "Preface." *Road to Wigan Pier*. New York: Harcourt Brace Jovanovich, 1958.

Orwell, George. *Animal Farm*. New York: Harcourt, Brace and Company, 1946.

———. *Down and Out in Paris and London*. San Diego: Harcourt Brace Jovanovich, 1933.

———. *Homage to Catalonia*. San Diego: Harcourt Brace Jovanovich, 1993.

———. *The Lion and the Unicorn. The Collected Essays, Journalism, and Letters of George Orwell, Volume II*. Ed. Sonia Orwell and Ian Angus. 4 vols. New York: Harcourt, 1968.

————. *The Road to Wigan Pier*. New York: Harcourt Brace Jovanovich, 1958.

————. "Why I Write." *Collected Essays*. London: Secker & Warburg, 1961.

5

Animal Farm and the Early Cold War
John Rodden

CHRONOLOGY

1939–45	World War II
1943	February 2: Hitler's armies surrender in Stalingrad November: Orwell begins writing *Animal Farm* November 28–December 1: Tehran Conference, attended by Allied war leaders of the "Big Three" (U.S. president Franklin D. Roosevelt, Soviet dictator Joseph Stalin, and British prime minister Winston Churchill)
1944	February: Orwell completes *Animal Farm* June 6: Allied forces land on the beaches of Normandy, France, which signals the invasion of German-occupied Western Europe; known as "D-Day"
1944–45	Soviet troops defeat Germans in Poland, Hungary, and most of Czechoslovakia and occupy all three countries
1945–49	USSR succeeds in promoting communist government takeovers in most East European countries
1945–53	Harry Truman serves as U.S. president
1945	April: Orwell travels to Germany and cables news reports on occupied Germany May 8: Germany unconditionally surrenders to the Allies, officially ending the European theater of World War II; known as "V-E (Victory in Europe) Day"

	August 6: First atom bomb dropped on Hiroshima, Japan
	August 17: *Animal Farm* published in United Kingdom
	September 2: Japan officially surrenders; known as "V-J Day"

1946–47   USSR–U.S. tensions over Soviet control of Eastern Europe lead to increasing East-West hostilities and beginning of Cold War

1946   August: *Animal Farm* published in the United States
            August: Orwell begins writing *1984*
            September: *Animal Farm* selected as a main choice of the Book-of-the-Month Club

1947   January: *Animal Farm* adapted by Orwell as a BBC radio play
            April: Dutch radio adaptation of *Animal Farm*

1948   February: Soviet invasion of Czechoslovakia
            June 18–21: West Berlin blockaded by the USSR; United States and Britain begin Berlin Airlift program to bring supplies to West Berlin
            September: USSR resumes anti-Semitic persecution campaign (until Stalin's death in 1953)
            November: Orwell completes *1984*

1949   January: West Germany founded
            February: Communist takeover in China
            April 4: North Atlantic Treaty Organization (NATO) formed, a twelve-nation Western alliance against the Soviet bloc
            May: Berlin Blockade lifted after 328 days
            June 8: Publication of *1984*
            July: *1984* selected as a main choice of the Book-of-the-Month Club
            September 25: USSR announces that it has tested an atom bomb
            October: East Germany founded

1950–53   Korean War

1950   January 21: Orwell dies of tuberculosis at the age of forty-six
            February 2: Joseph McCarthy, junior senator from Wisconsin, opens his anti-communist attacks on U.S. Army and other government agencies
            June: Korean War begins

1951	January: USSR launches "Hate America" campaign
1953–61	Dwight D. Eisenhower serves as U.S. president
1953	March 5: Stalin dies. Georgii Malenkov succeeds him as premier and first secretary of the Communist Party July: Korean War ends August 12: USSR explodes hydrogen bomb
1954	April–June: Television hearings on Senator Joseph McCarthy's accusations about widespread Communist presence in U.S. government agencies December 2: McCarthy censured by U.S. Senate Mid-December: *Animal Farm* released as animated cartoon film
1955	May 14: The Warsaw Pact, the military organization of the Soviet bloc nations, is formed—a seven-nation alliance to counter NATO June: *Animal Farm* cartoon receives award at the 1955 Berlin Film Festival

THE ORIGINS AND SUCCESS OF *ANIMAL FARM*

George Orwell once said that *Animal Farm* had been "in my mind for a period of six years before it was actually written." He added:

> Up to 1939 and even later, the majority of English people were incapable of assessing the true nature of the Nazi regime in Germany, and now with the Soviet regime, they are still to a large extent under the same sort of illusion . . . it was of the utmost importance to me that people in western Europe should see the Soviet regime for what it really was.[1]

Just after completing *Animal Farm*, Orwell wrote to a friend in 1944: "I consider the willingness to criticize Russia and Stalin to be *the* test of intellectual honesty."[2] Orwell soon put his fellow intellectuals and the reading public to the test. Orwell was not the first Western writer to satirize or condemn the USSR as a betrayal of revolution and socialism. André Gide in *Return from the USSR* (1937) and Arthur Koestler in *Darkness at Noon* (1941) had done the same. Orwell circulated the manuscript among four British publishers in 1944–45; all rejected the manuscript. He considered bringing out *Animal Farm* as a two-shilling pamphlet when he was unable to publish it as a book during the war. That turned out to be unnecessary.

Orwell's critique of the USSR was an extremely unpopular viewpoint among intellectuals in the mid-1940s. *Animal Farm* was written between November 1943 and February 1944. This was the period between the great Nazi defeat by the Russian army at Stalingrad and the launching of the invasion of Normandy. During these months, the Allies first became victorious, and there was a strong feeling of solidarity with the Russians, who even in retreat had deflected Hitler from a conquest of Britain. Orwell later explained: "I wrote it immediately after the Tehran conference [November 1943] which everybody thought had established the best possible relationship between the USSR and the West. I personally did not believe that such good relations would last long."[3]

Orwell was right. Within two years, the Western Allies and the USSR had split into hostile rival camps. The key idea of *Animal Farm* is contained in the preface to the Ukrainian edition written in 1947:

> Nothing has contributed so much to the corruption of the original idea of socialism as the belief that Russia is a Socialist country and that every act of its rulers must be excused, if not imitated. And so for the past ten years I have been convinced that the destruction of the Soviet myth was essential if we wanted a revival of the Socialist movement.[4]

Orwell invented a fable to fight a myth. Ultimately the fable won: *Animal Farm* is the best-known fable written in the twentieth century. It has sold more than 20 million copies in five dozen languages since its publication in 1945 and has been the subject of numerous dramatizations and even a celebrated animated cartoon-film.

Why has *Animal Farm* become both a best-selling book and a classic? One reason is that it speaks to the key issues to the latter half of the twentieth century, specifically socialism and communism. *Animal Farm* struck a nerve when it appeared just as World War II was closing and the postwar world was dawning. In Great Britain and the United States, as well as in other Western countries, the topic of anti-Communism became the dominant news headline. The postwar battle between Communists and anti-Communists, and between the USSR and the Western democracies, replaced the wartime battle between the democratic nations and the fascist powers led by Adolf Hitler in Germany and Benito Mussolini in Italy.

But *Animal Farm* has continued to be a best-seller because it possesses universal and lasting appeal as a work of art. It is not just a satirical treatment of the Russian Revolution and its aftermath, but also a fable about the betrayal of revolutions generally. To illustrate the enduring relevance of *Animal Farm*, one need only recall that some of its sentences have entered the popular imagination of the English-speaking world and are often quoted by people who do not even know that their source is Orwell's little fable. For instance, the sentence "All animals are equal, but some are more equal than others," appears on a popular brand of American greeting cards, known as Animal Farm Greeting Cards. There is no mention of Orwell anywhere on the cards.

Animal Farm sold well from its initial edition in August 1945 in Britain. It was named the main choice of the Book-of-the-Month Club in the United States in August 1946, when it sold more than a half-million copies. It has never stopped selling. In the early 1950s, it entered the junior and senior high school canon in Britain and the United States. Since that time, it has been one of the ten most commonly read books in British and American high schools. It was also adapted for the screen as an animated film in the 1950s and for the stage as a play in the 1960s. In 1996, on the fiftieth anniversary of its American publication, new editions and new stage adaptations of *Animal Farm* were released.

To understand this extraordinary success of *Animal Farm* as a school classic and top-selling book, one needs to appreciate the historical context of the fable. Because anti-Communism as a political issue is largely dead in the United States and other Western countries today, it is vital to recall the significance of that issue in the early postwar era. Otherwise it is difficult to understand the success, or even the basic meaning, of *Animal Farm* at all.

ANIMAL FARM AND "THE CRUCIAL DECADE"

Animal Farm was published on August 17, 1945. In the previous four months, Roosevelt, Mussolini, and Hitler had died; Churchill had been voted out of office; Germany had surrendered, and on

August 6, the atom bomb had exploded over Hiroshima. The time was ripe for a fantasy written from an anti-Stalinist stance. Of the leaders of the major wartime powers, only Stalin survived in power. And, indeed, *Animal Farm* would come to have its greatest influence in the following decade, during the early years of the international hostilities between the capitalist West and communist East known as "the Cold War."

Stretching from the mid-1940s to the late 1980s, the Cold War was characterized by intense hostilities between capitalist and communist world powers—hostilities that stopped just short of direct military conflict between the two superpowers: the United States and USSR.

These two nations were at war, but they did not fight each other by direct military means. Sometimes they fought through substitute nations ("proxy wars," such as in Korea in the 1950s and Vietnam in the 1960s and 1970s). Or their battles took the form of intense ideological, political, and economic rivalries. These rivalries remained keen for several decades, but they did not—as had happened in the cases of international rivalries before World War I and World War II—escalate into a "hot" or shooting war. Hence the term "cold" war. (The term was first used by the American financier and presidential adviser Bernard Baruch during a congressional debate in 1947.)

But the possibility that the Cold War might lead to World War III was ever-present. And after the United States dropped the atom bomb on Japan in August 1945 and the Soviets developed their own atomic weapons in 1949, the world feared that a third world war might destroy the planet. The next world war, said military experts, might be the last.

The years of greatest risk of escalation were the late 1940s and early 1950s. This was the period of Stalin's last years in power. During this time, Stalin became increasingly power hungry and paranoid. His armies marched in to occupy much of Eastern Europe and imposed communist regimes. These Eastern European nations—among them Hungary, Bulgaria, Czechoslovakia, Rumania, Albania, and eastern Germany—became communist dictatorships and satellites of the USSR.

Animal Farm was used by anti-Stalinists to attack the USSR. For instance, it was quickly translated into many Eastern European languages. Radio plays of *Animal Farm* were aired in Britain and Germany in 1947–48; even a ballet of *Animal Farm* was performed in Berlin.

The Cold War reached its peak during 1948–53. In this period the Soviets unsuccessfully blockaded the Western-held sectors of West Berlin (1948–49); the United States and its European allies formed the North Atlantic Treaty Organization (NATO), a unified military command to resist the Soviet presence in Europe (1949); and the Soviet-supported communist government of North Korea invaded U.S.-supported South Korea in 1950, setting off the Korean War, which lasted until 1953 and ended in a truce that divided North and South Korea into separate nations.

Stalin's death in March 1953 did not immediately reduce East-West tensions. His successors vied for power and conducted many political intrigues. The USSR was ruled by a triumvirate of three Communist Party leaders. Not until 1956 did a single leader, Nikita Khrushchev, emerge with sole power as the new dictator. But his ascendancy led only to a temporary lessening of hostilities between the capitalist and communist nations. The stand-off remained. A unified military organization among the Soviet bloc countries, the Warsaw Pact, was formed in 1955, and West Germany was admitted into NATO that same year.

So this first postwar decade constituted the "warmest," most dangerous years of the Cold War. Historian Eric Goldman termed the years 1945–55 "the crucial decade" in his book of that title (*The Crucial Decade* [1960]).

This characterization is helpful for our understanding of *Animal Farm*. Goldman used this phrase "the crucial decade" in broad terms. He argued that political and technological developments of the early postwar era—the Cold War, the spread of Communism throughout the world, the atomic and nuclear bombs, the birth of the computer and network television, and other major events— had set developments in motion that would have far-reaching and long-lasting consequences.

We are concerned here with Goldman's claim chiefly in relation to *Animal Farm*, the Cold War, and the spread of Communism. Goldman's thesis is broadly valid. Consider just the case of Communism. Only in the 1990s, in the aftermath of the failed communist revolution in Nicaragua, was the forward march of Communism halted in the Third World. And not until 1991 was

Communism swept away in the birthplace of the communist state, the USSR, with the collapse of the Soviet Union and its breakup into fifteen separate, independent nations.

The far-reaching consequences of "the crucial decade" and *Animal Farm* in the 1980s and 1990s are the subject of Chapter 6. Here we focus on the period 1945–55. So let us now take a closer look at the treatment and impact of *Animal Farm* during "the crucial decade" after its 1945 British publication.

CONTEMPORARY RECEPTION: THE BRITISH RESPONSE TO *ANIMAL FARM*

Most British reviewers knew something of Orwell's previous books. They knew that Orwell was a socialist and a supporter of the British Labour Party, which advocated socialism. Those British intellectuals hostile or opposed to *Animal Farm* were generally well informed about his politics and critical of it. Yet because of its satirical and allegorical form, they sometimes misinterpreted *Animal Farm*. Its form made it difficult for readers to understand Orwell's precise political message. As one British friend, William Empson, noted in a letter to Orwell, the allegory is inherently a slippery genre. If one handles it as an artist, as Orwell did in *Animal Farm*, it is hard to make it hit a narrow target and serve a pointed political case.

But the subtleties of Orwell's allegory were not immediately obvious to most critics. For instance, not everyone realized that the hens' revolt in Chapter 7 stands for the brutally repressed 1921 mutiny of sailors at Kronstadt, who had challenged the new regime to release political prisoners and grant freedom of speech and the press. Or that Napoleon's deal with Whymper, who trades the farm's produce at market, represents Russia's 1922 Treaty of Rapollo with Germany, which ended World War I.

T. S. ELIOT

After receiving rejections from two leading British publishing houses in 1944, Orwell sent the manuscript of *Animal Farm* to the poet T. S. Eliot. An American expatriate living in London and the author of *The Waste Land* (1922), perhaps the most celebrated poem of the century, Eliot was also a partner in the publishing firm of Faber & Faber.

Eliot did not agree with Orwell's political viewpoint in *Animal Farm*. Eliot was a defender of elites. He advised that if the pigs were the smartest animals, they should run the farm. He suggested that Orwell should argue for "more public-spirited pigs" and characterized Orwell's criticism as negative. Orwell's opinion that Stalin had "betrayed" the Russian Revolution, said Eliot, was "Trotskyite."

(Eliot associated Orwell's position, somewhat inaccurately, with that of Leon Trotsky, who had made the same claim about Stalin in *The Revolution Betrayed* [1937]). But *Animal Farm* is certainly not Trotskyite. Snowball is hardly its tragic hero.

Eliot's loyalty to the British war effort overshadowed his contempt for Stalin's tyranny. Despite the fact that Eliot was a well-known conservative and a critic of the USSR, he shared the widespread reluctance among British publishers to offend a wartime ally. Speaking for his publishing house, he said that "we have no conviction . . . that this is the right point of view from which to criticize the political situation at the present time."

FROM T. S. ELIOT, LETTER TO ORWELL, 13 JULY 1944
(First published in *The Times* [London], 6 January 1969)

We agree that it is a distinguished piece of writing; that the fable is very skillfully handled, and that the narrative keeps one's interest on its own plane—and that is something very few authors have achieved since Gulliver.

On the other hand, we have no conviction (and I am sure none of the other directors would have) that this is the right point of view from which to criticise the political situation at the present time. It is certainly the duty of any publishing firm which pretends to other interests and motives than mere commercial prosperity, to publish books which go against the current of the moment: but in each instance that demands that at least one member of the firm should have the conviction that this is the thing that needs saying at the moment. I can't see any reason of prudence or caution to prevent anybody from publishing this book—if he believed in what it stands for.

Now I think my own dissatisfaction with this [fable] is that the effect is simply one of negation. It ought to excite some sympathy with what the author wants, as well as sympathy with his objections to something; and the positive point of view, which I take to be generally Trotskyite, is not convincing. I think you split your vote, without getting any compensating strong adhesion from either party—i.e. those who criticise Russian tendencies from the point of view of a purer communism, and those who, from a very different point of view, are alarmed about the future of small nations. And after all, your pigs are far more intelligent than the other animals, and therefore the best qualified to run the farm—in fact, there couldn't have been an Animal Farm at all without them: so that what was needed (someone might argue), was not more communism but more public-spirited pigs.

W. J. TURNER

Eliot's opinion was broadly echoed in conservative circles in London. A representative example is this review, which appeared in Britain's leading conservative magazine. Turner suggests that Orwell does not go far enough in his criticism of Stalinism. Orwell is a "reformer" who believes that great changes can occur without brutal suppression, says Turner, but Stalin is a realist who knows that only violence brings about such changes. Like the communist critics, Turner sees Orwell as a "pessimist." But Turner regrets that Orwell, who was an atheist, does not have more faith in Man as a creature of God—whereas the Communists condemned Orwell for lacking faith in the basically noble nature of Man himself.

FROM W. J. TURNER, *The Spectator* (17 August 1945)

. . . It is a ruthless exposure of a colossal deception done in a calm tone and reasoned terms. In this book we are told how the animals successfully rebel against man, but find their last state exactly the same as their first. The only animal who is not deceived is the donkey, and perhaps this is the sole acid touch of disgruntlement Mr. Orwell allows himself.

But for all its judicial calm, only a deeply disgruntled man would have written this book, and that is just what I fail to understand in Mr. Orwell. To me, who am not and never have been one of those communists or amateur bolsheviks who prefer the national anthem of Russia to that of their own country, it seems that Mr. Orwell is grossly unfair to Stalin in his account of him as "Napoleon," successor to "Old Major" (Lenin), the prize boar leader of the animal rebellion. I think Stalin could read this book and accept its terrible indictment with a smile and a clear conscience, for is the Russian Revolution the complete description of Mr. Orwell's *Animal Farm?* The fact is, I fear, that Mr. Orwell is of those who believe that an omelette can be made without the breaking of eggs. [This was Lenin's famous "recipe" for making a communist revolution.] In other words, Orwell is either a sentimentalist, or a man whose greatness of heart forbids his becoming a revolutionary. . . .

Perhaps some pig-like combination of cunning and aptitude in the lower forms of self-expression are the qualities essential in successful rulers; but even so I feel he is too pessimistic and too impatient. Like most ardent reformers who are mere rationalists, he thinks he understands the world better than its makers. I am willing to assume, for the sake of argument, that the world was not made by the God of any religion, but by the process of an unknown, as yet undefined and perhaps undefinable principle; but I am not ready to admit that Mr. Orwell, or any other human being, could do the job better, or even knows better how it should be done. I claim, indeed, that man is not quite such a pig as Mr. Orwell describes, and that is why I call him a pessimist. And, without being a pessimist, I am prepared for much worse things still to happen to mankind than those satirised by Mr. Orwell.

T. R. FYVEL

Orwell's friends showed deeper understanding of his motives in *Animal Farm*. T. R. Fyvel was a personal friend and close colleague of Orwell during the 1940s. Fyvel and Orwell co-edited a series of books during the war for Orwell's publisher, Fred Warburg, who later published *Animal Farm*.

The following passage is taken from Fyvel's memoir about his friendship with Orwell. It tells the story of Fyvel's learning about *Animals Farm*'s publication from Warburg. Fyvel recalls his immediately enthusiastic response toward Orwell's fable.

FROM T. R. FYVEL, *GEORGE ORWELL: A PERSONAL MEMOIR*
(London: Secker & Warburg, 1982)

I said: "It's just a fable, isn't it?" Yes, said Warburg, but it was a satire about a revolution of farm beasts, based on the Bolshevik revolution and its end in Stalinism, in which the Communists were depicted as pigs. He, Warburg, had faced all kinds of pressures against its publication, even from people in his own office and especially from his own very outspoken wife Pamela who evidently felt passionately that this was no time for ingratitude towards Stalin and the heroic Red Army who had played the main part in defeating Hitler.

I thereupon sat down in Warburg's office and read the typescript right through—with rising admiration.

This satirical, but more than that, this sad and haunting tale of how the domestic animals stage a successful revolution against Farmer Jones, only to fall under the much worse tyranny of the Communist pigs—this seemed to me a beautifully written allegory, with not a word too many or too few: at last Orwell had risen to his true stature as a writer.

I marvelled with that ease he seemed to have brought together the threads of his political thinking and of his literary imagination and in doing so had created a fable of such beautiful, inescapable simplicity. He had constructed his allegory in the manner of Swift. Employing the age-old folklore of talking animals, he had used his farming knowledge to create a whole world of recognizable animal characters. And withal, he had written a little fairy story in which children could weep over the end of the poor cart-horse Boxer, sent by the pigs to knackers.

At the same time he had succeeded in ingeniously tracing the fate of the Bolshevik revolution. The pigs walking upright and the tyrannical boar Napoleon were the ruling Communists and Stalin. The expulsion of the pig Snowball, too clever by half, was that of Trotsky. The pains of Boxer in building the twice destroyed windmill were those of the Russian people under the Five Year Plans. The ending where the animals look from men to pigs and cannot tell one from the other referred to the wartime Teheran Conference of 1943, where Churchill, Roosevelt and Stalin had toasted each other as allies. The whole scene was lit up by phrases of genius such as the often-quoted "All animals are equal but some are more equal than others", which precisely reflected the new class system in the Soviet Utopia.

Now, I don't know how far I saw all this at the first reading. As I realize now, I probably did not, but I certainly got the gist of Orwell's success. I felt that the special magic of *Animal Farm* lay in Orwell's loving and accurate description of the landscape and routine of work on the farm.

Returning to Fred Warburg, I recall that I made a pompous little speech. What was the matter with [the] other people who had sat out the war in London? I asked. Did they really think that Stalin, after victory in the bloodiest of all wars and already taking up a hostile stance against his wartime allies in a new global conflict, would let his policies towards Britain be affected by a little fable? I told Warburg how the Allied soldiers moving up from Italy had advanced eagerly to meet their Soviet comrades-in-arms only to be faced with extended bayonets. Warburg was indeed cynically amused by the whole row and had not the slightest intention of letting himself be deterred from publication in August. . . .

But if on today's reading, *Animal Farm* is still a most convincing political satire, one can also see why it survives even more as the supreme modern intellectual fairy tale for children. Oddly, it was not Orwell's intention to provide children's reading. . . . After the successful publication, Orwell spent a full day rushing from bookshop to bookshop, asking for *Animal Farm* to be moved from the shelves of children's books where he often found it automatically placed.

Ultimately of course in vain. So successfully had he thought himself into the age-old European folk tradition of talking animals, that for children who read him he turned the domestic animals on the farm into immediately recognizable and memorable and sometimes lovable characters. Lovable above all was Boxer, the great cart-horse, poor in intellect but large in muscle, who could only say "Comrade Napoleon is always right" and "I must work harder." With Boxer, as a child's favourite there is Clover, the gentle, maternal mare; there is the cynical old donkey Benjamin who observes everything with detachment. There are the savage dogs, the recognizably silly sheep—it is the believability of these characters which has turned *Animal Farm*, like *Gulliver's Travels*, into favoured children's reading: perhaps this is the fate of all the best satires.

CYRIL CONNOLLY

Cyril Connolly, a prominent British intellectual during the middle decades of this century, attended prep (elementary) and public (secondary) school with Orwell. He reviewed *Animal Farm* and also praised the book. Connolly knew that Orwell had admired Jonathan Swift's *Gulliver's Travels* (1667) and stressed that "the feeling, the penetration, and the verbal economy of Orwell's master Swift" are apparent in *Animal Farm*.

But Connolly also described the USSR in terms more positive than did Orwell. Connolly considered Orwell a somewhat naive political thinker. He called him "a revolutionary in love with 1910." In Connolly's eyes, Orwell was a romantic opposed to "progress" who would have preferred to live in the simpler, pre–World War I era of their schooldays.

Connolly reviewed Orwell's book in *Horizon* magazine, which was then the leading literary journal in England and which Connolly edited. (Orwell's second wife, Sonia Brownell, was an assistant editor of *Horizon* at this time.)

FROM CYRIL CONNOLLY, *Horizon* (September 1945)

. . . It truly is a fairy story told by a great lover of liberty and a great lover of animals. The farm is real, the animals are moving. At the same time it is a devastating attack on Stalin and his "betrayal" of the Russian revolution, as seen by another revolutionary. . . . But it is arguable that every revolution is "betrayed" because the violence necessary to achieve it is bound to generate an admiration for violence which leads to the abuse of power. A revolution is the forcible removal of an obsolete and inefficient ruling-class by a vigorous and efficient one which replaces it for as long as its vitality will allow. The commandments of the Animal Revolution, such as "no animal shall kill any other animal" or "all animals are equal" can perhaps never be achieved by a revolutionary seizure of power but only by the spiritual operation of reason or moral philosophy in the animal heart.

If we look at Russia without the particular bitterness of the disappointed revolutionary we see that it is an immensely powerful managerial despotism—far more powerful than its Czarist predecessor—where, on the whole, despite a police system which we should find intolerable, the masses are happy, and where great strides in material progress have been made (i.e. independence of women, equality of sexes, autonomy of racial and cultural minorities, utilization of science to improve the standard of living, religious toleration, etc.).

If Stalin and his regime were not loved as well as feared, the Animal Farm which comprises the greatest land-mass of the world would not have united to roll back the most efficient invading army [from Germany in World War II] which the world has ever known—and if in truth Stalin is loved, then he and his regime cannot be quite what they appear to Mr. Orwell.

KINGSLEY MARTIN

Not all readers agreed with these essentially positive assessments of *Animal Farm*. Kingsley Martin, editor in chief of the *New Statesman and Nation*, had already rejected Orwell's reports as a foreign correspondent in Spain during the 1930s. Martin claimed that Orwell's news stories, which were highly critical of the communist role in the Spanish Civil War, were anti-Stalinist tirades. Martin considered Orwell a "disillusioned idealist" and a "Red baiter," who lashed out at Communists ("the Reds") at every opportunity.

But Martin falsely stated in his *Animal Farm* review that Orwell had only recently begun to criticize the USSR. Martin regarded *Animal Farm* as "historically false and neglectful of the complex truth about Russia." Orwell's criticisms, Martin believed, proved that he had "lost faith in mankind." Martin misinterpreted Orwell, asserting that *Animal Farm* lionizes Snowball—and that Orwell therefore wanted Trotsky to lead the USSR. Moreover, said Martin, for all its flaws, the Soviet Union under Stalin was much better than Russia under the czars.

FROM KINGSLEY MARTIN, *New Statesman and Nation*
(8 September 1945)

In a world choked everywhere with suffering, cruelty and exploitation, the disillusioned idealist may be embarrassed by the rich choice of objects for denunciation. He runs the risk of twisting himself into knots, as he discovers enemies, first to the Right, then to the Left and, most invigorating, at home amongst his friends. He may try to solve his dilemma by deciding on some particular Power-figure as the embodiment of Evil, concentrating upon it all his wealth of frustration and righteous indignation. If he remains only a critic and fails to turn his talent to the search for a practical remedy for a specific evil, he is likely, in time, to decide that all the world is evil and that human nature is itself incorrigible. . . .

The logic of Mr. Orwell's satire is surely the ultimate cynicism of Ben, the donkey. That, if I read Mr. Orwell's mind correctly, is where his idealism and disillusion has really landed him. But he has not quite the courage to see that he has lost faith, not in Russia but in mankind. So the surface moral of his story is that all would have gone well with the revolution if the wicked Stalin had not driven the brave and good Trotsky out of Eden. Here Mr. Orwell ruins what should have been a very perfect piece of satire on human life. . . .

In short, if we read the satire as a gibe at the failings of the U.S.S.R. and realise that it is historically false and neglectful of the complex truth about Russia, we shall enjoy it and be grateful for our laugh. But which will Mr. Orwell do next? Having fired his bolt against Stalin, he could return to the attack on British or American Capitalism as seen through the eyes say, of an Indian peasant; the picture would be about as true or false.

TOM HOPKINSON

Published shortly after Orwell's death in January 1950, Hopkinson's critique is the first lengthy, serious assessment of *Animal Farm*. It is not a book review but rather an analysis of the literary merits and political significance of *Animal Farm*. Writing almost five years after the original publication of *Animal Farm*, Hopkinson has greater historical distance to judge Orwell's fable than did the original reviewers. Hopkinson pronounces it a classic that can stand beside Jonathan Swift's *Gulliver's Travels*. Like Connolly and other critics, Hopkinson pairs *Animal Farm* with Arthur Koestler's *Darkness at Noon*, both outstanding works of fiction with an anti-Stalinist thrust. (Koestler, a former Communist, was a close friend of Orwell.)

FROM TOM HOPKINSON, *World Review* (January–June 1950)

. . . For myself, I know only two present-day works of fiction before which the critic abdicates: one is Arthur Koestler's *Darkness at Noon*, the other Orwell's *Animal Farm*. Is it coincidence that both are concerned with Soviet Russia? Or is it that each of the two books tackles fearlessly the great theme of our day—which is also the great theme of human history—the struggle of individuals to assert their human values against the tyranny of mass. . . .

It is as delightful a children's story as *Gulliver's Travels* or the best of Aesop. It is manifestly an attack on Stalinism. It can be read as a lament—a wonderfully good-humoured and entertaining lament—for the fate of revolutions. It is a profound and moving comment on man's divided nature—forced to combine, but compromising with truth in every combination that he makes.

Orwell's knowledge of farming helps to maintain the necessary faint illusion of reality. Nothing is shirked—even the relations of "Animal Farm" with its human neighbours. Everything is treated with the combined lightness and assurance that suspend disbelief. Each detail of the story suggests to the reader a parallel, or whole set of parallels, in the modern world. . . .

Animal Farm is a work of genius in the lofty tradition of English humorous writing.

CONTEMPORARY RECEPTION:
THE AMERICAN RESPONSE TO *ANIMAL FARM*

Difficulties with understanding Orwell's intentions in *Animal Farm* were even greater in the United States. This had to do with ignorance of Orwell's politics by American readers. Many American reviewers did not know much about Orwell's previous work or current ideas. For the majority of them, reading *Animal Farm* was their first encounter with Orwell's work.

Orwell was not sure whether one could count on the American public grasping what the fable was about. He advised his American publisher to give readers some idea on the dust jacket about the anti-Stalinist thrust of the book. Nonetheless, because of their unfamiliarity with the British context of his work in wartime London, many readers still misread *Animal Farm* as an attack on socialism generally, not just on the Soviet Union's "betrayal" of socialism. Thus, American reviewers sometimes mistakenly read *Animal Farm* as anti-revolutionary and anti-socialist.

Animal Farm was selected as a September 1946 Book-of-the-Month Club choice. The Club's selection of *Animal Farm* is probably the single most significant event for expanding its international reputation. Extolling the fable's "worldwide importance," Club president Harry Scherman issued a special statement: "Every now and then through history, some fearless individual has spoken for the people of a troubled time. . . . Just so does this little gem of an allegory express, perfectly, the inarticulate philosophy of tens of millions of free men. . . . Wherever . . . men are free to read what they want, this book and its influence will spread."

As if to guarantee that outcome, Scherman also asked subscribers to pick *Animal Farm* rather than any alternate Club choice. The fable sold 460,000 copies during 1946–49 through the Club and soon became a runaway best-seller. By 1947 it had been translated into nine languages (and titled *Comrade Napoleon* in at least one language, thereby unmistakably informing readers about its anti-communist intent).

As in the United Kingdom, comparisons with Jonathan Swift's *Gulliver's Travels* were common. *Animal Farm* soon became a classic. Some American readers saw it as simply anti-Stalinist propaganda and praised it on those grounds. Most British reviewers knew that Orwell was a socialist, but many American critics did not know this. American conservatives, who were largely unaware of Orwell's politics, often embraced the book wholeheartedly as being anti-socialist and anti-revolutionary. Or they took Orwell to be an ex-socialist.

These conservatives read *Animal Farm* therefore, as a criticism of the Soviet Union from the Right. Orwell reportedly told his friend Stephen Spender, the well-known English poet, that he "had not written a book against Stalin in order to provide propaganda for capitalists." Nevertheless, he fell victim to a process whose dangers he often discussed in conversation: how difficult it is to take up any political position without being presumed to hold (or being deliberately tagged with) the current string of "party line" views conventionally associated with the position. It was not well understood outside London that Orwell was an internal critic of the Left and yet not a bitter ex-socialist.

This section opens with Orwell's letter to Dwight Macdonald, who edited *Politics*, a New York anti-Stalinist left-wing journal. Orwell makes clear his intention and the political purpose of *Animal Farm* in this letter: It is followed by the review of *Animal Farm* in *Politics*, which showed a keen understanding of Orwell's intentions, and by several other examples of American responses to Orwell's fable. These include a favorable response by the leading U.S. literary journalist of the period (Edmund Wilson) and three negative critiques. These disapproving reviews show a rising level of hostility to Orwell, relative to the critic's level of support for Stalinism. The section closes with an excerpt by Peter Viereck. It points out how such pro-Stalinist intellectuals tried to prevent the U.S. publication of *Animal Farm* altogether. Having failed in their efforts, they condemned Orwell in their book reviews.

GEORGE ORWELL

FROM GEORGE ORWELL TO DWIGHT MACDONALD,
5 DECEMBER 1946
(Quoted from Michael Shelden, *Orwell: The Authorized Biography*
[New York: HarperCollins, 1991])

Re. Your query about "Animal Farm". Of course I intended it primarily as a satire on the Russian Revolution. But I did mean it to have a wider application in so much that I meant that *that kind* of revolution (violent conspiratorial revolution, led by unconsciously power-hungry people) can only lead to a change of masters. I meant the moral to be that revolutions only effect a radical improvement when the masses are alert and know how to chuck out their leaders as soon as the latter have done their job. The turning-point of the story was supposed to be when the pigs kept the milk and apples for themselves (Kronstadt). If the other animals had had the sense to put their foot down then, it would have been all right. If people think I am defending the status quo, that is, I think, because they have grown pessimistic and assume that there is no alternative except dictatorship or capitalism. . . . What I was trying to say was, "You can't have a revolution unless you make it for yourself; there is no such thing as a benevolent dictatorship."

(By "Kronstadt" Orwell meant the 1921 mutiny of the sailors at that naval base in support of strikers in Leningrad over shortages of food. The sailors were folk heroes of the Russian Revolution because they initiated the 1917 uprisings. Their mutiny therefore was a cruel blow to Lenin and the Bolshevik leaders.)

BEN RAY REDMAN

Redman was an outspoken anti-communist liberal and stronger defender of civil liberties. In the early postwar era, he wrote for a variety of conservative and left-wing publications, such as Dwight Macdonald's *Politics*.

FROM BEN RAY REDMAN, REVIEW OF *ANIMAL FARM*
(*Politics*, March 1946)

That *Animal Farm* is vastly amusing is a fact that may be already apparent to readers of this review. That it is truly brilliant is a fact that can be dodged by no reader of the book itself. That it will infuriate all those who believe in Stalinism is a fact as certain as is the existence of the U.S.S.R. It will infuriate. . . .

Statistics are sometimes deadly, but the lethal range of satire is deeper, wider, more comprehensive than that of statistics can ever be. And George Orwell has managed his medium with sure judgment, with steady precision. His satirical parallels and correspondences are just numerous enough and clear enough to serve his purpose; not so numerous nor so obscure as to divert the reader's interest from the narrative's course to the demands of a possible puzzle. Avoiding exaggeration of manner as well as distortion of matter, the author has scored consistently by his evenness of tone and his power of understatement. It almost seems that he has used his skill merely to arrange for truth to show itself in satire's mirror; a mirror that, performing an act of translation, simultaneously performs acts of interpretation and illumination.

It is more than likely that George Orwell's story of the great revolution that went wrong is destined to become a minor classic.

EDMUND WILSON

Wilson was probably the most influential American intellectual around midcentury. Given Wilson's own high reputation, this glowing review amounted to a crowning of Orwell from the American intelligentsia. Wilson compared *Animal Farm* to the work of leading satirical writers of earlier centuries (Voltaire's *Candide* and Jonathan Swift's *Gulliver's Travels*). Wilson predicted, accurately, that Orwell "is likely to emerge as one of the ablest and most interesting writers that the English have produced in this period."

FROM EDMUND WILSON, *The New Yorker* (7 September 1946)

. . . it is absolutely first-rate. . . . Mr. Orwell has worked out his theme with a simplicity, a wit, and a dryness . . . and has written in a prose so plain and spare, so admirably proportioned to his purpose, that "Animal Farm" even seems very creditable if we compare it with Voltaire and Swift.

Mr. Orwell, before the war, was not widely known in America. . . . He is one of several English writers who were only just beginning to be recognized in those years of confusion and tension and whose good work was obscured and impeded while the war was going on. But I think that he is now likely to emerge as one of the ablest and most interesting writers that the English have produced in this period.

GEORGE SOULE

Soule was a frequent book reviewer for *The New Republic*, which defended the policies of Stalin's Russia throughout the 1930s and 1940s. *The New Republic*, like Kingsley Martin's *New Statesman and Nation*, treated Orwell as a socialist renegade. In this review, Soule does not directly criticize Orwell's political position. Rather, he asserts that *Animal Farm* is flawed artistically—"dull," "creaking," "stereotyped."

FROM GEORGE SOULE, *The New Republic* (2 September 1946)

. . . the book puzzled and saddened me. It seemed on the whole dull. The allegory turned out to be a creaking machine for saying in a clumsy way things that have been said better directly. And many of the things said are not instantly recognized as the essence of truth, but are of the sort which start endless and boring controversy. . . .

Part of the trouble lies in the fact that the story is too close to recent historical events without being close enough. Major, the aged pig who on his deathbed tells the animals of their oppression and prophesies revolution, must be Karl Marx. His two followers who lead the revolution, Napoleon and Snowball, are then readily identified as Lenin and Trotsky. This identification turns out to be correct in the case of Snowball, but the reader soon begins to puzzle over the fact that Napoleon disapproves the project of building a windmill—an obvious symbol for electrification and industrialization—whereas this was Lenin's program. The puzzlement is increased when Napoleon chases out Snowball as a traitor; it was Stalin who did this. . . .

The thoughtful reader must be further disturbed by the lack of clarity in the main intention of the author. Obviously he is convinced that the animals had just cause for revolt and that for a time their condition was improved under the new regime. But they are betrayed by their scoundrelly, piggish leaders. In the end, the pigs become indistinguishable from the men who run the other nearby farms; they walk on two legs, have double and triple chins, wear clothes and carry whips. *Animal Farm* reverts to the old Manor Farm in both name and reality.

No doubt this is what George Orwell thinks has happened in Russia. But if he wants to tell us why it happened, he has failed. Does he mean to say that not these pigs, but Snowball, should have been on top? . . .

It seems to me that the failure of this book (commercially it is already assured of a tremendous success) arises from the fact that the satire deals not with something the author has experienced, but rather with stereotyped ideas about a country which he probably does not know very well. The plan for the allegory, which must have seemed a good one when he first thought of it, became mechanical in execution. It almost appears as if he had lost his zest before he got very far with the writing. He should try again, and this time on something nearer home.

ISAAC ROSENFELD

Rosenfeld, a young anti-Stalinist Jewish intellectual, considered Orwell a good liberal. He respected Orwell for his insistence on individual rights and freedom of expression. Still, Rosenfeld found *Animal Farm* lacking in sufficient creative imagination. The book is "disappointing" in its failure to "seriously deal" with Soviet history, claims Rosenfeld. His position reflects the generally negative editorial policy of *The Nation* toward Orwell and toward most anti-communist criticism during this period.

FROM ISAAC ROSENFELD, *Nation* (7 September 1946)

What I found most troublesome was the question that attended my reading—what is the point of "Animal Farm"? Is it that the pigs, with the most piggish pig supreme, will always disinherit the sheep and the horses? . . .

Though Orwell, I am sure, would not seriously advance the bad-man theory of history, it appears that he has, nevertheless, drawn on it for the purpose of writing "Animal Farm." There are only two motives operating in the parable (which is already an oversimplification to the point of falsity, if we take the parable as intended); one of them, a good one, Snowball's, is defeated, and the only other, the bad one, Napoleon's succeeds, presumably because history belongs to the most unscrupulous. I do not take this to be Orwell's own position, for his work has shown that he knows it to be false and a waste of time in historical analysis; it is, however, the position of his imagination, as divorced from what he knows—a convenient ground, itself a fable, to set his fable on. . . .

It is at this point that a failure of imagination—failure to expand the parable, to incorporate into it something of the complexity of the real event—becomes identical with a failure in politics. The story, which is inadequate as a way into the reality, also falls short as a way out; and while no one has a right to demand of "Animal Farm" that it provide a solution to the Russian problem—something it never set out to do—it is nevertheless true that its political relevance is more apparent than real.

MILTON BLAU

Blau reviewed literature regularly for *New Masses*, a mouthpiece of the American Communist Party. American Communists were hostile toward Orwell throughout his career. *New Masses* condemns Orwell's "utter contempt for Mankind." It misrepresents *Animal Farm* as the product of a "warped fascist-Trotskyist mind" that "seethes with hatred for Man."

FROM MILTON BLAU, "PIG'S EYE VIEW"
(*New Masses*, 10 September 1946)

As a form the fable is a very difficult one to work in. It has a peculiar nature inasmuch as it demands from the author the greatest understanding of life and people, an unfailing insight into what is true. Perhaps for this reason fable tellers are of two kinds: very wise men or just plain liars.

The fable has another quality. When it is good, great masses of people make it a part of their lives. When it is bad it dies, because the durability of a fable is its truth. Orwell's fable, having no truth, digs its own grave in the cow-flops which covers the contrived acre of "Animal Farm."

George Orwell relates the adventures of *Animal Farm* as a fable because his brand of slander is directed against all of mankind and against any possible visions man may have for a better world. Even Trotskyites and fascists know that you can't sell a lie of the Orwell dimension without a measure of dressing in pig-latin.

Mr. Orwell's zoological treatise of Soviet history has as its task the defining of Leon Trotsky as the betrayed hero of socialism and Stalin as the betrayer. . . . Throughout his dull fable Orwell's utter contempt for mankind spews forth. How man's wretched mind works! Orwell reduces the world and the struggle of man for a better world to a barnyard filled with stupid animals. But this is not enough: once having turned man into beast Orwell contrives to show what an ugly beast he is. Along with Orwell's blanket hatred is his "love," which in his fable he bestows, Judas-like, on the horse Boxer.

In Boxer he portrays the working-class, conscious and loyal, but so stupid that he can only learn the first four letters of the alphabet. Orwell argues through Boxer that the more the working-class fights for its own interests the more surely it will be defeated! He concludes, of course, that it is better to accept all the tragedy of capitalism than to see the "stupid" working class rise to power. . . .

Orwell makes his little contribution toward the general preparation of reaction for an anti-Soviet war. *Animal Farm* displays the warped fascist-Trotskyite mind worming its way back into literature; a mind which seethes with hatred for man and argues for nihilism, for the destruction of both man and art.

PETER VIERECK

Viereck, a young conservative, blasted American publishers for having rejected *Animal Farm*. Writing in a magazine edited by a Harvard Ph.D. student named Henry Kissinger, who would go on to become Secretary of State in the Nixon Administration, Viereck pulled no punches. He speculated that publishing houses had been infiltrated by "Stalinoid sympathizers" who hated Orwell and his democratic socialist convictions. Viereck was criticizing pro-Russian intellectuals (such as Kingsley Martin, George Soule, and Milton Blau), whose hostile Marxist-oriented reviews of *Animal Farm* we have already read. (It is likely that his estimate of "eighteen to twenty" American rejections is a bit high, but historians are divided about the precise number.)

FROM PETER VIERECK, "BLOODY-MINDED PROFESSORS"
(*Confluence*, September 1952)

With the characteristic hatred of literary Stalinoids for genuine democratic socialists (a hatred more frenzied and frothing than any they expend on fascists), [Angus] Cameron also was among those who after the war prevented Little, Brown from publishing George Orwell's anticommunist satire, *Animal Farm*. Some 18 to 20 publishers, almost all the leading ones, turned down the best anti-Soviet satire of our time. In view of its wit, its readability, its saleability, and its democratic outlook, the most likely motive for these rejections is the brilliantly successful infiltration (then, not now) of Stalinoid sympathizers in the book world.

THE AMERICAN INTELLECTUAL CLIMATE

The following interviews feature three leading American intellectuals who were Orwell's younger contemporaries in the 1940s. These men shaped American opinion about Orwell in the postwar era. The interviews give the flavor of the climate of opinion that *Animal Farm* entered in the 1940s and 1950s. They provide a deeper context for understanding the wide range of response to *Animal Farm* in the preceding book reviews. They also make clear that Orwell stood high in the estimate of American intellectuals who were not pro-Stalinist.

NORMAN PODHORETZ

Norman Podhoretz was a teenager when he first read *Animal Farm* in the 1940s. Later, as a leading intellectual and editor of *Commentary* magazine in New York, Podhoretz took Orwell as one of his literary and political models. Podhoretz came ultimately to admire Orwell most as a "Cold Warrior," that is, for his anti-communist criticism during the Cold War. Podhoretz praised Orwell for his outspoken opposition to Communism. He suggests that Orwell, if he had lived into the 1980s, might have become a conservative like Podhoretz himself.

FROM NORMAN PODHORETZ INTERVIEW (1986)

I think I have more in common with Orwell than Irving Howe. If someone asked you in the '50s who Orwell was, you would say—not to put too fine a point on it—"an anti-Communist. . . ."

So the name "Orwell Press" adopted by the Committee for the Free World is accurate: it's an anti-Communist organization and Orwell was the patron saint of anti-Communism. He is the neoconservative "guiding spirit" in that he was one of the first to fight the lies of the Communists. If you break with the Left, you are read out of existence. That's the price you must pay: you no longer can hope to have influence in that world. That's the way it was for the neoconservatives in the early '70s—and though it's changed today because we've built up a community of our own, the Left still dominates intellectual life.

Certainly Orwell wasn't ready in the late '40s to break.... In fact, to an extent, it had already happened with *Homage to Catalonia* and *Animal Farm*. I don't know if Orwell would have ever broken—he cherished his identification with the Left....

I don't think it's necessary or proper to look for ancestors who aren't your ancestors, and if I believed that Orwell were not what I've portrayed him—anti-pacifist, anti-neutralist, and on America's side in the Cold War—I'd give him up. But Orwell *is* an ancestor on the issues that concern me: democracy versus totalitarianism.

IRVING HOWE

Irving Howe was in his mid-twenties when he began to read Orwell. Before World War II, Howe had joined a Trotskyist group in New York. But after the war, he gradually distanced himself from Trotksyism and ultimately dropped even his Marxist politics. Nevertheless, he retained his commitment to socialism until his death in 1993. Like Pohdoretz, Howe saw Orwell as a great writer and a political model—but as a model of a socialist intellectual, not an anti-communist cold warrior.

FROM IRVING HOWE INTERVIEW (1984)

I saw Orwell as a fellow spirit—a radical and engaged writer. For a whole generation—mine—Orwell was an intellectual hero. He stormed against those English writers who were ready to yield to Hitler, he fought almost single-handed against those who blinded themselves to the evils of Stalin. More than any other English intellectual of our age, he embodied the values of personal independence and a fiercely democratic radicalism.

The loss [of Orwell's presence] seems enormous.... He was one of the few heroes of our younger years who remains untarnished. Having to live in a rotten time was made just a little more bearable by his presence.

He is the greatest moral force in English letters during the last several decades: craggy, fiercely polemical, sometimes mistaken, but an utterly free man. He saw the workers neither as potential revolutionaries nor savage innocents nor stupid clods. He saw them as ordinary suffering human beings; quite like you and me....

Orwell's deepest view of life was his faith in the value and strength of common existence: "The fact to which we have got to cling, as to a lifebelt, is that it *is* possible to be a normal decent person and yet to be fully alive." Let *that* be inscribed on every blackboard in the land!

RUSSELL KIRK

Unlike Podhoretz and Howe, both New York Jewish intellectuals, Russell Kirk was a conservative Midwestern intellectual. He too admired Orwell strongly. But he also emphasized the sharp political differences that separated him from Orwell. Unlike Podhoretz and Howe, Kirk's identification with Orwell does not lead him to minimize his differences with Orwell or emphasize his similarities to Orwell. Kirk regards Orwell as a socialist who ultimately, in *Animal Farm* and *1984*, despaired that socialism would lead to a better world.

FROM RUSSELL KIRK INTERVIEW (1983)

Orwell was a socialist only nominally. Really it was a despairing form of socialism that he was finally led to. But I wouldn't say most people were clear on that. There were persons who looked on Orwell as a thorough-going conservative, because they were unacquainted with his previous writings and background. I suppose that the average American reader knew nothing about the man. He appeared to Average Americans as someone who speaks up for American principles against communism. That kind of naive attitude prevailed. Among persons of some education, who were familiar with Orwell, the attitude was somewhat different. I suppose the typical American liberal, who dominated the American campus then as now, was friendly to Orwell.

Beginning with *Animal Farm*, conservative intellectuals who were familiar with his work certainly didn't conceive him in any way to be a socialist or a conservative or tending toward conservatism. They saw him more as a disillusioned socialist.

Orwell was, in the mid-fifties, a dramatic force for turning people away from socialism and progressivism. That was the key period of his influence. That was a period of painful reflection for Americans, who no longer believed left-wing ideas about the much-promised benefits of bigger government or the welfare state. Orwell's disillusion with socialism assisted such reflections.

THE U.S. GOVERNMENT AS A SPONSOR OF ORWELL'S WORK

Orwell was indeed a strong anti-Stalinist. The reviewers and intellectuals of his day were agreed on that point. But many of them would have been surprised that Orwell cooperated with secret British intelligence agencies, and those in other nations, to translate and distribute his work. For example, without asking for any fees, Orwell licensed translations and radio broadcasts of *Animal Farm* in Eastern Europe and Asia. The American government was heavily, and secretly, involved in these activities. Beginning with the Korean edition of *Animal Farm* in 1948, the U.S. Information Agency sponsored translations of Orwell's books in more than thirty languages, including Afrikaans, Danish, Dutch, Finnish, French, German, Greek, Icelandic, Indonesian, Italian, Maltese, Norwegian, Polish, Portuguese, Serbo-Croatian, Sinhalese, Czech, Slovene, Spanish, Swahili, Swedish, Ukrainian, and Vietnamese. The Voice of America also broadcast *Animal Farm* (1947) and *1984* (1949) in Eastern Europe.

In a May 1947 memorandum to J. Edgar Hoover, head of the Federal Bureau of Investigation (FBI), an FBI agent noted that *Animal Farm* was one of a half-dozen books that the CIA was vigorously promoting in the West to combat Communism. Perhaps this induced a vice president of Orwell's American publisher, Harcourt Brace, to take a bold step. In 1949, Harcourt Brace went so far as to request an endorsement of *1984* from Hoover. Apparently with Orwell's support, the publishing house appealed to Hoover that his endorsement of Orwell's work would "help to halt totalitarianism." (Hoover declined.) (This information is taken from an FBI memo to Hoover, 8 May 1947; a letter to Hoover from Eugene Reynolds, 22 April 1949; and Hoover's negative reply, 29 April 1949. Information about the foreign translations and Voice of America broadcasts comes from John Rodden, *The Politics of Literary Reputation* [Oxford, 1989], pp. 204, 434.)

DEAN ACHESON

Acheson served as U.S. Secretary of State from 1949 to 1953, in the first Eisenhower Administration. He was a strong anti-communist who believed in the power of Western values and ideas (individual freedom, economic liberty, constitutional rights) to combat Stalinism. Hence he energetically supported various programs to translate and circulate Western books in Communist nations.

FROM DEAN ACHESON, "PARTICIPATION OF BOOKS IN
DEPARTMENT'S FIGHT AGAINST COMMUNISM"
(State Department Memorandum, 11 April 1951)

Animal Farm and *1984* have been of great value to the Department in its psychological offensive against Communism. . . . On account of the possible psychological value, the Department has felt justified in sponsoring translations, either overtly or covertly.

McCARTHYISM, COMMERCIALISM, AND THE RECEPTION OF THE *ANIMAL FARM* FILM

Joseph Raymond McCarthy entered Congress in 1946. By 1950 he was loudly proclaiming that the U.S. Army and other government agencies had been widely infiltrated by Communists and Soviet agents. He publicly charged in February 1950 that 205 Communists had infiltrated the State Department, a claim that created a furor and catapulted him into headlines across the country.

McCarthy has gone down in history as an outspoken, unscrupulous, unprincipled critic of Communism. After 1950 he turned his passionate search for communist traitors in the United States into a blind crusade. He made many wild accusations against decent, law-abiding American citizens. His investigative techniques were shoddy and based on intimidation. During his testimony before the Senate Committee on Foreign Relations, he proved unable to produce the name of a single "card-carrying Communist" in any U.S. government department.

Historians have determined that McCarthy's accusations about the communist affiliations and subversive activities of American citizens were largely unfounded. Nevertheless, he gained increasing popular support for his campaign of accusations by capitalizing on the frustrations of a nation weary of the Korean War and appalled by communist advances in Eastern Europe and China. To his supporters, he appeared as a dedicated patriot and guardian of hallowed American traditions; to his detractors, he was an irresponsible, self-seeking politician who was undermining the nation's traditions of civil liberties.

McCarthy's irresponsible accusations gave rise to the term *McCarthyism*: the practice of making accusations of disloyalty, especially of pro-communist activity, which are supported by slight, doubtful, or irrelevant evidence.

Some historians compare McCarthyism and postwar Stalinism as similar developments. Although the two phenomena did arise during the same historical era and partially in response to each other, such an analogy is false. The abuses of freedom experienced in the United States under McCarthyism were slight and limited compared to the tyranny and severe oppression that millions of Soviet and Eastern European citizens suffered. McCarthyism never caused injustices comparable to Stalinism. It did not result in the murder of 60 million people, as did Stalin's concentration camps. Nor, unlike Soviet Communism, did it lead to a tyrannical dictatorship imposed for decades on hundreds of millions of people in Russia and Eastern Europe.

But McCarthyism did violate the civil liberties of many Americans, and it represents a low point in the level of public tolerance in the United States. McCarthyism, which enjoyed its heyday in the United States between 1950 and 1954, caused many Americans to feel that their rights to freedom of speech were being violated. At its worst, it caused several thousand people—including many teachers, librarians, and professors—to lose their jobs and hundreds of immigrants and other people with suspect backgrounds to flee the United States or to receive jail terms.

McCarthyism was not limited to the activities of Senator McCarthy. Rather, it constituted a comprehensive hostile climate toward Communists and socialists. It consisted of attacks in the press and broadcast media as well as in the political sphere. The U.S. Congress also passed many pieces of legislation that formally restricted the civil liberties of American citizens and alien residents. For instance, in 1947, Congress passed the Taft-Hartley Act, which substantially curtailed the rights accorded to trade unions by the legislation of the 1930s. Another major piece of legislation was the McCarran-Walter Act, also known as the Immigration and Nationality Act. Passed by Congress in 1952, it empowered the Department of Justice to deport immigrants or naturalized citizens who engaged in subversive activities. It was primarily used against Communists and socialists who had fled Nazi Germany and other nations in fascist Europe in the 1930s.

McCarthy was officially censured by the Senate in December 1954 for questionable financial dealings and persistent accusations against high-ranking officials. (McCarthy's increasingly irresponsible attacks came to include President Dwight D. Eisenhower and other Republican and Democratic leaders.) The move followed thirty-six days of televised hearings between April and June 1954 on McCarthy's largely groundless charges that the U.S. Army "coddled communists." This detailed television exposure of his brutal and truculent interrogative tactics discredited him and helped to turn the tide of public opinion against him.

McCarthy's fall from grace was as meteoric as his ascension. When he first took the national stage in 1950, many Americans had supported his relentless quest to ferret out Communists; now the media and the public branded his formerly popular anti-communist crusade a "witchhunt."

JOHN RODDEN

As the following historical account by the cultural historian John Rodden indicates, the public's ambivalent attitude toward McCarthyism was reflected in the confused reception of the *Animal Farm* film. The film adaptation of *Animal Farm*, made in 1954, has also been frequently used in schools and has influenced postwar thinking about Orwell's fable.

FROM JOHN RODDEN, *THE POLITICS OF LITERARY REPUTATION*
(New York: Oxford University Press, 1989)

The 1954 Christmas season brought to the screen an animated cartoon version of *Animal Farm*. The cinema posters announced: "Pig Brother Is Watching You."

Created by the British husband-and-wife team of John Halas and Joy Batcheler, *Animal Farm* was the first non-American feature-length cartoon. It was also the first animated cartoon of a "serious" work of art. Halas and Batcheler were touted as cinematic pioneers. One critic wrote a book about the film's production; the film also received an award at the 1955 Berlin Film Festival. . . .

The film portrayed Orwell's story as a general fable about the evils of power and lifted it clean from its historical context. Unsurprisingly, therefore, the adaptation was assaulted in political organs from one end of the ideological spectrum to the other. On the far Left, the *Nation* used the film as an occasion to reopen the attack on Orwell and judged it a crude anti-Communist polemic. Conservative and anti-Communist critics, possibly still caught up in McCarthy's accusations about Communist control of Hollywood, implied that the British directors harbored "Trotskyite" sympathies. One reviewer noted that Halas (an anti-Nazi war refugee from Poland) and Batcheler, had made numerous anti-Nazi propaganda films for the British government during the war. The critic suggested that the filmmakers had engaged in leftist subversion of Orwell's message: they had deliberately redirected the fable's satire away from the Bolshevik Revolution. Noting the lack of any clear historical correspondences in the film to Russia under Lenin and Stalin, the reviewer asked, "Has truth become a luxury no longer available to liberals?" Delmore Schwartz observed in *The New Republic*: "To a Rip Van Winkle or a Martian Man, the film might seem to be on the British Labour Party." Another critic did mistakenly describe the film as "a bitter satire on the Welfare State."

Admittedly, Halas and Batcheler made no attempt to remind viewers of the special relevance of Orwell's fable to Soviet history. One pig clearly resembled recently deceased [British] Labour leader Ernest Bevin. In promotional ads, a fat-bellied pig wearing a string tie and smoking a cigar was clearly a caricature of a U.S. political boss, apparently a southern senator cut in the mold of Huey Long. Old Major was given the voice and face of Winston Churchill. A pig with bushy eyebrows and a rude scowl resembled Joseph McCarthy. There was also a porcine Hermann Goering [the Nazi commander of the German air force]. This prompted at least one critic, in apparent ignorance of the book, to write that *Animal Farm* was a direct attack on fascism.

Other cinematic decisions by Halas and Batcheler were found questionable. Only the pigs talked, giving ammunition again to the Communist charge that *Animal Farm* (and Orwell) considered "the People" mere "dumb beasts." Widely deplored was the film's happy ending, implying that popular revolutions can succeed. The film closes with Benjamin leading animal revolutionaries from the far reaches of the globe in a triumphant march to oust the pigs from power. But I found that, when Benjamin and the other animals join hands in the final frame, the film inadvertently evokes memories of the opening scenes. It reminded me of the solidarity of the first Animal Revolution led by the pigs. Thus it reawakened, rather than refuted, Orwell's doubts about the inevitable course of violent revolution.

GERALD WEALES

McCarthyism was not the only context in which the *Animal Farm* film was received in the United States. The omission of certain minor characters arguably robbed the fable of its historical context and its complexity. For instance, Clover, the mare who remains loyal to the Revolution even after Boxer's death, is dropped from the film. So too is Mollie, the pretty horse who deserts the Revolution for lump sugar and ribbons. All these facts are noted by Gerald Weales in his review. Weales attributes these simplifications to the filmmakers' excessive concern to make money. The alterations lead Weales to criticize the film for resulting in what he called "the transformation of the prophet Orwell into the profit Orwell."

FROM GERALD WEALES, "FILMS FROM OVERSEAS"
(*Quarterly Journal of Film, Radio and TV* [Fall 1955])

The film version has completely discarded the message of the fable and has focused its attention on the processes. The five writers who worked out the story for the film became so interested in how the animals could master the mechanics of running a farm that Orwell's few descriptive paragraphs are spread across half the film. As much attention is given to the work of the farm—scenes, such as the one in which the ducks, wielding sickles in their beaks cut the hay and drag it into an oblong heap which turns out to be two sheep balancing a ladder between them, an improvised haywagon—as is given to the growing power and corruption of the ruling pigs.

As if the farming sequences were not sufficiently like ordinary cartoons, the producers have introduced a fluffy gauche duckling as cute and as saccharine as any character that ever came out of the Disney Studios, who is pointlessly underfoot for most of the picture. Otherwise, the film has reduced the number of characters, preferring to focus its attention upon the pigs Napoleon, Snowball, and Squealer, on Boxer the horse, and on Benjamin the mule. . . .

Of greater harm to Orwell's intention is the change that some of the characters undergo in their transference to the screen. The pigs come off best: they retain their essential viciousness, although it is inevitably softened by the fact that most of them seem unable to keep from resembling Porky Pig. Boxer, however, is no longer the stupid mass of muscle power that he is in the book: he still works himself to death for Animal Farm, but in the film he would never be capable of coining his famous maxim, "Comrade Napoleon is always right." Benjamin, the sardonic, unbelieving mule, who has a little of Orwell in him, is still taciturn in the film, but he works as hard as Boxer does for the farm, and he commands the counterrevolution—the film's most foolish invention, an enterprise that would hardly appeal to the mule of the book who expects that conditions will be bad under any circumstances. . . .

When at the end of the book, the animals look in the window of a farmhouse and see the pigs and the neighboring farmers enjoying a game of cards, they discover that they cannot tell the pigs from the men. This is the moment for which the book was written: this is the message, the failure of the revolution on which Orwell insists. The producers, however, are not satisfied to end in despair, even though the despair be a warning, the animals in the film must knock the house down and overthrow the pigs.

If it were possible to accept this film simply on its own terms, to forget that it is based on a source outside itself, one could find the cartoon an occasionally interesting, occasionally amusing essay in naive political optimism. But inevitably, one imagines that the sugar coated ending (maybe Moses the raven worked on the script too) was devised in the hope that the film would be appealing to more people, and it is difficult not to resent the transformation of the prophet Orwell into the profit Orwell.

SPENCER BROWN

Brown shares Weales's misgivings about the *Animal Farm* film, but he emphasizes more the possible political motives of the movie's promoters. Writing in the Jewish magazine *Commentary*, which was strongly anti-communist in the mid-1950s, Brown voices suspicions about the unpolitical treatment of the *Animal Farm* film by its American promoters. Why, asks Brown, did the promoters fail to mention in their advertisements for the film that it is a satire on Soviet communism? Brown implies that the answer has two reasons: (1) the promoters did not want to alienate sympathizers of the USSR, and (2) they figured that *Animal Farm* would be more commercially successful if they downplayed its politics.

FROM SPENCER BROWN, "STRANGE DOINGS AT *ANIMAL FARM*"
(*Commentary*, February 1955)

The film has many merits, stemming chiefly from Orwell's ingenuity in incident and his marvelous knack of securing the suspension of disbelief by sympathetic and detailed realism.

It has certain defects, too, worst among which is the animators' revision of the ending: the sorrow of Orwell's animals is unrelieved, intensified finally by the realization that their revolution and suffering have been in vain, that their pig-exploiters are no different, even in appearance, from Mr. Pilkington. In the Halas-Batchelor film, however, it is not human exploiters who attend Napoleon's orgy, but other pig-bureaucrats from pig satrapies elsewhere. They all get drunk, the animals of the world unite in revolt and converge on Animal Farm, Napoleon whistles to his dogs for help, but they too are sodden in liquor and unable to prevent the overthrow of the tyrant. . . .

Another detail that might be objected to is the excessive prettying up of the animals' toil. When they are getting in the harvest and when Boxer prances as he pulls stone for the windmill, one almost expects the Seven Dwarfs to pop round the barn, singing "Hi-Ho" and pitching in with right good will. The temptation to Disneyize must have been irresistible, but Disney is not Orwell.

Yet with these and other flaws the film has not seriously damaged Orwell and may have the merit of bringing his satire to those who do not know the novel. In the promotion of the film, however, and in the responses of the critics, something happened that is worthy of note.

What, according to critics and advertisers, is Orwell's anti-Communist *classic Animal Farm?*

It is, says Bosley Crowther in the New York Times, "a pretty brutal demonstration of the vicious cycle of tyranny"; it presents "the leaders of the new Power State as pigs" and conveys "a sense of the monstrous hypocrisy of the totalitarian leader type." In a lengthy review, Mr. Crowther never comes closer than this to mentioning Russia. . . .

Can the parable of *Animal Farm* be applied equally to all forms of totalitarianism? My "reinterpretation" of this fable as it would apply to Nazi Germany should, I think, stand as a sufficient answer. Those who unmention Russia are asking us to believe that so sophisticated an anti-Communist as George Orwell wrote a book in which *by mere accident* every event and every character can be shown to correspond *exactly* to some fact, general or particular, of Soviet history. . . .

Why do people spend three years of painstaking labor on an anti-Communist film only to deny, when the job is finished, that it *is* anti-Communist? I have no answers to these questions. Advertising is a mysterious business, and liberalism these days seems to be a mysterious business too; when you put the two mysteries together, you get something like the kind of story I have been telling.

CONCLUSION

Animal Farm is a classic. But that is not so because it is an endearing animal story. Or a perfect little fairy story. It is a classic because of its adult themes and profound intellectual questions, which have been the subjects of academic conferences and scholarly books.

No, *Animal Farm* is not a typical animal story. Nor is it a happy tale. It was the first literary masterpiece to attack what Orwell called "the myth that the Soviet Union is a socialist country." *Animal Farm* was a "countermyth"—a myth created to fight a myth—

and the critical issue was its form: the allegory. Orwell's message was universal, but his subjects had precise referents: the USSR and its history.

At the same time, *Animal Farm* is set in England (which is why the animals sing "Beasts of England"). Orwell meant to show that his book was primarily about the history of the USSR. The "fairy tale" of *Animal Farm* was happening in the USSR, Orwell said. *Animal Farm* was not only a critique of the USSR, however. It was also a warning to Britain, America, and other nations.

The warning was simple: It can happen here, too.

STUDY QUESTIONS

1. *Animal Farm* continues to be a best-selling book long after the international events that it satirized have passed. Why is this so?

2. How did the Cold War contribute to the continuing relevance of Orwell's warning in *Animal Farm?*

3. Both T. S. Eliot and W. J. Turner offer conservative critiques of *Animal Farm*. Outline the similarities and differences in their responses.

4. Assess Kingsley Martin's view that Orwell's satire in *Animal Farm* reflects an attitude of cynicism and disillusion. Martin criticizes Orwell for distorting "the complex truth about Russia." In light of our discussion of Soviet history and Soviet leaders in Chapters 2–4, do you agree with Kingsley Martin? Or is it Martin himself who is "historically false"?

5. Why did British readers and reviewers generally understand *Animal Farm* better than did their American counterparts?

6. Identify the typical American reviewer's mistakes in reading *Animal Farm*. How did Orwell try to clarify his political position in *Animal Farm* for American readers? Does Orwell's letter to Dwight Macdonald seem sufficiently clear to avoid confusion? If so, do you think that the confusions were partly deliberate? Did readers want to turn *Animal Farm* to their own political advantage?

7. In our excerpt by Peter Viereck, the author claims that eighteen to twenty American publishers rejected *Animal Farm*, mostly on political grounds. What were their reasons? How do these reasons relate to the intellectual climate of the period?

8. What is the role of religion in *Animal Farm?* Why does Moses the raven disappear and suddenly return?

9. Both Russell Kirk and W. J. Turner are conservatives who emphasize the role of religion in Orwell's political beliefs. Describe their treatment of themes such as despair and revolutionary idealism in relation to their comments about religion.

10. Why did Orwell cooperate with secret government efforts to circulate *Animal Farm* behind the Iron Curtain?

11. Why did Orwell title the revolutionary hymn of *Animal Farm* "Beasts of *England*"?

12. Do you think Orwell's warning in *Animal Farm* also applies to the Western democracies? Or should we read *Animal Farm* exclusively as an attack on the USSR?

13. Is *Animal Farm* perhaps better understood as a warning about the

dangers of violent revolution and tyranny in general? Support your answer with specific examples from the book.

14. Identify the Seven Commandments of Animalism and the revisions that the pigs made to them. Which of the Seven Commandments do you consider to be the most important? Explain your answer.

TOPICS FOR WRITTEN OR ORAL EXPLORATION

1. In 1944 the Soviet Union was still a wartime ally of the United States and the United Kingdom. What do you think would have been the reception of *Animal Farm* if it had been published soon after Orwell finished it in February of that year? Would the book have been ignored, or would it have caused even greater debate? Why? Speculate freely, based on our summary of U.K. and U.S. wartime attitudes toward the USSR.

2. Evaluate T. S. Eliot's criticism of *Animal Farm*. Do you agree with Eliot that the animals' rebellion would have proceeded humanely if "more public-spirited pigs" than Napoleon had been in power?

3. Many readers of *Animal Farm* consider Snowball to be a decent pig. Using your own definition of "decent," explain why you agree or disagree.

4. Did Napoleon betray the animals' revolution, or was the betrayal carried out by the pigs themselves? What significance does this question have in relation to debates about Trotsky and Stalin? (Trotsky's supporters usually considered Stalin to be the villain for the weaknesses and crimes of the Soviet regime rather than Communism itself.)

5. Do you think the controversies surrounding *Animal Farm* in the postwar era have helped or hurt its popularity and sales figures?

6. Both T. R. Fyvel and Cyril Connolly were good friends of Orwell. They see *Animal Farm* in a different light from the other critics, and they seem to understand Orwell's intentions at a deeper level. What are the similarities and differences in their views of *Animal Farm*? Do you think that Fyvel's greater admiration for the book is partly due to the fact that he is writing in the 1980s, long after *Animal Farm* has proved to be a success?

7. Compare and contrast the difference between Ben Ray Redman's book review in the journal *Politics* and Orwell's letter to that journal. (Redman was one of the few early American reviewers of *Animal Farm* who seemed to understand Orwell's basic intentions.)

8. Compare and contrast the hostile book reviews of *Animal Farm* by George Soule and Kingsley Martin.

9. Isaac Rosenfeld sharply criticizes *Animal Farm*, but his objections are artistic rather than chiefly political. Explain how his "disappointment" with *Animal Farm* differs from the other negative reviews in this chapter.

10. Does Milton Blau, in his anti-Orwell and pro-communist review of *Animal Farm*, distort the book and Orwell's intentions? How does Blau's review reflect the basic doctrines of Marxism-Leninism, outlined in Chapter 2?

11. The American book reviews of *Animal Farm* are best understood in the context of the intellectual climate of the early postwar era. Using statements by Norman Podhoretz, Irving Howe, and Russell Kirk, how would you characterize the thinking of American intellectuals of the 1950s? What are the similarities and differences between conservatives and radicals?

12. Norman Podhoretz stated that the name "Orwell Press" is a good one for an anti-communist organization. Do you agree?

13. Do you think Podhoretz is fair to characterize Orwell as "the patron saint of anti-Communism"? Or does that seem too narrow?

14. Orwell died in 1950 and claimed to be a socialist right up until the end. Comment on Norman Podhoretz's statement that if Orwell had lived into the 1980s and had seen the evolution of the Cold War, he would have changed his politics and become a capitalist or a neo-conservative.

15. Despite their opposed political positions, why do you think that Norman Podhoretz and Irving Howe both admire Orwell so strongly? How is that possible? Do you find either man's view of Orwell to be more persuasive? Do you think Orwell would have supported one man's interpretation over the other?

16. Summarize the influence of McCarthyism on the reception of the *Animal Farm* film adaptation.

17. Outline the conflicting interpretations of the *Animal Farm* film that emerged during the McCarthy era.

18. View the *Animal Farm* film adaptation. Now respond to the original reviewers. For instance, both Gerald Weales and Spencer Brown express reservations about the film in their reviews. Weales is more concerned with the artistic issues in the film. Brown, on the other hand, focuses on ideological matters. Do your own opinions about the film correspond more closely to Weales or Brown? Explain.

19. Compare and contrast the *Animal Farm* film adaptation with the movie *Babe* (1995), directed by Chris Noonan. For instance, both

films have farm settings and feature talking pigs in the leading roles. But the pigs in *Babe* are portrayed favorably and the farm animals achieve a working democracy by the film's closing. Discuss these similarities and differences. What does *Babe* imply about power relations, revolutionary politics, the possibility of social equality, and the natures of human beings and animals?

SUGGESTED READINGS

Atkins, John. *George Orwell: A Literary and Biographical Study*. New York: Frederick Ungar Publishing Co., 1954.

Brander, Laurence. *George Orwell*. New York: Longmans, Green, 1954.

Connolly, Cyril. *Enemies of Promise*. London, 1938; revised and reset, 1949: Routledge & Kegan Paul, Ltd.

Hollis, Christopher. *A Study of George Orwell*. Chicago: Henry Regnery Co., 1954.

Koestler, Arthur. *Darkness at Noon*. Reprinted 1958. New York: Signet Books, The New American Library. Written 1938–40; published 1941. An account of the Moscow Purge Trials of the 1930s in fictionalized form, of special interest for comparison with *1984* and *Animal Farm* especially with respect to brainwashing and "reality control."

Meyers, Jeffrey. *A Reader's Guide to George Orwell*. London: Thames & Hudson, 1975.

Milosz, Czeslaw. *The Captive Mind*. Translated by Jane Zielonko. New York: Knopf, 1953.

Rees, Sir Richard. *George Orwell: Fugitive from the Camp of Victory*. Carbondale: Southern Illinois University Press, 1961.

Rieff, Philip. "George Orwell and the Post-Liberal Imagination." *Kenyon Review* (Winter 1954): 49.

Vorhees, Richard J. *The Paradox of George Orwell*. West Lafayette, Ind.: Purdue University Studies, 1961.

NOTES

1. *CEJL*, p. 406.
2. *CEJL*, vol. 3, p. 203.
3. *CEJL*, vol. 3, p. 406.
4. *CEJL*, vol. 3, p. 405.

6

The 1980s and 1990s: Soviet *Glasnost,* Third World Communism, and Orwell

John Rodden (with translations from the Russian by Cristen Carson Reat and translations from the German by John Rodden)

CHRONOLOGY

1978	USSR and Afghanistan sign a twenty-year treaty of friendship that calls for military cooperation between the two nations
1979	The Nicaraguan Communists, the Sandinistas, gain power in a successful coup December 27: USSR invades Afghanistan
1980	Lech Walesa organizes the Polish independent trade union that will come to be known as Solidarity July 19: The XXII Summer Olympic Games open in Moscow; many nations, including the United States, boycott the Games in protest of the 1979 Soviet invasion of Afghanistan
1981–89	Ronald Reagan serves as U.S. president
1981	Spring: *Animal Farm* serialized in a Nicaraguan newspaper opposed to the Sandinistas December: Martial law declared in Poland; lifted one year later
1982	Poland bans Solidarity November 10–12: Soviet dictator Leonid Brezhnev dies of a heart attack; Yuri Andropov succeeds him

1983	December: Orwell's last novel, *1984*, reaches #1 on American, British, and West German best-seller lists
1984	January: In response to Western attention accorded *1984*, Orwell is widely denounced in Soviet and East European media
	February: The 1984 Winter Olympics are held in Sarajevo, Yugoslavia; forty-nine countries participate in the first Games to be held in Eastern Europe
	February 9: Soviet dictator Yuri Andropov dies; he is succeeded by Konstantin Chernenko
	April: A stage musical of *Animal Farm* opens in London and plays later in Finland, Spain, Austria, Switzerland, Canada, and the United States
	July 28: The XXIII Summer Olympic Games open in Los Angeles; the USSR, East Germany, and Bulgaria refuse to participate in retaliation for the U.S. boycott of the 1980 Games in Moscow
1985	March 10–11: Konstantin Chernenko dies; Mikhail Gorbachev is declared General Secretary of the USSR Communist Party
1987	September 7–12: Erich Honecker is the first East German leader to visit West Germany
	September: Customs officials at the Moscow International Book Fair remove *Animal Farm* from the British bookseller exhibits
1988	April: USSR agrees to withdraw all 115,000 Soviet troops from Afghanistan within nine months
	October: Gorbachev becomes chairman of the ruling legislative body of the USSR
1989–93	George Bush serves as U.S. president
1989	February 15: Soviet troops complete withdrawal from Afghanistan
	June: Pro-democracy demonstrators occupy Tiananmen Square in Peking, China; the government kills thousands, which leads to the end of the seven-week demonstration
	July: After objections from the USSR, a stage adaptation of *Animal Farm* is dropped from the International Theatre Festival, held in Baltimore

August 24: First non-communist government in post-war Poland

November 9: The Berlin Wall, a symbol of the Cold War and communist repression, is taken down, resulting in free travel between East and West Germany

December 25: Rumanian leader Nicolae Ceausescu and his wife are found guilty of genocide against the Rumanian people and sentenced to death; they are shot immediately

1990   May 29: Boris Yeltsin wins election for president of Russia

July 5–6: NATO leaders declare that the Cold War is over

October 3: Germany is officially reunited

December: Lech Walesa becomes president of Poland

1991   January–April: The Persian Gulf War

July 1: Warsaw Pact formally dissolved

August 19–21: High-ranking Soviet leaders launch an unsuccessful coup to oust Gorbachev from power

August–September: Fourteen Soviet republics declare independence and secede from the USSR

November 6: Yeltsin bans the Communist Party in Russia

December 8: Yeltsin and leaders of eleven former Soviet republics join together to form the Commonwealth of Independent States (CIS), replacing the USSR (four former republics refused to join CIS)

December 25: Gorbachev resigns as president of the USSR, which now formally ceases to exist

1992   February 1: George Bush and Boris Yeltsin jointly declare a formal end to the Cold War

ANIMAL FARM SINCE THE 1950s

As one can see from the timeline above, George Orwell and *Animal Farm* were subjects of much controversy and influence in the decade following its publication. Historian Eric Goldman has termed the years 1945–55 "the crucial decade" in his book of that title (*The Crucial Decade* [1960]). This chapter covers the tremendous reception and impact of *Animal Farm* in the communist world since "the crucial decade."

Let us first place *Animal Farm* within the historical context of the years since the mid-1950s. As we saw in Chapter 5, the Cold War did not end at that time. The Soviet Union sent troops to preserve communist rule in East Germany (1953), Hungary (1956), Czechoslovakia (1968), and Afghanistan (1979). For its part, the United States helped overthrow a left-wing government in Guatemala (1954), supported an unsuccessful invasion of Cuba (1961), invaded the Dominican Republic (1965) and Grenada (1983), and undertook a long (1964–75) and unsuccessful effort to prevent communist North Vietnam from bringing South Vietnam under its rule.

The late 1970s saw an easing of Cold War tensions, as evinced in two disarmament treaties in 1972 and 1979 (known as SALT I and SALT II). In these agreements, the two superpowers set limits on their strategic missiles capable of carrying nuclear weapons. This was followed by a period of renewed Cold War tensions in the early 1980s as the two superpowers renewed their arms build-ups. But the Cold War began to dissolve in the late 1980s during the administration of Soviet leader Mikhail S. Gorbachev. He made efforts to democratize the Soviet political system. When communist regimes in the Soviet bloc countries of Eastern Europe collapsed in 1989–90, Gorbachev acquiesced in their fall. The rise to power of democratic governments in East Germany, Poland, Hungary, and Czechoslovakia was quickly followed by the unification of West and East Germany, again with Soviet approval.

Gorbachev's democratic reforms had meanwhile weakened his own Communist Party in the USSR. In December 1991 the Soviet Union collapsed. Fifteen newly independent republics emerged in the aftermath, including a Russia with a democratically elected, anti-communist leader. The Cold War had come to an end.

That sequence of international events forms the larger historical context in which readers have encountered *Animal Farm* since the 1950s. *Animal Farm* continued to sell well and influence Western public opinion deeply, especially American and British readers, after the 1950s. The main reason was that the Cold War endured: the battle between Communism and anti-Communism still raged in the West. Orwell's book, which attacked Communism without reservation, became a mouthpiece for its anti-communist admirers.

Animal Farm's extraordinary success began with the book-buying public. More than 1 million copies were sold through the Book-of-the-Month Club in the 1940s and 1950s. By 1972, sales of hardcover and paperback editions had reached 11 million. By the 1990s, the sales total exceeded 20 million in seventy languages, placing *Animal Farm* among the top twenty best-sellers in the history of publishing.

These phenomenal sales figures are due in part to the entry of *Animal Farm* into the curriculum of junior and senior high schools. By the late 1950s, *Animal Farm* was being widely taught in schools in Britain and the United States. It has since become one of the ten most popular works of literature in American junior and high schools. A former college chairman of the Advanced Placement Program noted in the 1970s that Orwell's beast fable was the only book previously read by every student of the eighty-five in his freshman literature class. The enduring impact of Orwell's book is well illustrated by the popular "Animal Farm" greeting card series, which features a piglet on the back cover, straddling a fence and uttering the famous words from Orwell's book, "All animals are equal . . ."

Animal Farm has been frequently dramatized on radio, television, and the stage. The most popular stage adaptation has been Nelson Bond's *Animal Farm* (1961). Written near the height of the Cold War, the play makes clear that the USSR is Orwell's object of satirical attack. Its preface opens: "You will meet beasts whose prototypes have dominated news headlines for a half hundred years. . . . The entire action of the [play] takes place in England. . . . You may decide for yourself that the real scene is set several hundred miles further to the east." In 1996, which witnessed the fiftieth anniversary of its American publication, a new adaptation for the stage was produced in the United States.

Animal Farm aroused heated debate when it was first published, and international debates still continue about the book. For instance, the stage adaptation of *Animal Farm*—whose satiric songs included "Four Legs Good, Two Legs Better," "Beasts of England," and "Sugar Candy Mountain"—was removed from the international theater festival in Baltimore in 1989 because it was deemed offensive to the USSR and other communist countries; the capitalist West had been drawing frequent comparisons between "the ruling pigs" in *Animal Farm* and the communist leaders of the Soviet Union, Poland and Nicaragua ever since the early 1980s. President Ronald Reagan had even dubbed the Soviet-led communist nations as "the Evil Empire."

We will draw special attention here to the book's impact in the 1980s. During this decade, Orwell and *Animal Farm* received press attention because Orwell's novel *1984* was in the news, the USSR was beginning to crumble, and President Reagan and his administration voiced outspoken criticism that evoked the anti-Soviet rhetoric of the early Cold War era. During 1982–83, editors began a "countdown to 1984" that brought Orwell and his two books much publicity. (*1984* even rose to #1 on British and American best-seller lists in late 1983 and early 1984.) A stage musical adaptation of *Animal Farm* opened at the National Theatre in London in 1984, directed by Peter Hall, which brought Orwell to the attention of a wider range of people. Meanwhile, *Animal Farm* and *1984* were still banned in the Soviet Union and Eastern European countries (except Yugoslavia). Both books circulated widely in prohibited areas in underground editions. In 1988, *Animal Farm* was officially published in the USSR.

Orwell always maintained that *Animal Farm* was directed against Soviet Communism. He intended a preface entitled "The Freedom of the Press" to introduce *Animal Farm*, but it was never used and remained unpublished until 1971. The preface included this paragraph: "If liberty means anything at all, it means the right to tell people what they do not want to hear. The common people still vaguely subscribe to that doctrine and act on it. In our country it is the liberals who fear liberty and the intellectuals who want to do dirt on the intellect. It is to draw attention to that fact that I have written this preface." Orwell sought to show the Soviet system in its true colors. Despite its pretensions to greater liberty, it reintroduced tyranny in a new guise.

We have selected three formerly communist nations in order to show the relationship of *Animal Farm* to recent international events: the USSR, East Germany, and Nicaragua. The excerpts that follow indicate the continuing relevance of Orwell and *Animal*

Farm from its publication to the present: commentaries about *Animal Farm* and Orwell in the Soviet state-controlled press, interviews with Soviet and East German readers of Orwell, and the use of *Animal Farm* as anti-communist propaganda in Nicaragua.

FIRST OFFICIAL PUBLICATION OF *ANIMAL FARM* IN THE USSR

Mikhail S. Gorbachev served as General Secretary of the Communist Party of the USSR from 1985 to 1991. Gorbachev was the first (and last) Soviet leader to rise through the ranks of the Communist Party after 1953, in the post-Stalinist era. This, in part, made him more open-minded than his predecessors.

Upon taking power, Gorbachev embarked on a program of cultural, political, and economic reform referred collectively to as *glasnost* ("openness") and *perestroika* ("restructuring"). Due to *glasnost*, a major cultural thaw took place. Freedoms of expression and of information were significantly expanded. For example, the press and broadcasting were allowed unprecedented liberties in their news reports and editorials. Under *perestroika*, the first modest attempts to democratize the Soviet political system were undertaken. For instance, multiple candidates ran for elected office (not just the hand-picked Communist Party choice). The secret ballot was also introduced in some elections. Some limited free market mechanisms were also introduced into the Soviet economy.

Gorbachev was hailed as a great reformer in the West, but many Soviet officials and citizens believed his reforms either went too far or that he was too timid. One of the most controversial areas of his reforms was in the publication of literature. During 1986–88, as part of Gorbachev's policy of *glasnost*, formerly banned literary works began to appear in newspapers and books in the USSR. Among these was *Animal Farm*, which was first serialized in Soviet newspapers and then published separately as a book.

Following are four documents that deal with issues connected to the Soviet publication of *Animal Farm*: an overview of the complicated political scene in the USSR when *Animal Farm* was published in 1988–89 and reviews and commentaries of the book that appeared in the late 1980s. They have been translated from the Russian for this volume by Cristen Carson Reat.

JOHN RODDEN

The official Soviet interpretations of Orwell's work in the main government publications were evasive about *Animal Farm*'s meaning. Soviet critics sought to muffle the fact that the book was an allegory about the early decades of USSR history. Indeed the official efforts to soften the satirical edge of *Animal Farm*, which are notable in the selection by John Rodden, resemble the euphemisms in *Animal Farm* itself. Orwell uses these euphemisms to satirize the distortions of language by Soviet and Communist Party officials.

Consider, for instance, the following three passages from *Animal Farm* in light of the language of Soviet reviewers in the next document.

> The work was strictly voluntary, but any animal who absented himself from it would have his rations reduced by half. [Chapter 4]

> Napoleon had commanded that once a week there should be held something called a spontaneous demonstration. [Chapter 5]

> Once again all rations were reduced except those of the pigs and dogs. A too rigid equality in rations, Squealer explained, would have been contrary to the principles of animalism. Squealer always spoke of it as an adjustment, never a reduction. [Chapter 7]

Glasnost advocated "openness," but that did not amount to full honesty. Communist officials feared that if they told the full story of Soviet Communism, they would be ousted from power.

Although the publication of *Animal Farm* exemplified the new climate of Soviet openness, the presentation of *Animal Farm* by Soviet cultural officials stopped short of fully admitting the truth about Orwell's fable. Between the lines, however, Soviet intellectuals did sometimes admit the truth of *Animal Farm* as a story about Stalinism's horrors, as the last two translated selections in this chapter demonstrate.

FROM JOHN RODDEN, "ORWELL IN THE USSR:
GORBACHEV'S *GLASNOST*"
(*La Salle Magazine*, Spring 1989)

This summer the leading Soviet literary journal, *Novy mir* [*New World*], published the most influential political novel of the twentieth century, George Orwell's *1984*. That event was accompanied by the publication in recent months of several chapters of Orwell's *Animal Farm* in three different Soviet publications, among them *Nedelia*, the literary supplement to the official government newspaper *Izvestiia*.

These publication events are only two of the many cultural reforms undertaken by Soviet President Mikhail Gorbachev. But Orwell's pair of satires have sold more than 40 million copies in 65 languages [more than any other pair of books by a single author in history]. And he is the keenest Western critic of the Soviet system under Stalin. So the publication of *Animal Farm* and *1984* possesses much wider significance. When it comes to *samizdat* [underground literature] some books are more equal than others.

The belated appearance in the U.S.S.R. of *1984* (1949) and *Animal Farm* (1945) represents a new epoch for the Soviet Union as well as for Orwell's reputation in the Communist world. Indeed, in recent months *glasnost* has moved far beyond the realm of literature and art to Soviet history and politics, with 1989 already witnessing public criticism of everything ranging from the Soviet space program to Stalin's tyranny and even the fundamentals of Marxist-Leninism.

But the Soviet presentation of certain artworks—especially the example of the disingenuous treatment of Orwell's books by the Soviet press—can also serve as timely "criteria for gauging the credibility of *glasnost*," in the phrase of Milan Simecka, the Czech translator of *1984*. Simecka spent 1981–82 in prison for translating Orwell in pre-Gorbachev days. His words are a cautionary reminder that the much-touted transformation of Soviet political life may be calculated to preserve the Soviet system by obtaining Western loans, trade, and technology transfers. Likewise, the press discussions of *Animal Farm* and *1984* show that USSR leaders are not yet willing to come to terms with the Lenin-Stalin era. Despite the enthusiasm of Western intellectuals for Gorbachev, it is worth remembering that *glasnost* literally means "publicity" as well as "openness." The Soviet response to Orwell in 1988–89 remains less than fully honest.

In earlier years, Orwell's anti-Communism repeatedly carried him *Pravda*'s prize curse, "Enemy of Mankind," bandied with special gusto during the Stalin years. Not the least of the wry ironies of his Soviet reputation has long been that, despite the frequent condemnation of his work in Communist Party publications, none of his books had until 1988 ever been officially published in the U.S.S.R. Numerous references to and even reviews of *Animal Farm* and *1984* have appeared in the Soviet press since the late 1940s. But until recently, an official import ban existed on Orwell's work. Soviet citizens were jailed for possessing his books, and tourists had their copies seized on entry to the U.S.S.R. . . .

"The time has come," concludes the *Literary Gazette* "to free ourselves from the stagnant prohibitions, to discard the myths, to shatter the crooked mirrors, and to read George Orwell thoughtfully and without prejudice."

Has it?

Or as Sergei Zalygin, editor of *Novy mir*, put it: "It's possible that Orwell wrote his book with a concrete address—the address of socialism. But the time has passed when the book, to put it delicately, embarrasses us."

Again: has it?

Not quite yet, it would seem. Most embarrassing for the Soviets is *Animal Farm*, whose "concrete address" could not be clearer. Indeed one might have assumed that the one-to-one correspondences between USSR history and this biting satire would have been inescapable. But the September 1988 *Nedelia* notes only that *Animal Farm* is "surprisingly contemporary." It is "directed against those who make a mockery of [socialist] ideals, openly or in a disguised way, against political demogoguery and political adventurism." No mention is made of the fable's historical referents.

Likewise the March and July 1988 issues of *Rodnik*, published by the Latvian Communist Party, blatantly contradict Orwell's famous statement (in the original *samizdat* Ukrainian preface of 1947) that his main goal in *Animal Farm* was to "expose the myth" that "Russia is a socialist country." Instead the March *Rodnik* notes (falsely) that *Animal Farm* alludes to the Night of the Long Knives in Nazi Germany (Hitler's June 1934 purge of Ernst Rohm and the S.A.) and to the 1937–38 liquidation of the anarchist militias in the Spanish Civil War. In a single passing phrase, the editors mention that *Animal Farm* also refers to "the Moscow trials of 1937." But then come the old appeals to justify Stalin. Readers "can well imagine the true picture of that period, with all its tragedies, and with the great stress and strain of the struggle." They will find it "impossible to support" the fable's portrait of a time of "tyranny," the editors maintain.

Indeed the *Rodnik* editors conclude by pointedly arguing for the "universality" of *Animal Farm* as a fable about tyranny in general. "People have tried many times to connect *Animal Farm* to our history, but such efforts are biased, not to mention that they water down the author's intention." Orwell's "grotesque animal paradise" is "by no means open to a single interpretation."

All this involves much more than misleading literary criticism or historical inaccuracies. The case of "Comrade Orwell" is significant precisely because it shows the anxious jumble of hopes, fears, and tensions pressing upon Soviet attempts to confront the past.

Opening the books on the Soviet past, that is, is not just a matter of dumping "stagnant prohibitions." Orwell's writings have everything to do with the Soviet present—and future. . . .

These deceitful introductions to Orwell are representative of much Soviet cultural criticism during the *glasnost* age. They alert us to how far *glasnost* has still to go before it truly signifies "openness"—and toward precisely what has *not* yet happened in the U.S.S.R. The Soviet leadership has shown no signs of permitting a free press. (The Soviet "Index" of forbidden literature has shrunk by a third, but it still exists. Nor is the state's fundamental right to suppress "undesirable" material in question.)

"There should be no forgotten names and blank pages in Soviet history," declared Gorbachev in a much-quoted statement last year. The task of remembering and blank-filling, however, is not so easy as that call implies. (Last year Soviet schools even canceled Russian history exams, because the Soviet education ministry could not agree on a satisfactory explanation of post-1917 events.) . . .

So at all events, we are witnessing at present not a cultural revolution, but a very partial reclamation project.

NEDELIA

The following excerpt (discussed in the selection above), is taken from the introduction of the first Soviet publication of *Animal Farm*. It originally appeared in the widely read Sunday magazine *Nedelia*, of the USSR's major state newspaper (*Izvestiia*). Although the editors accurately describe Orwell as a socialist, they omit any mention that the special target of *Animal Farm* is Stalin's USSR.

FROM *NEDELIA* (16 September 1988)

In 1945, George Orwell (pseudonym for Eric Blair) wrote a fable about how animals destroy the tyranny of man and become victims of a much harsher tyranny. *Animal Farm* is one of the brilliant examples of social anti-utopias of the twentieth century.

Orwell's biography (1903–1950) is quite unusual. Orwell was a Socialist. It is good that the prose of this prominent English writer is coming late to us, but it is especially beneficial to our readers. Orwell's satire does not deride Socialist ideals, as some of our critics until recently have thought. It is directed against mockery of them, direct or veiled, against social fanaticism and politically reckless actions. This satire remains surprisingly contemporary in today's political world, both in Russia and elsewhere.

VICTORIA CHALIKOVA

The following selection appeared in *Rodnik* in 1988 shortly after several chapters of *Animal Farm* were published for the first time in the Soviet Union. Victoria Chalikova rightly emphasizes that Orwell remained "on the Left and an enemy of capitalism" throughout his life. But she recognizes that *Animal Farm* and *1984* constituted warnings to the West about the dangers of socialist ideals gone astray. She attributes the political critique reflected in *Animal Farm* and *1984* to psychological factors. She speculates about Orwell's psychology and his allegedly "pessimistic" temperament. By the 1940s, claims Chalikova, "Orwell's optimistic attitude" of the 1930s was "exhausted."

FROM VICTORIA CHALIKOVA, "MEET GEORGE ORWELL"
(*Rodnik*, 1988)

In the 1930s, Orwell was an optimist—as much as it is possible for a writer with a pessimistic temperament. Orwell's optimism was based on three convictions:

1. Every repressive regime devises its own punishment.
2. The progress of mankind is not an illusion.
3. The hunger for power, revealed by repressive regimes is not a characteristic of human nature, but the consequence of poverty, of insufficiency and gives rise to competition (we remember the apples and the milk that went only to the pigs!). . . .

By the end of the 1940s Orwell had not experienced any kind of political upheaval: he remained on the Left and an enemy of capitalism.

But his optimistic attitude was depleted, and the three major premises forming the basis of his convictions were not crossed out or replaced. They simply became maybes:

1. The progress of mankind, perhaps, is only our illusion.
2. Perhaps the appearance of repressive regimes is firmly established forever by those who are capable.
3. The hunger for power, maybe, is not a reaction to a situation, but a characteristic of human nature.

Thus, *Animal Farm* was born. It is necessary, Orwell wrote, "to destroy the Stalinist myth in the name of reviving the Socialist movement. A myth destroys a myth, as fire fights fire." So this had to be done allegorically, in the form of a fable.

To understand the conception of *Animal Farm* one must know fundamentally that Orwell was an exception among his peers, not only in his judgment of Stalinism, but in his relationship to the USSR. Never once did he allow himself one contemptuous word or condescension toward the Russian working-class. (Only the corrupt Communist leaders.)

A. ZVEREV

As the previous selections make clear, some of Orwell's Soviet interpreters during the *glasnost* era tried to misrepresent or downplay Orwell's target in *Animal Farm*. Orwell himself witnessed similar attempts during his lifetime and left no doubt about his purpose. As he wrote to his agent: "If they question you again, please say that *Animal Farm* is intended as a satire on dictatorships in general, but *of course* the Russian revolution is the chief target. It is humbug to pretend anything else."

The following excerpt comes from Russian literary critic A. Zverev. This essay appears in *Anti-Utopias of the Twentieth Century* (1989), which features a new Russian translation of *Animal Farm*. Zverev stresses, fairly, that Orwell's main "goal" in writing *Animal Farm* was "the dethroning of Stalinism" from its sympathetic place in the eyes of Western intellectuals and the general public. But Zverev misleadingly says that *Animal Farm* is "directed at the Stalinist system, not at the USSR." Zverev also criticizes Orwell for believing that Lenin—not just Stalin—was responsible for creating the brutal; tyrannical Soviet "system."

FROM A. ZVEREV, "MIRRORS OF ANTI-UTOPIAS"
(Anti-Utopias of the Twentieth Century [New York: Scribner's, 1989])

Much of *Animal Farm* is recognizable to us: Hardly anyone doubts which historical models are used for Napoleon and his rival. . . . However, the content of this work cannot be reduced to a mere summary of the first decade of Soviet history. It gave Orwell his raw material, but then history is not so simple. After all, a totalitarian dictatorship was not for Orwell a synonym only for Stalinism. Rather, he sees the circumstances and growth of such a dictatorship not at all unique to Russia and as having taken on other forms: It grew in Hitler's Germany, in Spain, in the Latin American banana republics.

One cannot forget about all of this when reading *Animal Farm*. The model of the dictatorship described by Orwell is objectively more important than any given parallels which are present in this story. . . . Written at the very end of the war, *Animal Farm* today reads like one of the books already anticipating a great deal in the postwar social experiment, although this, of course, was not Orwell's aim. His goal was the dethroning of Stalinism, which—from lack of knowledge, from illusions, from the ascribed genius of the Leader, from the victory in the Great Patriotic War—possessed a particular attractiveness for many and for many in the West.

[Upon translation and publication of *Animal Farm* in the Ukraine in 1947, Orwell wrote in the preface the following:] "Nothing was so conducive to the misrepresentation of initial socialist ideas, than the belief, as though present-day Russia is a model of Socialism and therefore, any action her rulers perceive to follow are necessary and serve as an example for imitation. That's why for the last ten years I have been convinced that the sooner we shatter the myth about the USSR, the sooner we can strive to resuscitate the Socialist movement."

It turns out that these words are directed not at the USSR per se, but at the Stalinist system. The myth about this system has not been shattered even today. Orwell's books are helping with this task.

Orwell wrote from inside the thick of the events of the mid-twentieth century. He did not have any historical distance. He didn't understand the reasons for the existence of the forced-labor camps or the tragedy of its human losses.

Unlike Orwell, however, we can understand why he was convinced that the development of the Russian state after 1917 was unavoidable and why he rejected any thought of an alternative. At that time it was really difficult to identify any alternative, but we know that an alternative did exist. A careful reading of Lenin's last articles possibly would have convinced Orwell himself of this.

SERGEI TASK

The following excerpt is a note from a recent Russian translator of Orwell's work, Sergei Task. It appeared at the end of his 1989 translation of *Animal Farm*. Like earlier Russian commentators, Task strives to underscore that *Animal Farm* attacks the "mockery" of socialist ideals, not socialism or its socialist ideals themselves. Among his most interesting points is that he felt compelled to change Snowball's name to Cicero, the famous Roman orator, in order to give a sense of Trotsky's eloquence and smooth talk. Orwell meant the name "Snowball" to suggest that Trotsky could "snow" his listeners and roll his words into a verbal "snowball" that overwhelmed his opponents. But there is no equivalent in the Russian language for this English metaphor.

FROM SERGEI TASK, "NOTE FROM THE TRANSLATOR"
(Anti-Utopias of the Twentieth Century [New York: Scribner's, 1989])

What drama did George Orwell have in mind in 1945 when composing this fable? As to the bloody swinishness occurring on the farm and the terminology itself—animal committees, meetings, the form of address "comrade"—there is no doubt that Orwell means the USSR. Therefore, the usual question for a Russian translator—what difficulties with language will be particularly problematic—did not arise.

But Orwell's boar had the nickname Snowball, which doesn't communicate the same idea in Russian. I decided to call him Cicero, so that he could be a worthy rival to Napoleon. Cicero, the last orator, the truest rhetorician.

Our [Russian] readers are most likely the most sensitive readers in the world. There are those who think we are being assaulted for "our ideals" in *Animal Farm*. I would like to reassure our readers immediately: Orwell's satire is not directed against "our ideals," or more accurately, against the ideals common to all mankind. It is against mockery of them, direct or veiled. It is against all social fanaticism and politically reckless actions which succeeded in the twentieth century. (We do not remain completely blameless and will not pull the whole blanket over ourselves.) It was not only in our country. Dictatorship of any variety can awaken savage instincts. Totalitarianism is universal. All forms of it are different masks on a single face.

INTERVIEWS WITH TWO SOVIET READERS OF ORWELL'S WORK

Who would risk a lengthy prison term to read a forbidden work of literature? What did an average Soviet citizen think about *Animal Farm?* The following accounts feature the personal experience of two Soviet women who read *Animal Farm* when it was a crime in the Soviet Union to do so.

Natasha, a fifty-six-year-old electronics engineer from Moscow, agrees with "most of Orwell's ideas," but she doesn't think that it altered her ideas about Stalinism "in any significant way." She too believes that *Animal Farm* is broader than "just depicting Stalinism," and she states quite firmly that *Animal Farm* was written too early to "evaluate fully Stalin's brand of dictatorship."

FROM INTERVIEW WITH NATASHA (1997)

In 1970 I read *Animal Farm* in the middle of the night because in those days it was illegal to read it. We called it "reading under the blanket" because we could only read such things behind closed doors. Often my husband and I would get forbidden literature by means of *samizdat*. In Russian, *samizdat* literally means "self-published." It was a system that existed in the Soviet Union by which manuscripts that were denied official publication were circulated secretly. Often that meant barely legible mimeographed copies that were read by hundreds of people. We had to read *Animal Farm* in one night so that we could pass it on to the next person.

I saw *Animal Farm* as having a broader purpose than just depicting Stalinism. I think that it portrayed the evils of dictatorship, not just in my country, but any place where repressive regimes exist. I also think that *Animal Farm* was written too early to evaluate fully Stalin's brand of dictatorship. I agreed with most of Orwell's ideas, but I don't think it altered my ideas about Stalinism in any significant way.

We knew many people who had heard about *Animal Farm*, but didn't have any desire to read it. For instance, two friends of ours, a freelance writer and an engineer who were members of the Communist Party, only read it when it was published legally in Russia in 1988. We didn't know much about George Orwell or any of the anti-Communist writers in the West, because we just weren't exposed to western writers in school. I might have believed some of what they wrote.

I was born in 1943 and started school in 1950. It was when I started school that I was exposed to the most powerful image of Stalin in the media. He was portrayed as Stalin "The Inspirer" and "The Great Organizer." I would say that most of the Soviet people at that time firmly believed in Stalin and the Soviet rhetoric. Stalin united them. He advocated peace and progressive thinking. Stalin created the mechanism in industry and agriculture for accomplishing specific goals. He took into account the history and nature of the people and urged them to improve and perfect themselves. In other words, Stalin incarnated and animated the dreams of the majority of the people.

When I think back to what I knew about the Bolshevik Revolution, I believe that it was the cornerstone for rebuilding Russian society. The Revolution took into account progressive western thinking and was a catalyst for great change in Russia. One of its main goals was to create the necessary conditions for the rebirth of our nation which in turn would assist world progress. In Russia, the repression of the 1930s—as was everywhere around the world—was part of the preparation for World War II. It started out as a combination of revenge-seeking for the chaos of our Civil War in the early 1920s and the restructuring of order in society. Later, it became a political war within the Communist Party, a battle for power among rival factions of Communists.

Overall, I think that the Communist Party played a beneficial role in the USSR. It waged war against darkness and savagery by advocating progressive ideas of brotherhood, justice, and equality. It reflected a desire to safe-guard all that is good.

I must mention, however, that I was not a member of the *Komsomol*, or Communist Youth League. The *Komsomol* was the Communist organization for youth in the Soviet Union that was the stepping stone for eventual Party membership. Being a member of this organization often gave its young members preferential treatment over non-members in areas such as employment and education. Because I was not a *Komsomol* member, I just barely succeeded in gaining employment at a machine-building factory for defense.

It was at my first job in 1959 at this compound that I was strongly advised to join the *Komsomol*. They told me that if I didn't, I would be like a "white crow," which is the Russian equivalent of a "black sheep." Because there was so much pressure on me, after being there only a few months I decided to join the *Komsomol*. I did the minimum I needed to in order to get by.

It was in 1960, after I joined the *Komsomol*, that for the first time in my life I became aware of the fact that they were feeding us propaganda. I began to question the image of Stalin, the Bolshevik Revolution, and the way in which I was raised. There were numerous clashes among people about these issues. I was actually very lucky. At the time, such people were called "rabble" or "soft-faced dandies." Later many of them were labeled dissidents.

I gradually began to have doubts about the kind of life that our leaders had promised to bring to us. The farther I got away from the time period of 1917–1953, the more I was inclined to think that they were making great fools out of all of us. Now I am fully aware of what they did to us— this crime they committed in front of us all. They took away the most important thing: freedom.

In the mid-1980s, given this orientation, I considered *glasnost*, or openness, to be a doubled-edged sword. At first it seemed as if it were what many of us had dreamed of and talked about for so many years. *Glasnost* relaxed bureaucratic controls on information and allowed for more open discussions. Such loosening of control enabled us to learn and to discuss more about the past and present. I believe that Gorbachev encouraged a reassessment of some features of Soviet life. However, *glasnost* degenerated, in my opinion, because it called *everything* into question. Its standards were lowered. Often *glasnost* is understood as "the cruder, the better."

Ultimately, I think that *glasnost* was deficient. It overlooked generosity, brotherhood, and equality. It did not allow for the preservation of the integrity of our past. *Glasnost* pushed the ethical boundaries in journalism and the arts, often degenerating into vulgarity. It sought to break all historical ties in the name of truth-telling and openness. Often *glasnost* brought lies. It was for individualism and against international brotherhood, against the idea of Communism. It created the conditions for the flourishing of "cut-throat capitalism," the awakening of savage and parasitic capitalist instincts, the return of brutish and bestial laws of the capitalist struggle for survival, the battle for private property, and elements of fascism instead of elements of socialism.

• • •

Elena Lifschitz, a fifty-four-year-old professor of Russian from St. Petersburg (formerly called Leningrad), remembers her first encounter with *Animal Farm* well. Like Natasha, Lifschitz agreed with much of what Orwell wrote and felt that the use of pigs to represent the Communist Party leaders "was a very fitting image." Although she felt that "Stalin had betrayed the revolution," she came to realize that the "revolution itself was a crime, not only what Stalin did after the revolution." Although *Animal Farm* did not change Lifschitz's overall image of Stalinism, it did help her to "see more clearly what was happening around me."

FROM INTERVIEW WITH ELENA LIFSCHITZ (1997)

I first read *Animal Farm* in 1968 when I had my son, Sasha. When we were living in Leningrad, several copies of the Russian translation of *Animal Farm*, published in the West, were smuggled in by some courageous American tourists. We were fortunate to have had a friend who knew someone who received the books in Leningrad.

My husband and I read it together in our communal apartment. We had obtained an actual copy of the translated book, which at the time was even more dangerous than having photocopies of it. The authorities had classified Orwell's books as "anti-Soviet propaganda." Possessing and giving such books to others was punishable by a long prison term. We never wanted to know any names of the people involved in the process of passing illegal books in order not to get anybody in trouble in case we were summoned to the KGB. We were very careful when reading the books. We wrapped them in newspaper so that nobody could see the cover.

We read it in one night. I would have the baby in one arm and would read a page and then the my husband would read a page while I did something else, such as cooking or changing the baby. With every knock on the door we would hide the forbidden book in a secret place.

I really liked what Orwell wrote. For example, I felt that the use of pigs to represent the Communist Party leaders was a very fitting image. Orwell's "all Animalism" (i.e. four legs good two legs bad, all animals are equal but some are more equal than others) certainly corresponded to my experience of the privileged treatment accorded to Communist Party members in the supposedly "classless" society. I think that the continuous rewriting of the 7 Commandments of Animalism accurately represents the Soviet Constitution: It was a farce that could be rewritten at Stalin's behest.

On the other hand, I don't think that Orwell's portrayal of Boxer the carthorse—as naive and all-believing in Napoleon—was an accurate depiction of the working class. It just wasn't very close to what I saw around me in real life. Reasonable persons from all walks of life could see that the official propaganda was not truthful. You didn't need a college degree for that.

My overall image of Stalinism didn't change very much after reading Orwell because it had always been very negative. When I was quite young I felt that Stalin had betrayed the revolution. It was later I came to realize that the revolution itself was a crime, not only what Stalin did after the revolution. I think that Trotsky might have been better for Russia only in the sense that fewer people would have been exterminated. He would have probably established a slightly different totalitarian system.

I cannot say that the satirical representation of Communism in *Animal Farm* opened my eyes to the horrors of the Soviet system, because its perversity had become clear to me long before. But Orwell's ridicule of the pretensions of Communists to social justice and to superior morality did help me see more clearly what was happening around me, and it helped me to survive the pressures of the totalitarian regime. The oppressors are not so frightening when you see that they can be laughed at!

Now Russia is a very different country, of course. Since the time of Gorbachev's reforms, Russians have been free to read what they want. Orwell's books are available in Russian bookstores. We try not to forget, however, that there are places in the world—China, North Korea, Vietnam, and Cuba—where even today life is governed by the laws of Orwell's *Animal Farm*, and where reading Orwell can still be treated as a crime.

INTERVIEW WITH AN EAST GERMAN READER
OF ORWELL'S WORK

Wolfgang Strauss, a retired professor of British and American literature and linguistics, taught at the universities of Leipzig and Jena in East Germany. Strauss was a member of the East German Communist Party. But he was also an outspoken critic of some of its policies, and for that reason he was blacklisted by the East German government and not permitted to travel abroad. He was one of the few top-ranking professors who marched in the protest demonstrations against the East German communist regime in the autumn of 1989. After the fall of the Berlin Wall in November 1989, Strauss began to teach Orwell's work in his English classes at the University of Jena.

In the following passage, he reports on an incident from the 1950s, in which the mere possession of Orwell's work cost a young East German his freedom.

FROM INTERVIEW WITH WOLFGANG STRAUSS (1995)

Comparisons between the vision of George Orwell and the former East Germany are very compelling to me. I always begin my lectures on Orwell by reading from some declassified documents compiled by the GDR's secret police. They tell the story of a young man who was sentenced in the 1950s to two and a half years in jail because he obtained copies of Orwell's books "illegally" from West German relatives. They had mailed the books to him, and he had circulated them among his friends.

That was the entirety of his "crime." This "crime" was officially termed: "Illegal importation and Distribution of Writings Hostile to the Regime." That wording was the terror that the East German government felt about this *true* socialist!

Fortunately, the imprisoned student has lived to tell his tale. He published his horrifying story in 1998 and entitled his book: Orwell's East Germany.

So I always conclude my seminars on Orwell with excerpts from this unjust case. The students of today are always very moved. Invariably they remark: "Thank God, we are glad to be so young. We have been spared the ordeal of living through that terrible time."

ANIMAL FARM AND THE NICARAGUAN REVOLUTION

In 1981 the anti-Sandinista newspaper *La Prensa* ("The Truth") serialized Orwell's fable near the height of the Nicaraguan civil war. *La Prensa* was edited by supporters of the Nicaraguan contras, the rebel force that aimed to overthrow the Marxist (Sandinista) government under President Ortega.

By serializing *Animal Farm* in its pages, *La Prensa* was implying that the Sandinista revolution had been betrayed and corrupted, just as the Russian Revolution had. Although the newspaper editors did not make the analogies explicit, readers were meant to draw the appropriate comparisons: Nicaragua was the dictatorship of *Animal Farm*, President Ortega was Napoleon, the Sandinistas were the pigs, and so forth.

The following news account of the serialization of *Animal Farm* in Nicaragua is from a conservative American newspaper opposed to Marxism and the Sandinista revolution.

FROM NICK FRAZIER, "SANDINISTAS TESTING IN AILING
NICARAGUA"
(*Wall Street Journal*, 4 May 1981)

The independent forces want free elections, which they are convinced would unmask the Sandinistas as an armed minority. But the Sandinistas have announced that such elections won't be held for several years, and then only to affirm their role as leaders of the revolution. . . . The brightest note is that so many of Nicaragua's troubles are out in the open. Despite restrictions on what newspapers can publish, the three dailies here are filled with the ongoing political debate, ranging from serious discussions of economic systems to trivial potshots at the other papers. . . . The independent *La Prensa* showed a drawing of a poor peasant family quizzically watching a Sandinista official whiz by in a shiny Mercedes-Benz marked "property of the people." *La Prensa* published another implicit comment on the revolution when it inserted in all its editions newsprint copies of George Orwell's *Animal Farm*, the scathing fable of a socialist barnyard revolution in which the revolutionaries became corrupted by new-found power.

Indeed, critics of the Sandinistas worry most that, by repressing political activity, the new government will take on more and more characteristics of the deposed Somoza regime. "I can still hear in my ears when the Somoza masses shouted 'Somoza forever'—in English," says Pedro Joaquin Chamorro Jr., the combative editor of *La Prensa*. "Now you hear the Sandinista masses shouting, 'Sandino yesterday, Sandino today, Sandino forever.'"

CONCLUSION

Cyril Connolly, a close friend of Orwell, described *Animal Farm* as "a fairy story told by a great lover of liberty and a great lover of animals." As we suggested in the Introduction, Orwell's subtitle, "a fairy story," was an ironic comment on the book's historical relevance. That is, *Animal Farm* was no fairy story. It was about the reality of Soviet Russia.

Now that the USSR has collapsed, Soviet Russia is no more. But the themes of *Animal Farm* that generated such controversy during the wartime and early postwar eras are still relevant and controversial: the abuse of power, the erosion of civil liberties, democracy versus dictatorship, and many others. These are universal themes, not time-bound ones. *Animal Farm* is not merely about Lenin and Stalin, or even just about the Russian Revolution and the history of the Soviet Union. As Chapter 7 will demonstrate, it has much to say to us today about revolution in general, about power and equality, and about the relations between government leaders and followers.

STUDY QUESTIONS

1. The rebellion led by the pigs failed to turn Manor Farm into the ideal society that Old Major anticipated in *Animal Farm*. Why does the animals' rebellion fail? Are the reasons similar to those that accounted for the ultimate failure of the Russian Revolution?

2. Identify the major distortions or inaccuracies in the Soviet publications that introduced *Animal Farm* to the Soviet public. Do these seem to be minor, unintentional mistakes that are due to cultural and political differences between the USSR and the Western democracies? Do they seem to be deliberate attempts to mislead the Soviet public about Orwell's main intention in *Animal Farm?*

3. Do you consider *Animal Farm* to be chiefly a satire of Soviet history? Why or why not?

4. Now that the Soviet Union has collapsed and the Cold War waged between the United States and the USSR is over, are the political lessons of *Animal Farm* no longer pertinent?

TOPICS FOR WRITTEN OR ORAL EXPLORATION

1. Chapter 2 discussed the main principles of Marxism. Do you see similarities between those principles and Gorbachev's policy of *perestroika?* Do you think that *perestroika* was a deceptive or genuine amendment to the key doctrines of Soviet Communism?

2. Given *Animal Farm*'s treatment of the dangers of revolution, what do you think Orwell's opinion would have been about the ultimate fate of the USSR? Would he have believed that his prophecy turned out to be true? Would he have been surprised that the USSR turned out to be so much weaker than *Animal Farm* under Napoleon?

3. In Chapter 3 of *Animal Farm*, the cat tries to re-educate the sparrows. The pigs constantly try to re-educate other animals. Does it seem to you that Gorbachev's policies were similar attempts to "re-educate" the Soviet public?

4. Does the death of the USSR imply that no government can survive a history of deceit and lying to its people? Or does it mean that all violent revolutions must ultimately end in failure and collapse from within?

5. Many U.S. citizens believe that politicians lie all the time and governments mislead the public as a matter of policy. Do you agree? Is the difference between the policies of most governments, including the

United States and *Animal Farm*, more a difference of degree or of kind?

6. *Animal Farm* caricatured a totalitarian society—a nation whose government had total power and control over the main opinion-making institutions (the media, the schools). Do you think it is possible to control public opinion without the explicit use of totalitarian tools (e.g., by using enticing advertisements, control of the government budget)?

7. Many observers of Soviet history attempt to defend Trotsky and denounce Stalin. They imply that the USSR would have been much more humane if Trotsky had triumphed in his battle for power with Stalin. What do you think?

8. Many critics of Gorbachev claim that he betrayed Communism. Do you think his policies violated the spirit of the Seven Commandments of Animalism?

9. Compare Squealer's twisting of factual events in *Animal Farm* with the presentation of *Animal Farm* during *glasnost* in the late 1980s in the Soviet media. Are there close similarities?

10. If you were a leader of the USSR in the 1980s, would you have demanded that the stage version of *Animal Farm* be banned from international theater festivals? Does such a demand seem consistent with the principles of *glasnost*—a sign of openness to criticism?

11. Consider Elena Lifschitz's observation: "Reasonable persons from all walks of life could see that the official propaganda was not truthful. You didn't need a college degree for that." If the propaganda was so transparent, even to uneducated people, why didn't the USSR collapse from within earlier? Why didn't its people revolt openly? Does Lifschitz's observation imply that Orwell was wrong to imply in *Animal Farm* that the "intelligent pigs" could easily deceive "dumb beasts" such as Boxer?

12. Our two Soviet interviewees read *Animal Farm* at roughly the same historical moment, within just two years of each other. Whose experience of *Animal Farm* seems to you more frightening? More compelling? More relevant to post-1991 Russia? What are the main differences in the lives of these two readers? For example, how do they differ in their evaluation of the Communist Party of the USSR?

13. *Animal Farm* was officially prohibited in most communist countries until the late 1980s. If you were one of the two Soviet interviewees in this chapter, speculate on what it must have been like to obtain a copy of the *Animal Farm* through the underground network. Would you have been terrified? Would you have refused to read it? Would

you have informed the government about the person who offered it
to you?

14. Do you think *Animal Farm* is strongly relevant to communist countries besides the USSR, such as Nicaragua? What about other former
communist nations such as East Germany, Hungary, and Romania?

15. The excerpt in this chapter by John Rodden notes that in 1988 "Soviet schools even canceled Russian history exams, because the Soviet
education ministry could not agree on a satisfactory explanation of
post-1917 events." Think about any controversial issues in American
history such as the Civil War and Reconstruction in the nineteenth
century or the civil rights and feminist movements in the 1960s and
1970s, respectively. Can you imagine American school officials' can-
celing history exams because educators could not agree about the
interpretation of these events? Pick one of these events, and analyze
the controversies about it. Have there been attempts to hide the truth
about these events, such as the efforts made by Stalin to conceal the
realities about the crimes of post-1917 Soviet Communism?

16. In your opinion, does the biographical treatment of Orwell by Soviet
reviewers seem accurate? Identify the main differences between their
presentation and the biographical summary of Orwell in Chapter 4.

17. Do you think that the name "Cicero" captures an important aspect
of Snowball? This example illustrates one of the difficulties that trans-
lators encounter (remember, the name "Snowball" does not make
sense in Russian). Do you think such differences in translation substantially affect the way that readers respond to a book?

18. Do you think that the newspaper *La Prensa* really expressed "the
truth" when it serialized *Animal Farm* to attack the Sandinistas in
Nicaragua?

19. The *Wall Street Journal* was a fierce critic of the Sandinista Revolution in Nicaragua. Does its comparison of *Animal Farm* with the
Sandinistas seem accurate or biased to you?

SUGGESTED READINGS

Adler, Les K., and Thomas G. Paterson. "Red Fascism: The Merger of Nazi
Germany and Soviet Russia in the American Image of Totalitarianism, 1930s–1950s." *American Historical Review* (1970): 1046–
64.

Anisimov, I. "Enemies of Mankind." *Pravda*, 12 May 1950, 3; translated
in *Current Digest of the Soviet Press*, 1 July 1950, 14–15.

Dallin, David J. *From Purge to Coexistence*. Chicago: Henry Regnery Co., 1964.

Fischer, Louis. *The Life and Death of Stalin*. New York: Harper and Co., 1953.

———. *The Life of Lenin*. New York: Harper & Row, 1964.

Franck, Thomas N., and Edward Weisband. *World Politics: Verbal Strategy Among the Superpowers*. Vol. 1. New York: Oxford University Press, 1968.

Hunter, Lynette. *George Orwell: The Search for a Voice*. Suffolk: Open University Press, 1984.

Kroll, Jack. "The Politics of the Stage." *Newsweek*, 30 June 1986, 67.

Mendel, Arthur P. *Essential Works of Marxism*. New York: Bantam Books, 1961.

Patai, Daphne. *The Orwell Mystique: A Study in Male Ideology*. Amherst; University of Massachusetts Press, 1984.

Stansky, Peter. "The Orwell Year." In Jean W. Ross, *DLB Yearbook*. Detroit: University of Detroit Press, 1984.

Sturua, Melor. "An Orwellian America." *Izvestia*, 15 January 1984. Translated in *World Press Review* (March 1984): 53.

Venclova, Tomas. "I Am Grateful to Orwell." *Index on Censorship* (August 1984): 11.

Wilson, Edmund. *To the Finland Station: A Study in the Writing and Acting of History*. New York, 1940; reprinted 1953 by Doubleday Anchor Books.

Woodcock, George. *The Crystal Spirit*. Boston: Little, Brown, 1966.

Zalubrowski, Sonay. "*1984* in Rumania." *Chicago Sun-Times*, 1 January 1984.

7

Animal Farm Themes in Light of Late–Twentieth–Century Public Issues

William E. Shanahan III

The various themes Orwell addressed in *Animal Farm* continue to be relevant. While reading *Animal Farm* as a critique of Stalinism is essential, reading it in the light of contemporary concerns is also revealing and rewarding. The microcosm Manor/Animal Farm (here exemplifying all animals) was designed to evoke more than just some Stalinist brand of Marxism-Leninism. Issues of power, freedom, rights, truth, and the like were selected to rise above the specific context and remain relevant for years to come.

Such issues have played themselves out in various and, at times, intriguing ways over the intervening half-century since *Animal Farm*'s writing. Power, for example, permeates almost all aspects of our society. Power both produces and destroys, is both good and evil. Power circulates, moves, in most everything that we do, strikingly coming to light in the near-constant cry from all quarters for conformity. Politics is a frequent battleground over the proper balance between public welfare and individual rights. Cherished freedoms come under close scrutiny whenever society clamors about some perceived threat to its members, especially its children. Fundamental questions about basic liberty are raised if national security is at stake. Orwell's political concerns perhaps have become even more relevant since their publication.

Potential comparisons between contemporary issues and *Animal*

Farm abound. If *Animal Farm* effectively treats these and other relevant issues within the fairy story's context, then perhaps it continues to have something to say to us. Taking heated political issues out of their own context and putting them into a seemingly more disinterested narrative context potentially allows for a less involved, emotional engagement. Of course, taking so-called disengaged, innocuous issues about animals and putting them into hotly contested social issues can make for a charged, heated exchange. *Animal Farm* is a wonderful political vehicle. One can ride around in it and be completely enchanted with admiring the car itself. Or one can ride and be so taken in by the view that the car disappears from view. Who decides?

POWER: ITS POLITICAL ABOLITION?

> They were just coming down the stairs when Mollie was discovered to be missing. Going back, the others found that she had remained behind in the best bedroom. She had taken a piece of blue ribbon from Mrs. Jones's dressing-table, and was holding it against her shoulder and admiring herself in the glass in a very foolish manner. The others *reproached her sharply*, and they went outside. (31; emphasis added)

Revolution does not beget all the revolutionaries' utopias. Radically altering one's world brings inevitable risks. Some of the changes almost certainly will not be to everyone's liking. The example provided in this section's epigraph might seem trivial to some. To others, the importance of one's presentation and especially one's ability to choose that presentation might be integral to one's identity. Irrespective of how you value such questions of appearance, what needs to be recognized in this example is how power is at work.

Power is a difficult word and requires investigation, if not strict definition. For Mollie, power makes itself known by sharply reproaching her for wanting to wear Mrs. Jones's ribbon. This is no small matter for Mollie, who is not generally fond of postrevolutionary Animal Farm. She is unhappy with the hours, the work, the lack of human affection and attention, and the overall ethic on the farm. The community of animals is concerned with her behavior and her attitude, fearing the most serious of crimes: fraternization with humans. Clover goes so far as to *search* her stall for contraband. Eventually, Mollie leaves the farm in favor of the old-style cart life: light work, good grooming, pretty ribbons, and plenty of sugar. Once her whereabouts were known, not one of the animals ever spoke her name again. The shunning was complete. If she were unable to live within Animal Farm's increasingly stringent and arduous environment, then she was not wanted. The power of the group to dominate and dictate the lives of the group was near total.

Given the difficulty of defining power, contextualizing power within an ongoing debate about power might help to gain some insight into power. Orwell wrestled with questions of power throughout his life. His rejection of fascism and Stalinism were tied intimately to his views on power. However, in order to understand power generally and Orwell's views specifically, a broader view of power is needed. In addition to Orwell's relationship to more overt forms of power's negative force (for example, Stalinism in *Animal Farm*), he had an active relationship with power's supposed positive force, anarchism: "Orwell had noted the growing resemblance of communism and fascism, which had convinced him of the anarchist tenets that the centralized state was evil and that liberty was human being's first, inalienable birthright. Orwell further agreed with the anarchists, and against the Marxists, that power was psychologically addictive and inherently corrupting."[1] The themes of Stalinism, socialism, and anarchism come together in power. Orwell's treatment of power in anarchism will complement the earlier discussion of the abuse of power on Animal Farm and in Stalinist Soviet Union. Anarchism presents a unique case, especially with respect to political power. What about other forms of power? How do different forms of power relate to one another? Can power be abolished? What about political power? Is the abolition of power an oxymoron? Rather than rushing to a definition, this section of the chapter will embed the undefined concept into a contemporary political debate consumed with issues of power: anarchism versus the government.

Laws are not required for power to be felt. In fact, one of Orwell's chief objections to the anarchist utopia is the "problem" of public opinion and censure or ostracism. The question of the state provides us with an excellent space in which to examine power. Anarchy comes from the Greek word *anarchos*, which means "without a ruler." Anarchists oppose government:

> To be governed is to be watched over, inspected, spied on, directed, legislated, regimented, closed in, indoctrinated, preached at, controlled, assessed, evaluated, censored, commanded. . . . To be governed means that at every move, operation, or transaction one is noted, registered, entered into a census, taxed, stamped, priced, assessed, patented, licensed, authorized, recommended, admonished, prevented, reformed, set right, corrected. Government means to be subjected to tribute, trained, ransomed, exploited, monopolized, extorted, pressured, mystified, robbed; all in the name of public utility and the general good. Then at the first sign of resistance or word of complaint, one is repressed, fined, despised, vexed, pursued, hustled, beaten up, garroted, imprisoned, shot, machine-gunned, judged, sentenced, deported, sacrificed, sold, betrayed, and to cap it all, ridiculed, mocked, outraged and dishonoured. *That* is government, *that* is its justice and its morality![2]

Pierre-Joseph Proudhon, the first to call himself an anarchist, eloquently and forcefully presents at least part of the argument against government. Some anarchists, like Proudhon, believe that the government corrupts the natural cooperative tendencies of individuals and that its abolition would allow for those capacities to flourish. Law, according to this view, is not only unnecessary; it is extraordinarily dangerous. Others believe that humans are not naturally cooperative, and thus we must not let "irrational" individuals govern. Individuality prevails in this version of anarchy. Law, here, also corrupts. Interestingly, one of Orwell's objections to anarchism was its belief in the innate goodness of humans or of their perfectibility: "Orwell's pragmatic streak dismissed anarchism as hopelessly utopian. Anarchism 'aimed at the impossible feat' of human 'perfectibility'. . . . Unlike the anarchists, Orwell did not believe in the innate goodness of human beings."[3] Importantly, there are many different forms of anarchy (some have suggested that there are as many anarchisms as there are anarchists), so one must be careful not to reduce its diversity and complexity into a singular concept. For the purpose of our investigation, however, the anarchist attack on hierarchy, authority, and government in defense of freedom, autonomy, and liberty is the focus.

Orwell wrote an essay on Jonathan Swift and his *Gulliver's Travels*. In that work, Swift portrays an anarchist society inhabited by the Houyhnhnms. Rather than law, they employ "exhortation," the incitement of good deeds, to maintain societal order. Orwell objects to this form of compulsion, arguing that it is more destructive than the rule of law. He goes so far as to liken it to "totalitarianism":

> In a Society where there is no law, and in theory no compulsion, the only arbiter of behaviour is public opinion. But public opinion, because of the tremendous urge to conformity in gregarious animals, is less tolerant than any system of law. When human beings are governed by "thou shalt not," the individual can practise a certain amount of eccentricity; when they are supposedly governed by "love" and "reason", he is under continuous pressure to make him behave and think in exactly the same way as everyone does.[4]

Internal discipline, motivated by external exhortation, risks taking advantage of human nature. For Orwell, however, human nature is at least in part governed by gregariousness, a fondness for social interaction. Of note, many anarchists also argue that humans are social creatures. For them though, this innate sociability allows for the *possibility* of an anarchist society. According to Peter Kropotkin, a major anarchist theorist and a Russian prince, observations of nature reveal that humans are social creatures. Nature, he argues, is *"the first ethical teacher of man*. The social instinct, innate in men as well as in all the social animals,—this is the origin of all ethical conceptions and all subsequent development of morality."[5] Thus, Orwell and Kropotkin agree on human social nature but disagree on the implications of this nature. Does a human willingness to conform with society's needs and wants make law more or less necessary? More or less desirable? Are humans even sociable by nature?

Obviously, the world of Animal Farm is not strictly analogous, representing, instead of anarchism, a totalitarian style of socialism. Still, our understanding of power should begin to develop as we compare and contrast each "totalitarian" society. Animal Farm had explicit rules in the form of the Seven Commandments. It also had leaders—though the leaders emerged rather than were chosen. The pigs, who possessed more intelligence and knowledge, seemed to be natural leaders. The leaders did not always give orders, however. Much as in anarchy, the leaders exhorted their comrades: to bring in the hay faster and more efficiently, to produce more grain, to carry more rocks faster, and the like. The leaders used many different forms of incitement to action. Especially early on, the task was easy since the animals required direction and not much encouragement. After all, most of the animals were behind the revolution, and so they wanted it to work.

Also as in anarchy (where there are no "leaders" per se), the leaders are not the only ones involved in exhortation and censure. Boxer is a leader by example. Through his example, he exercises power. He influences other animals by his enormous effort. Already working longer days than any other animal, what does he do when enough work is not getting done? He gets up earlier. Boxer's example allows him to direct the other animals into more work. He controls them not directly but indirectly through his influence. For whatever reasons, animals are moved to more work as a result of Boxer's effort. Is he responsible for their actions? Can this use of power even be considered "control"?

The control employed on Animal Farm was not always so seemingly benign. The other animals' treatment of Mollie was harsh. She was deeply affected by their behavior toward her. Increasingly as the postrevolution society was formed, the rules became more stridently enforced and the demands on the animals increased.

The power we are concerned with here in this section also includes that form of power, of course. That was especially one of the focuses in the Marxism chapter, however. Marx himself raised questions about what the world would look like in a postrevolutionary society when he coined the phrase "dictatorship of the proletariat." He believed that as a result of the forces and relations of production, there would be an inevitable revolution. This revolution would invert the status quo class relationship such that the proletariat would become dictator over the bourgeoisie. Marx insisted that this dictatorship would be only temporary. After the transition from capitalism to communism, all classes would be abolished. Lenin was totally committed to the notion of a proletarian dictatorship, and so it became a guiding concept for the Russian Revolution. The experience on Animal Farm, and by Orwellian analogy in the Stalinist Soviet Union, was that the proletariat was indeed dictatorial and the disastrous consequences were not transitional.

What if instead of a socialist society with commandments, Animal Farm was an anarchist society with no rules? What implication would that have for power relationships on the farm? The hay would still need to be brought in. Grain would still need to be grown. The windmill might even be built. How would the animals motivate each other to get the work (especially the unpleasant work) done? Orwell's argument is that there would either be no difference, or it would be worse for the individual. The pressure toward conformity with the group would be overwhelming on a farm without rules. Clearly an animal like Boxer, once on board, will perform beyond his or her limits, no matter what the rules or who the ruler. Maybe the gregarious Mollie would be cajoled into giving up her ribbons without leaving the farm. What would be the implications of that for Orwell's argument about the totalitarian tendencies of an anarchist society? After all, Mollie's choice would have been "free." Or would it? If Orwell is correct, Mollie's sociability would have worked against her on a farm with no rulers. In fact, the only way that such a farm could function, according to both Orwell and many anarchists, is if Mollie and others internalized a strong measure of discipline. Does Orwell's argument collapse in on itself, though—that is, if no ruler allows for the least individualistic deviance from the norm, does the strongest (for example, a totalitarian dictator) allow for the most?

Anyone familiar with high school culture is aware of the imposing pressure of public or peer pressure. The calls for conformity are overwhelming: from clothes to music and movies, from friends to intimates and enemies, to language and beyond. Individuality frequently is viewed as weird and to be avoided. High school is an excellent testing ground for Orwell's argument about conformity, and high school students are particularly suited to engage it. Somewhere between authoritarianism and anarchy lies high school. The authoritarianism is easy to demonstrate. The remarkable lack of legally protected freedom associated with minor status in our society generally and the unique form of license associated with high school authority specifically combine to form a potent brew of potentially repressive state apparatus. On the other hand, the culture of high school students creates an almost anarchic social milieu.

There are no rules per se, and the rulers emerge variously and change frequently. If one does not like the dominant culture, one is free to inhabit or initiate one's own. Despite the apparent freedom of these various subgroups, conformity reigns. Or, does it? Is high school more anarchic or authoritarian? Is conformity the hidden dictator in high school? Or does freedom reign? Should it? Why do "adults" deserve more freedom and liberty than "children"? Why should teachers rule students in school?

Anarchism and socialism present political critics with excellent proving grounds for the various questions concerning coercion, conformity, and power. *Animal Farm* provides readers with a safe environment in which to examine these questions. This chapter is aimed at putting some of these questions into different contexts. Power is an elusive concept. Ultimately we have not gone very far toward defining it. Our purpose in this section, however, has been to look for instances of power in order to begin a discussion about it. Though elusive definitional examples of power are easy to come by. Look no further than the front of your classroom or cut of your hair.

• • •

Emma Goldman is one of the foremost anarchists in its history. As both a theorist and an activist, Goldman brought anarchism to the people with an astonishing force and commitment. Born in 1869 in Russia, she moved with her family to Rochester, New York, in 1886 and was transformed by the government execution of four anarchists in Chicago in 1887. The details of her career, which take her into such controversial areas as women suffrage and birth control, are not relevant for our immediate concerns (though they are recommended highly for those whose interest is piqued). Suffice it to say, Goldman speaks from a career completely devoted to the pursuit of anarchist ideals in all facets of life.

Like Kropotkin and others, Goldman believes that a harmonious social existence is natural for humans, likening it to food and air. Government interferes with the natural development of that innate characteristic by its enforcement of laws with violence. So runs the theory that if the government is eliminated, intrinsic sociability will arise spontaneously and freely. Orwell believes in the gregariousness of humans by nature, but disagrees with their harmonious-ness. These arguments might work against his earlier arguments. If his totalitarian view of anarchist society is accurate, then the individuals in it conform more completely than in totalitarian societies to public dictates (as a result of their gregariousness). Yet this conformity is the cornerstone of Goldman's anarchist society: one that coexists harmoniously *as a result of* just that social pressure to conform. Thus, the real problem Orwell raised is the value underlying that conformity. Is it totalitarianism or natural law? Natural law means that such sociability is inescapable (similar to Orwell's view of human gregariousness) and the attack of totalitarianism would be far off the mark. Are humans social animals by nature? Is there any such thing as "human nature"? If there is, how could we *humans* come to understand humanness? Do Orwell's arguments about human gregariousness and anarchist societies unravel (contradict) themselves? How does power enter into the equation? If power is inescapable, what happens to questions about the value of democracy or totalitarianism?

In *Animal Farm*, the animals seemed to start out harmoniously enough. Although there was grousing by some, Benjamin the donkey for example, the animals generally agreed about the overall direction of the revolutionary Animal Farm. There was nonetheless quite a bit of disagreement on the particulars of everyday farm policy, at least among the pigs. These disagreements brought about the explicit reign of dog-inspired terror by Napoleon, eventuating in his "election" as president and Snowball's physical expulsion from the farm.

Returning to our earlier example, what if, instead of being disciplined into rejecting human ribbons, Mollie had been exhorted or coaxed into conforming with the majority of animals on the farm? Assuming that the gregariousness or sociability of the animals was similar to humans as formulated by Orwell and some of the anarchists, Mollie would have given up her ribbons in order to conform to the group, if only the "government" (in the form of commandments and de facto leaders) had not been present. Is Mollie better off on Orwell's farm or the anarchists'? Does the Animal Farm government interfere with or secure Mollie's freedom? Is freedom even possible if all the animals are compelled to conform by their nature? Is there any difference in the way power is employed during the late reign of Napoleon on the farm and hypothetically on the anarchist farm sketched out in this section's pages?

FROM EMMA GOLDMAN, "ANARCHISM: WHAT IT REALLY
STANDS FOR"
(in *Red Emma Speaks* [New York: Schocken Books, 1972; original,
1911])

A natural law is that factor in man which asserts itself freely and spontaneously without any external force, in harmony with the requirements of nature. For instance, the demand for nutrition, for sex gratification, for light, air, and exercise, is a natural law. But its expression needs not the machinery of government, needs not the club, the gun, the handcuff, or the prison. To obey such laws, if we may call it obedience, requires only spontaneity and free opportunity. That governments do not maintain themselves through such harmonious factors is proven by the terrible array of violence, force, and coercion all governments use in order to live. Thus Blackstone is right when he says, "Human laws are invalid, because they are contrary to the laws of nature."

• • •

Mikhail Bakunin was one of the most influential anarchists in the history of political thought. His noble Russian lineage was discarded in favor of an international revolutionary enterprise and an intervening prison stay. Born in 1814 in Russia, Bakunin served in the artillery for a couple of years before devoting himself to revolutionary causes. His participation in a revolt in Dresden, Germany, landed him in jail. He eventually ended up in a Russian prison for six years, emerging as a physically embattled but spiritually energized revolutionary force with which to be reckoned, indeed a revolutionary forceful enough to rival Marx in his prime.

The excerpt that follows is from a basic writing of Bakunin on the nature of education in a revolutionary society. An all-round education extends to all "children" and continues throughout their life. Interestingly, early education is obligatory for younger children. Should education be obligatory for anyone? Your high school once again is an excellent place to interrogate Bakunin's contention that "public opinion" is the most powerful influence on every individual. Once again, here the "natural influence" (as compared to Goldman's natural law) of human solidarity is at work. In order to work more morally, public opinion first needed to be moralized and humanized. Is high school corrupted by the immoral hand of government (teachers, administrators, rules, and the rest)? Are your peers born of solidarity and just waiting for the abolition of authority structures to act coolly and rationally? What would happen if students successfully overthrew the power structures of your high school? Should education be equated with the most restrictive influence exerted on humans? If public opinion's influence is exerted irrespective of particular government or lack of any government, what difference does it make if public opinion is moralized? Would your public opinion be moralized if your school government were abolished? How would you act?

Despite what Orwell might argue to the contrary, *Animal Farm* also reads in favor of the harmoniousness of animals (including humans). Return to our example of Mollie. The underlying reason discernible for her behavior was her desire for affection. Though she was used to human affection, what would have happened if the other animals had treated her more kindly and tried to accentuate her appearance by other-than-human means (for example, braiding her mane)? Mollie's great offense was allowing a human to stroke her nose. What if instead of having to seek such physical attention outside the farm, Mollie had been able to receive her needed dose of affection from her comrades? Perhaps Orwell's fairy story is actually a tale of an anarchist, not a Marxist, revolution run amok.

FROM MIKHAIL BAKUNIN, "ALL-ROUND EDUCATION"
(in Bakunin, *From Out of the Dustbin* [Ann Arbor, Mich.: Ardis, 1985; original, 1869])

The natural influence which human beings exert on each other is only one of the conditions of social life against which revolt would be impossible and useless. This influence is the very material, intellectual, and moral basis of human solidarity. . . . Life outside all society and outside all human influences—absolute isolation—is intellectual, moral, and material death to a human being. Solidarity is not the product of individuality but its mother, and the human individual can be born and develop only in human society.

The sum of the dominant social influences, as expressed by the common or general awareness of a more or less outspread human group, is called *public opinion*. And who is unaware of the all-powerful influences of public opinion on every individual? Compared to it, the effect of the most draconian and restrictive laws is nothing. Public opinion is thus the preeminent educator of human beings. From this it follows that for individuals to be moralized, society itself must be moralized before all else; its public opinion, its conscience must be humanized.

TRUTH: A POLITICAL AMBITION?

> Man demands truth and fulfills this demand in moral intercourse with other men; this is the basis of all social life. One anticipates the unpleasant consequences of reciprocal lying. From this there arises the *duty of truth*. We permit epic poets to *lie* because we expect no detrimental consequences in this case. Thus the lie is permitted where it is considered something pleasant. Assuming that it does no harm, the lie is beautiful and charming.[6]

Friedrich Nietzsche, a famous German philosopher, lends us his insight on the origin of truth. Truth is one of humanity's highest values. Wars have been fought over it. Lives and reputations have been destroyed as a result of transgressing it. Whole societies have been built on it. Despite this seeming unwavering commitment to truth over human history, we regularly lie. Truth, despite the lip-service paid to it, especially in our society, constantly is subjugated to other goals. For instance, the president of the United States, as a matter of course, misleads, misdirects, and outright lies in order, for example, to protect the national interest. Any of us could imagine any number of possible situations in which we would lie unhesitatingly—for example, if our own or loved one's safety was in danger and lying was required to save her or him. Truth, despite being viewed in the abstract as vital, is frequently devalued. Why, then, do we profess it to be? And what happens when truth is violated in the public domain?

Lying is one of the central themes of *Animal Farm*. The pigs engaged in a systematic campaign of misinformation aimed at the neighboring farms, the town's folk, and their own comrades on the farm. By misinformation, what is meant is information known to be false by those disseminating it. Although we cannot know necessarily what the various animals on the farm are thinking, we can assume that they were aware of what we as readers were aware. Thus, the flagrant rewriting of the farm's history, the constant revisions of its operating principles, and the attempts to persuade other animals at all costs are examples of lying. Once again, the justification for such lying, no doubt would be tied to pragmatic concerns: the success of the revolution on the farm, the need to spread the revolution to other farms, and the general well-being of animals everywhere. Despite these claims, other motivations can be seen: the desire for power, control, and general selfishness. Truth is not the most important value after all. In fact, as in all societies where truth is professed to be the highest value, Animal Farm ends up defiling its own values. Nietzsche provides useful insight into this phenomenon as it occurs throughout history: "We still do not yet know where the drive for truth comes from. For so far we have heard only of the duty which society imposes in order to exist: to be truthful means to employ the usual metaphors. Thus, to express it morally, this is the duty to lie according to fixed convention, to lie with the herd and in a manner binding upon everyone."[7]

The remainder of this section considers some questions of truth (and lying) from within several different perspectives that will help to contextualize the questions and shed some light on the particular controversies. We will consider the regularly revisited battle over textbooks and textbook censorship. Truth is the watchword from both sides. Truth also demands its due when considering the very real battles engaged when this country goes to war. Specifically, we will lay bare some of the concerns that the press corps had with what they perceived as the government's intrusion into their ability to report the truth. The most recent foray into such territory was the Persian Gulf War. Finally, we will return to a time when truth was at the forefront of this nation's consciousness. Watergate, as it came to be known, shook the foundations of the U.S. government. The president was accused of breaking the law and lying to conceal his transgression. In each controversy, we will use the insight gathered from Orwell's treatment of similar issues so many years ago in *Animal Farm*.

SCHOOLBOOK SELECTION OR CENSORSHIP?

Textbook and other schoolbook selection is one of the most fundamental concerns we have as a nation. Since young people in our society attend school for a sustained part of their youth, those in charge must maintain constant vigilance over what is taught and how. Also, the purpose of this schooling is to prepare the future citizenry of the nation, thus increasing the stakes. There are many facets to the questions concerning textbooks and other schoolbooks. The line between selection and censorship is fine and often depends on what one's ideology is going into the process. Unfortunately, the extreme cases of book censorship can be found regularly in our society's schools:

> As I thumb through stacks of press clippings that report book bannings and book burnings in America, I cannot block out of my mind the atrocities that followed the torching of books in Nazi Germany. As I studied literature in the late forties and early fifties, I never dreamed that I would be reading about book burnings in this country in the seventies and eighties, but people who distrust writers are throwing books into flames during scheduled immolations every Friday night.[8]

Is the analogy to Nazism strained? Do book burnings necessarily end in Nazi-style atrocities? Is schoolbook censorship the same as book burning? Do any differences make the former less offensive than the latter? Book selection is an inevitable aspect of teaching school. Since our society would never allow students to choose their own books, somebody must. Who should do it? Teachers and librarians? Administrators? Parents and concerned citizens? What is at issue here?

In *Animal Farm*, the question of book selection and censorship is not raised explicitly. However, the underlying concerns are very similar. Ironically, the question of books is not relevant due to the literacy rate among the animals, while the lack of literacy accomplishes part of the book censor's agenda—that is, book censors attempt to shape the book readers through exclusion, while the pigs literally exclude content (on the side of the barn with the governing principles, for example) in order to shape their comrades. Orwell certainly is making an argument about literacy: being able to read can restrain governmental abuse. Snowball's attempts to teach literacy were abandoned quickly in his absence. The wholesale revision of history (truth) allowed the pigs to distort the path of the revolution. The inability of many animals to read meant that the government's words could be changed without scrutiny by the governed. This led to many of the abuses perpetrated by the pigs on the farm.

The development of a responsible, principled citizenry in a representative democracy demands that the citizenry be able to evaluate their choices critically and understand what those choices are. On the farm, they were able to do neither. Their illiteracy interfered with both their understanding of their choices and ability to think critically about them. Set aside the cause of this interference briefly, and compare its results with those accomplished in selection and censorship.

If we are never exposed to the possibility that, for example, the government is not a given but must be defended, how will we ever be informed about the legitimacy of anarchism? How do most people respond to the very idea of no government? Do they immediately dismiss the possibility as impossible or idealistic? Are they open to the anarchists' arguments? Quite possibly, their level of education (inculcation?) on the necessity of the government is very high. In the United States, we are taught about the need for government to fight crime, protect us from foreign invasion, protect freedom and accomplish other goals. This knowledge comes out in a variety of ways: through classroom instruction, the textbooks selected, the availability of alternative sources of information, and what is taken for granted in many subject areas. The question of whether to have a government is subjugated to what that government should do. This framing of the question such that certain issues are never discussed is one of the dominant aspects of education in the United States. You could substitute capitalism or democracy for government in the example. Education functions on the backs of its assumptions by bending its students to those assumptions. Similarly, the revolutionary course on the farm was changed by altering the consciousness of the people. Only drinking alcohol *to excess* was prohibited, and that is the way that it always has been.

The control that elementary and secondary schools exercise over students is also enormous. What is the difference between educational control in the United States and the pigs' control on Animal Farm? Do inclusion and exclusion of materials function in the same way? How do they differ? If the goal is to make an agreeable citizenry, why not select and censor toward that end? Does truth matter? Should we teach students to search after truth or "lie according to convention"? Does truth even make sense? What is the truth: evolution or creation? Did the European explorers and settlers commit near-genocide of the native populations in the Americas?

. . .

Michael Schudson, the author of the excerpt that follows, focuses on textbooks and the questions of selection and censorship. One of the central concerns raised by opponents of many current textbooks is their refusal to embrace religious truths. Rather than attempting to instill universal spiritual values, textbook authors apparently are embracing a form of secular humanism. Basically, secular humanism avoids the religious and praises humanity. Living a good life on this earth is the goal of secular humanism. Humans are seen as special and deserving of a unique place in the world. This position is a result not of divine intervention but of our own making and of our nature. Education is a major emphasis for secular humanists, along with freedom of thought. Although humans are special, we must cultivate these traits in order to help us to become better people. This movement away from the transcendent realm directly conflicts with, for example, the Christian right's desire to reinscribe Christian values in their children and in their country.

Schudson is unabashed in his support for secular humanism over any explicitly religious perspective. He embraces what he sees as tolerance and diversity in the humanist tradition. His fear about Christian control over textbooks is that they would repeat our history of intolerance, that "love thy neighbor" would extend only to thy Christian neighbor. The particular danger Schudson sees is embedding this Christian homogeneity in the schools. Our history with regard to diversity is mired in destructive exclusion. According to Schudson, we must not emulate such a past.

Once again, Mollie provides an excellent example of intolerance in *Animal Farm*. The community opposed her old-farm values: her desire for human companionship, her "frivolous" attention to appearance, and her refusal to work as hard as the other animals. Their refusal to accept her as she was led to her exclusion and eventual exit from the community. The success of the community after the revolution necessitated a strong, unified front. Since the conditions were difficult and the work arduous, the animals needed to be part of something larger than their immediate life. In other words, dissension was disastrous. Were the animals on the farm justified in their efforts to bring Mollie in line or hasten her exit? Does the good of the many outweigh the outcries of the few? Was that not the logic employed by Stalin during his wholesale slaughter of millions of his people? How much is one horse worth? One person?

FROM MICHAEL SCHUDSON, "TEXTBOOK POLITICS"
(Journal of Communication 44 [Winter 1994])

Suddenly, the poor textbook is hero, not goat. Dull that it is, capitalist commodity that it is, it is secular humanist and proudly so. Thank God for that! So is the state secular humanist, so is the legal system, so necessarily are the norms through which civil society becomes possible at all in a socially heterogeneous society. The trouble with the Christian right is not that it misreads textbooks but that it wants to establish a world no longer safe for diversity. The provisions in colonial America for prohibiting Jews and Catholics from voting; the ways throughout the 19th century of keeping women, blacks, and the propertyless from the franchise [the vote]; or the efforts, largely unsuccessful in the long run, to keep immigrants from voting—these are not the part of the American heritage we should be emulating.

• • •

Robert Weissberg takes a different tack with regard to the schoolbook controversy. He focuses on the objects of citizen scorn. The problem is not that people simply fail to see the "truth" of diversity claims or of free inquiry's value. Instead, according to Weissberg, there exists a stranglehold on academic publishing by the left. Rather than free thought, we have free thought along a very narrow spectrum on the left. The right is attacked for even making claims against the left's publishing control by public outrage directed at them. Since the left ostensibly is attempting to do "good" things, the right's response often is viewed as extreme.

Though arrived at through different means (a violent takeover), even more control over "publishing" characterized Napoleon's regime on the farm. Admittedly, given the paucity of written materials there, this control may seem largely irrelevant. Yet as we have seen, the ability to control, for instance, the barn with the farm's governing principles published on its wall, meant control of the revolution's direction. The importance of this control is obvious. The analogy to schoolbooks should be also. If a political ideology can control the nation's publishing (especially of the school's books), then it can help to direct the nation's course as well. Setting aside what they did specifically, are the pigs right to control the content of the words read by the other animals? If the fate of the revolution hangs in the balance, are the pigs not *obligated* to direct the farm in whatever way is necessary to secure a successful revolution? Still, if the pigs control the words (and history), what checks are there on them?

Weissberg raises another concern: "THE TRUTH." He caricatures the left's belief that it has the truth. Do you think this is a fair characterization? Look back at the passage above by Schudson. He disavows religious control over which textbooks are admitted into the classroom. What does he suggest instead? Secular humanism, of course. Is this not just another religion in different clothes? Another example of the truth hiding behind words like *tolerance* and *diversity?* In other words, does the defense of any ideology determining textbooks fall prey to the same objections Schudson raised against the Christian right? If such politics are inevitable, who should choose which books get into the classroom? Does *Animal Farm* help us to understand the dangers? How so?

FROM ROBERT WEISSBERG, "POLITICAL CENSORSHIP:
A DIFFERENT VIEW"
(*PS* 22 [March 1989])

Why do normally apathetic citizens get so worked up over school texts? It is too convenient to dismiss this hostility as uninformed opposition to

THE TRUTH. They are reacting to a leftish political vision, a vision so pervasive in publishing and leading departments that it is judged as politically neutral. And since this vision is so driven by honorable intentions, people who object to it can only be right-wing kooks.

INFORMATION MANAGEMENT OR PRESS RESTRAINTS?

In order to function appropriately, democratic decision making must have the consent of the governed. The manufacture of that consent is at the core of politics. Deception in the manufacture of that consent risks concentrating power in too few hands and still maintaining the illusion of a democracy. Concentration and abuse of this power can be checked by an informed citizenry, at least according to democratic theory. One of the linch-pins of that information is a free press. If the government is able to control what the press reports to the people, then it can shield itself from the rigors of the people's harsh eye.

One of the most crucial times for a nation is wartime. The decision to go to war is one of the most weighty decisions that a nation makes, with enormous consequences for its own people and those it might fight. When the nation has a military capability the size of that of the United States, extreme caution must be employed. When the perceived enemy has a military the size of that of Iraq, the potential carnage demands that the larger nation consider all the options. To consider those options and the war decision effectively, the government and its people must be informed properly. The history of the Persian Gulf War with respect to an informed citizenry demonstrates the huge gap between democratic theory and practice. In fact, the history of U.S. decision making regarding war makes a mockery of "rule with the consent of the governed," a cherished principle of democracies:

> During the Persian Gulf War many Americans felt as if they were experiencing something new in terms of suppression of dissent, restrictions on reporters, manipulation of information and the like. As . . . events . . . from the Revolution, the War of 1812, the Mexican War and the Civil War show, such an assessment of the situation could not be farther from the truth. In times of crisis, government leaders often feel that they can rule without the consent of the governed. That practice has a long heritage in this country and will take a long time to root out. Only by knowing this fact can Americans who care about participation in government be properly equipped

to fight the battle that needs waging to ensure informed involvement in all kinds of decision making. By treating each instance of
wartime restrictions as totally unexpected, we may indeed be per-
petually doomed to repeat our history.[9]

The wholesale censorship of the print and visual media during the
Gulf War, startlingly for many, is not an exception to otherwise
democratic wartime governing. Actually, this style of uninformed
government without consent is the rule.

Once again, *Animal Farm* offers some insight into the matter.
The manipulation of information by Napoleon and his cohorts is
the recurring theme in their battles with the humans. Orwell has
Napoleon's pigs directly contradict what we know as readers to be
true about the Battle of the Cowshed. This distortion of facts about
the battle allowed Napoleon to reap more accolades and to disparage his former nemesis, Snowball. The resulting praise helped
him govern, and the disparagement helped him to overcome the
specter of Snowball. Control of wartime information is crucial to
history that Napoleon is writing. He must write Snowball out of
their history in order to increase his own legitimacy. The only way
to do this, given that Snowball was the hero first class of the battle,
was to alter the historical consciousness of the other animals. This
is done through various means, though the specifics are not relevant for our comparison to U.S.-style wartime decision making.

Is it legitimate for a democratic government to conceal information from its people in order to make a war more acceptable to
them? What if their dissent interferes with the likelihood of success
in that war? How far can a government go in censoring the coverage of that war? How can the people check governmental abuse
if their main channel of information is shut off? How can one protest what one does not know about? What if the purpose of the
censorship is to prevent protest? Is this an acceptable course of
action in a democracy? What does *Animal Farm* contribute to his
discussion? Are the same issues raised on the farm relevant to, for
example, the Gulf War? Should Napoleon or President Bush be
able to govern without the consent of the governed?

• • •

In the following excerpt, Haig Bosmajian provides his readers with a history lesson in the hope that they will not be doomed to repeat it. The lesson consists of his detailing the history of governmental abuse of the press during wartime. The deviousness of this "sanitization" of the war effort is dazzling: exclude coverage of the dead. One of the greatest concerns during a war is the number of lives lost, on both sides. Usually the goal is not to kill as many enemies as possible but to kill as many as necessary. This desire is coupled with the need to keep one's own deaths to a minimum. A particularly distressing aspect of the media coverage during the Vietnam War was the explicit battlefield footage that exposed the U.S. public to the utter brutality of war. Many believe that the war coverage led to a lack of support among many living in the United States. (Interestingly, Margaret Blanchard, quoted above, disputes this claim with recall to "experts.") Irrespective of the truth value of this claim, the government does not want protest when it decides to take its nation to war. If the public believes that the war is being fought without a lot of lives lost, so the thinking runs, they are less likely to protest. Simply put by Bosmajian, the public did not see the bodies. The government conspired to censor the war's consequences. As anyone familiar with the war knows, the campaign was overwhelmingly successful.

Orwell appears in Bosmajian's text as a warning sign of what might come about if citizens fail to check the governmental excesses. In the "double speak" language of *1984*, he quotes the famous saying, "War is Peace." The public in Orwell's dystopian future is so inculcated into the thinking of the government that they are unable to expose even the most glaring instances of governmental abuse. Bosmajian predicts that the government's efforts were so successful during the Gulf War that they almost certainly will try it the next time. If we are to avoid such misinformation campaigns in the future, we must be on guard.

FROM HAIG BOSMAJIAN, "LYING TO THE PEOPLE"
(Western Journal of Speech Communication, Fall 1991)

So successful was the sanitizing of the war news that we as citizens were exposed through the print and visual media to a war where the casualties, our own and the enemy's, were for all intents and purposes never seen. The government did not restrict or prohibit just film and video coverage of battlefield deaths, but dead American soldiers were returned to the United States in coffins we were never shown. The thousands of dead Iraqi soldiers, along with the civilian casualties, were censored away. Surely, if we are capable of killing 150,000 people in several days, we ought to be technologically capable of visually recording their deaths so that all Americans could share in the full nature of the war. So successful was the government's censorship that questioning of the war or any opposition to the war could not be established on the basis of the human degradations, mutilations and deaths that resulted from political decisions made in Baghdad and Washington, D.C. Such a successfully managed censorship effort inevitably will be emulated by government in the future; we may be ready to enjoy war without any visible evidence of human suffering and death. We may have reached the Orwellian world where "War is Peace."

PRESIDENTIAL PRIVILEGE OR CRIMES
AGAINST THE STATE?

On 17 June 1972, five men were arrested for second-degree burglary at the Democratic Committee headquarters located in the Watergate complex in Washington, D.C. Thus, the controversy that ensued came to be known as Watergate. Some of the Plumbers, as they would come to be known, were eventually convicted. Before it was over, the resulting scandal sent shock waves that reached all the way up to the presidency. President Richard M. Nixon was not implicated immediately, and some of the burglars maintain to this day that he knew nothing of the break-in. Yet questions arose concerning the amount of knowledge the president had and when he obtained that knowledge. Televised hearings over the Watergate scandal began in the summer of 1973 with the now-famous question from committee chair Senator Howard Baker: "What did the President know and when did he know it?" A central question became whether the president lied to protect himself.

Enough evidence came forth to cast sufficient doubt about (or maybe convince of) Nixon's ignorance. For many, the only true question was just how much he directly orchestrated events in his administration's cover-up. Also casting doubt on his innocence was the subsequent conviction of cabinet members. The *Washington Post* received a Pulitzer Prize for its role in "breaking" and covering Watergate; this seems especially relevant to the previous discussion on press restraints, supporting the importance of a "free" press for governing with consent. The consequences of silencing the press during Watergate (or during a war, perhaps) are extraordinary and potentially tragic for the country and its people. The president's office was forced to admit knowledge of the break-in. The president resigned on 8 August 1974 in the face of impeachment proceedings against him. Vice President Gerald Ford, who was appointed by Nixon after previous Vice President Agnew resigned, took office the next day, after which, he promptly pardoned Nixon.

• • •

Marilyn Kressel, who wrote the following excerpts, does an excellent job of comparing *Animal Farm* and Watergate: "The pathology of Watergate parallels with striking accuracy the motifs endogenous to the totalitarian framework of *Animal Farm*."[10] Kressel proceeds to render a striking likeness of Watergate's ravages on the U.S. visage. She begins by examining the devices of the "scapegoat" or "fall guy." Throughout the article, the stylistic device Kressel uses is a back-and-forth between *Animal Farm* and Watergate. The scapegoat device, according to this comparison, was employed liberally by the pigs on the farm and the pig in the White House. Napoleon scapegoated Snowball. After driving him off the farm, Napoleon then blames everything that goes wrong on the absent, but always present, Snowball. This accomplishes much and no doubt contributes to the continuing rule of Napoleon. Whether his rule is advantageous to other animals on the farm does not appear to be a question for Orwell. Kressel makes the move to Watergate handily: "The transition from the world of simpleminded animals to our own experience is really not very farfetched. In examining the progression of the Nixon Administration's maneuvers on the Watergate front, the scapegoat motif emerges quite clearly. The variance is only in the tactical format of the imagistic transformation of former White House henchmen."[11] The benefits for any regime, let alone a totalitarian one, are obvious. Nothing sticks to such a regime, at least until the strategy is reduced to an embarrassment. Is this unique to totalitarianism? Does it matter to Kressel's argument, as you understand it? Have any recent presidents used this device to improve their image or divert attention from their image? Can the scapegoat device be useful in a democratic regime? What about on the farm? Was a strong, centralized government necessary for the transition from Manor to Animal Farm? Could the pigs ever have relinquished power? Even without pig control, does the scapegoat device help maintain the needed credibility of a governing regime, especially on a farm of animals who decide based on other-than-rational terms and credibility is crucial?

The second totalitarian motif Kressel explores is loyalism. She delineates two distinct loyalty levels: a tight core around the leader and an entire population. Both of these levels are present surrounding Napoleon on the farm. He has a devoted inner circle of pigs and a largely obedient populace. Animal Farm functions as a result of this loyalty, but at what cost? Is there a better way? Once again, the move from the book to the world is made easy by Kressel: "Extrapolated to the policies of Nixon's White House, the loyalist motif applies to the outright fidelity of the young men with whom the President surrounded himself. They were adherents to a Nixonism which would afford them to elitism of a select ruling class."[12] What happens when a president receives enormous support based on, for instance, character? The people follow their leader because they are convinced that he or she is worthy and would act in their best interest. Let us say this leader also inspires intense loyalty from those surrounding her or him, a willingness to preserve the long-term good despite a short-term failing (this is not to say that what Nixon allegedly did was merely a failing). Is loyalism inescapably a "totalitarian motif"? What about elitism? Should the elite govern with the consent of the masses? Is there any such thing as an elite? Was there an elite on Animal Farm? Should the more "intelligent" animals rule? Make policy? Was Boxer guilty of blind loyalism, as Kressel suggests?

The final comparison Kressel offers is "the rhetoric of propaganda." She defines propaganda as "the distortion of facts and events so that they reflect favorably on the ruling class." The use of distortion has been pointed out throughout this chapter. The pigs regularly and self-servingly distorted what they knew to be true. Kressel cites as a representative anecdote the pigs' consumption of the milk and apples as necessary for their health. This propaganda device was the most prominent vehicle for the pigs in their drive toward complete control. Kressel makes a strong case against the Nixon cabal:

> The propaganda of self-serving rhetoric by White House spokesmen had long been standard operating procedure as a means by which to obfuscate any suggestion of wrongdoing on the part of high officials. The degree to which misleading demagoguery was employed becomes more apparent as investigations progress. Retrospective evaluation indicates an incredible inconsistency between the evidence as it now exists and the facts as the White House presented them.[13]

The truth of the matter is apparent to Kressel as she reads the "evidence." By now, with our two-sided discussion of power and truth, truth is emerging as strongly dependent on power—that is, truth is not some neutral, objective reality waiting to be discovered, but directly depending on the forces at work in discovering that reality. Reality is called forth through the ideological, lived world of those professing it. Similarly, power in our society is reliant on truth. Truth claims enliven us. We see telling the truth as one of our paramount values, despite the lives we might live. Is it possible to tell the truth in an unbiased way? How does the answer to that question implicate the use of propaganda by a president? What is the difference between propaganda and persuasion? If a difference exists, is the use of propaganda by the president acceptable for a democracy? What if one's audience, as on Animal Farm, could not always understand difficult messages? Does this have an impact on how you try to persuade them? What if the simplified version of an argument does not work? Is the use of less truthful but more persuasive arguments acceptable? Who decides? Is this the role of the press in our society? Who could have accomplished it in *Animal Farm?*

Kressel is writing toward the end of the scandal and has the events of the day determining her reality. She is writing her opinion of what these events indicate for the future. She likens *Animal Farm* to Watergate one final time, comparing the frightening future of Animal Farm to the U.S. future. Does this comparison makes sense some twenty-five years later? How has Watergate affected you? Can you see similar issues concerning the presidency today or in the recent past? Is the future hopeless on the farm? Is this an indictment by Orwell of a particular form of revolution or of all revolutions? This "utopia" or all utopias? If Watergate turned out to be not as big a scandal as Kressel predicted, then can we learn anything about history from this example? Are historians or journalists caught up in the events of the day more or less reliable? How do we tell—that is, if what is in question is what happened, how do we judge which events are true? Is it possible for any historian, irrespective of when they write, to take an unbiased historical approach? Is the old saying true: History is written by the winners? How about just: History is written?

FROM MARILYN KRESSEL, "PIGS ON TWO FEET: GEORGE
ORWELL THROUGH THE PRISM OF WATERGATE"
(*Intellect* 103 [1974])

From the tumult of the Watergate ordeal, and its resultant massive body of evidence, has emerged both the crude characterization of entrusted officials and the cuckolding of the American public. . . . At this point of reckoning, when the blinds are up and we are given full view, we are compelled to acknowledge the same reality faced by unassuming beast-lings in a fanciful tale as they stood dumbfounded while the tenets in which they so firmly believed degenerated into the ultimate and pathetic irony: "All animals are equal, *but some are more equal than others.*" Their lamentable plight has now become indistinguishable from our own.

TOPICS FOR WRITTEN OR ORAL EXPLORATION

1. Have a roundtable discussion with some of your classmates on the desirability of truth in our society. Relate your discussion to examples from *Animal Farm*. Pick a moderator to facilitate the discussion, and make sure everybody gets a chance to talk. Set a time limit. Invite others to watch, and open it up to the audience after the discussion for questions and answers.

2. Friedrich Nietzsche wrote a considerable amount on the questions of truth and lying. Read some of his writings, and present some of his extremely controversial philosophy to the class.

3. Examine some of your textbooks. Try to find evidence of different perspectives on the world. For example, are there examples of capitalism? Democracy? Secular humanism? Christianity? Formulate some objection to the texts. Get time on a school board agenda. Present your evidence and your objection.

4. Research schoolbook censorship, and select an important court case. Find out the arguments each side made. Recreate parts of the trial for the class. For example, you could choose someone to be an important witness and someone else to be the other side's lawyer. You could cross-examine the witness or present closing arguments. You also could present the judge's decision and rationale. The judge could be part of the recreation.

5. The peace movement was impaired seriously by the federal government's campaign to control the information about the Persian Gulf War. Find out about the movement. Find out how press restraints hurt its ability to launch an effective counterattack against the government's war machine. Everyone in the class should imagine that they are policymakers during the war. Try to persuade the class that the government should allow the press to report freely about the war. Explain how the government is governing without proper consent, for example.

6. Give an unsanitized news report to the class about some part of the Gulf War. Use some of the information excluded from presentation during the war, but released subsequently. Choose your medium (e.g., radio, television, MTV). Adapt your presentation to your medium and your audience as you see fit.

7. Research executive privilege. Trace it from its inception, chronicling its use (and abuse) by various presidents. Lay out the advantages and disadvantages for the office and for the general public. Present your arguments in a way that allows an intelligent reader (or listener) to

make an informed choice. Choose an appropriate forum for your presentation.

8. Compare and contrast the Clinton presidential scandals with Watergate's. Are there any issues central to both? How does lying enter into the scandals? What about truth? Is the comparison between the scandals a politically motivated one—that is, does one side stand to benefit if the comparisons hold water? How are the scandals different? Can Watergate's lessons teach us anything about President Clinton's troubles?

9. Have a debate with one or more of your classmates on the desirability of government: "Resolved: That government in the United States should be abolished."

10. Create your own version of Animal Farm. Engage the issues of truth and power. How would your farm handle the questions raised about government in this chapter? How would decisions be made? Would truth be a paramount value? How would nonconformity be handled? Provide details and specific references to *Animal Farm*. Explain what went wrong on the farm and how your's rectifies the problems.

11. Choose an anarchist thinker. Research his or her particular brand of anarchism. Or formulate your own version. Examine this strain of anarchism with respect to some of the questions raised in this chapter about truth and power. How does this anarchism differ from the ones detailed in the chapter? How does it deal with the problem and solution of public opinion? How does truth function in this society? Does this theory assume anything about human nature?

12. The pigs exercised censorship in pursuit of a revolution. Is the government justified in employing the same tactics to *prevent* a revolution? Compare and contrast the events in *Animal Farm* to the possibility of such a revolution in the United States. Is a revolution even possible in the United States? What would be required for such an event to come about?

13. Using Mollie as an example, compare the power of ostracism, peer pressure, and public censure that is present in your classroom. Is it better or worse than on the farm? Are there parallels? Is such power desirable? Necessary? Is it even possible to eliminate such power, if it were desirable?

SUGGESTED READINGS

Blanchard, Margaret A. "Free Expression and Wartime: Lessons from the Past, Hopes for the Future." *Journalism Quarterly* 69:1 (Spring 1992).

Jenkinson, Edward. "When Readers Dislike the Works of Writers: Censorship in America Today." *South Atlantic Quarterly* 82 (1983).

Kressel, Marilyn. "Pigs on Two Feet: George Orwell Through the Prism of Watergate." *Intellect* 103 (1974): 192–95.

Marshall, Peter. *Nature's Web: Rethinking Our Place on Earth*. Armonk, N.Y.: M. E. Sharpe, 1996.

Nietzsche, Firedrich. "The Philosopher: Reflections on the Struggle Between Art and Knowledge." In *Philosophy and Truth: Selections from the Nietzsche's Notebooks of the Early 1870's*. Ed. and trans. Daniel Breazeale. Atlantic Highlands, N.J.: Humanities Press International, 1979.

Rodden, John. *The Politics of Literary Reputation: The Making and Claiming of "St. George" Orwell*. New York: Oxford University Press, 1989.

Woodcock, George. *Anarchism: A History of Libertarian Ideas and Movements*. New York: Viking Penguin, 1986.

NOTES

1. John Rodden, *The Politics of Literary Reputation: The Making and Claiming of "St. George" Orwell* (New York: Oxford University Press, 1989), p. 158.

2. Pierre-Joseph Proudhon in Peter Marshall, *Nature's Web: Rethinking Our Place on Earth* (Armonk, N.Y.: M. E. Sharpe, 1996), p. 307.

3. Rodden, p. 159.

4. George Orwell in George Woodcock, *Anarchism: A History of Libertarian Ideas and Movements* (New York: Viking Penguin, 1986), p. 72.

5. Peter Kropotkin in Marshall, p. 310.

6. Friedrich Nietzsche, "The Philosopher: Reflections on the Struggle Between Art and Knowledge," in *Philosophy and Truth: Selections from the Nietzsche's Notebooks of the Early 1870's*, ed. and trans. Daniel Breazeale (Atlantic Highlands, N.J.: Humanities Press International, 1979), p. 27.

7. Nietzsche, "On Truth and Lying in a Nonmoral Sense," in *Philosophy and Truth*, p. 84.

8. Edward Jenkinson, "When Readers Dislike the Works of Writers: Censorship in America Today," *South Atlantic Quarterly* 82 (1983): 351.

9. Margaret A. Blanchard, "Free Expression and Wartime: Lessons from the Past, Hopes for the Future," *Journalism Quarterly* 69:1 (Spring 1992): 16.

10. Marilyn Kressel, "Pigs on Two Feet: George Orwell Through the Prism of Watergate," *Intellect* 103 (1974): 193.

11. Ibid.

12. Ibid., p. 194.

13. Ibid., p. 195.

Glossary of Literary Terms
John Rodden

allegory   A fictional story in which the plot and characters are organized to make sense on both a literal level of meaning and other symbolic or conceptual levels of meaning. *Animal Farm* is a historical and political allegory that makes sense on both a literal and a symbolic level. On the literal level, it makes sense as a simple animal story. On the symbolic level, it makes sense as a commentary on the history and politics of the Russian Revolution and its aftermath (and all other revolutions and their outcomes). Some literary critics have amusingly referred to *Animal Farm* as an "animallegory."

didactic literature   Works intended chiefly to teach or enlighten (rather than to give enjoyment). *Animal Farm* does both, but it is sometimes classified as "didactic literature" because its satirical and allegorical functions dominate.

fable   A short narrative that embodies a moral thesis, often concluding with a "moral." Probably the most common example is the *beast fable*— for example, from Aesop's fable, "The Hare and the Tortoise": "Plodding wins the race."

fairy tale   A story, usually for children, about magical or fantastic events that are not just implausible but untrue. Orwell noted that he subtitled *Animal Farm* "a fairy story" precisely in order to stress that it *was* fantastic, but unfortunately, that it was *not* untrue. As Chapters 2, 5, and 6 make clear, history has largely borne out Orwell's claim that *Animal*

Farm is a "true" fairy tale about the history of the USSR—and that it also possesses much broader relevance to other governments in other places and times.

genre   A term derived from the French meaning "literary form." Depending on what the reader focuses on in Orwell's story, *Animal Farm* may be classified as belonging to many genres, or types, of literature: *satire, fable, fairy tale*, and *allegory*.

parable   A short narrative about human beings designed as an analogy to convey some truth, principle, or lesson. Christ's parables of the Good Samaritan and the Prodigal Son are well-known examples in Christianity. *Animal Farm* is sometimes discussed as a parable on the human condition that draws such lessons as "power corrupts."

propaganda   Strongly or exclusively didactic literature, written in an explicit, narrow way to convince the reader to adopt a particular attitude toward a pressing contemporary issue. *Animal Farm* has been criticized (mainly by pro-Soviet readers, Communists and, far left-wing readers) as propaganda against the Soviet Union and Communism. But this criticism is inaccurate, because Orwell's book is not just about the USSR or Communism; it transcends its time and place and remains pertinent for the twenty-first century. *Animal Farm* is a didactic work, but it is not propaganda.

satire   A form of literature that derides a subject by making it ridiculous, amusing, or contemptible. Satire usually implies a moral judgment and is written to correct wrongs or criticize injustice. *Animal Farm* renders the Soviet Union and its leaders both laughable and despicable. Orwell uses many *symbols* to effect this, such as depicting the main characters of the story—who symbolize the Soviet leaders—as pigs. In doing so, he delivers a severe judgment of the Soviet Union in particular and the betrayal of revolutionary ideals in general.

symbol   A word or phrase that signifies an object or event beyond itself. *Animal Farm* contains many literary symbols. For example, the windmill is a symbol of the building up (and destruction) of USSR economy via Stalin's Five-Year Plans.

Index

Contributors

JAMES ARNT AUNE is an associate professor of speech communication at Texas A&M University, where he teaches courses in the history of rhetorical theory. He is the author of *Rhetoric and Marxism* (1994) and the forthcoming *Beyond Economic Correctness: Studies in Free Market Rhetoric*.

CRISTEN CARSON REAT received her M.A. in Russian literature from the University of Texas at Austin. She has written on ideological issues relating to the teaching of Russian literature.

DANIEL REAT received his B.A. from Rice University in business and art history. He contributed two illustrations to this book and works as a lawyer in Houston, Texas.

JOHN RODDEN teaches at the University of Texas at Austin. He is the author of *The Politics of Literary Reputation: The Making and Claiming of "St. George" Orwell* (1989) and several other books.

PAUL RODDEN is a poet and fireman. He contributed five illustrations to this casebook and is the author of *Meager Knowledge* (1989), a poetry collection. He lives in Austin, Texas.

THOMAS G. RODDEN is a systems analyst and special consultant based in Palo Alto, California, and is a former executive in the European division of General Electric. He is the recipient of a Fulbright Scholar Award to Austria and contributed an illustration to Chapter 1.

JONATHAN ROSE is a professor of history and director of the Book History Program at Drew University. He is the former president and founder of SHARP (Society for the History of Authorship, Reading, and Publishing), an international scholarly organization devoted to issues connected with book history. He is the author of *The Edwardian Temperament, 1895–1910* (1986) and editor of *The Revised Orwell* (1992).

WILLIAM E. SHANAHAN III is a professor of communication and the director of forensics at Fort Hays State University, Kansas. He has been involved with academic debate for over two decades as both a competitor and a coach.

CRAIG THOMPSON received his M.F.A. from the University of Texas at Austin. He contributed two illustrations to this book and works as a graphic artist in Austin, Texas.

DENISE WEEKS is an assistant professor of English at Weber State University in Ogden, Utah. She currently teaches courses in technical writing, literature, and composition.